SEX, GOD, CHRISTMAS & JEWS

Intimate Emails About Faith and Life Challenges

Also by Gil Mann

How to Get More Out of Being Jewish Even If:
A. You are not sure you believe in God,
B. You think going to synagogue is a waste of time,
C. You think keeping kosher is stupid,
D. You hated Hebrew school, or
E. All of the above!

To order:
Call 800–304–9925 or visit www.BeingJewish.org.

SEX, GOD, CHRISTMAS &JEWS

Intimate Emails About Faith and Life Challenges

Gil Mann

Leo & Sons
PUBLISHING

Minneapolis, Minnesota, USA

A Friendly Copyright Notice

1st Edition

Library of Congress Control Number: 2005937916
ISBN 0-9651709-3-4

10   9   8   7   6   5   4   3   2

Printed in the United States of America by:
Leo & Sons Publishing
A Division of On Line Marketing, Inc.
175 Oregon Avenue South
Minneapolis, MN 55426

Phone: 763-545-3666
Book Orders: 800-304-9925
Fax: 763-542-0171
Email: LeoPublish@aol.com
Website: www.BeingJewish.org

Dedicated to Yael *z"l*

May her memory be a blessing

Table of Contents

Thank You!

This book had a long gestation period. In the course of the pregnancy, there were many midwives, doctors, clergy, friends, and family who gave support and assistance to the baby and to the mom (that would be me). I am grateful to them all.

Before a single word of this book was written, I was the fortunate beneficiary of the generosity and vision of Leslie and Abigail Wexner. Thanks to them, Rabbi Herb Friedman, Rabbi Nathan Laufer, and Rabbi Ramie Arian, I was able to spend three years advancing my learning about Judaism in the life-changing Wexner Heritage Foundation Jewish studies program. I am most grateful to them and the scholars and staff of the Foundation.

The first words of this book actually were written thanks in part to Marc Klein — though at the time, I did not realize I was beginning to write a new book. Mark managed the Jewish content area of America Online. He liked my first book so much that he suggested I create an area of AOL to respond to people via the Internet. Those responses were the genesis of this book as they evolved into a *Jewish Email of the Week* column that was widely distributed. I am grateful to him for his enthusiastic support of my work and for his help in turning his suggestion into a reality. Also, working on Jewish content at AOL was Rabbi Mark Diamond, who was in charge of AOL's *Ask a Rabbi* feature. We were in touch often and I appreciated his support and dedication.

For some time now, people have been sending email to me on my own website, www.BeingJewish.org. The website is a success thanks to my fantastic webmaster, Natalie Bensimhon. I love working with her. She is capable, fast, smart, artistic, and always a delight. Thank you, Nat!

I also thank the many newspapers, editors, websites, and webmasters who have published my column. In addition, I am grateful to UJC and Federations in 70 communities in the United

States and Canada who have arranged for me to lecture and hear questions and feedback in person from thousands of people from coast to coast.

Over the years of writing responses to emails, I regularly conferred with rabbis and scholars. Two of them, Rabbi Hayim Herring and Rabbi Yosef Shagalow, often provided me with answers when I had technical questions about Jewish law and ritual. Over the years, they've given me much-valued feedback on my columns and this book. They have challenged and broadened my thinking about Judaism and life in general. They've also given me the precious gift of their friendship, which I cherish dearly. A thank you to them must include my thanks to their wives, Terri Krivosha and Chana Shagalow.

Many other people have helped me in multiple ways in my work and on this project. Thanking them each in the detail they deserve would be like one of those endless speeches at the Academy Awards. I am grateful to these people for their influence, inspiration, and devotion of time, thought, concern, and help: Rabbi Kassel Abelson, Cantor Audrey Abrams, Lois Anderson, Michelle Anton, Michelle Basman, Sandi Berman, Andy Bloom, Corinne Booher, Rabbi Aaron Brusso, Rabbi Norman Cohen, Nora Contini, Rabbi Alexander Davis, David Epstein, Barb Field, Joshua Fogelson, Avinoam Gelb, Ehud Gelb, Rabbi Saadia Gelb (my uncle and hero), Bernie Goldblatt, Dr. Jane Goodall, Hana Gruenberg, Andy Halper, Bill Harrison, Steve Harrison, Carolyn Hessel, Rabbi Rob Kahn, Dr. Mel Konner, Rabbi Irwin Kula, Rabbi Harold Kushner, Laura Lazowski, Amy Hirshberg Lederman, Sue Levine, Mary Lewis, Yury Millman, David Mueller, Dr. John Nash, Cantor Neil Newman, Laura Nigro, Ellen Sue Parker, Donna Rosenthal, Betsy Sansby, Nadine Schneider, Dick Spiegel, Cathi Stevenson, Debbie Stillman, Dvora Tager, Jess Todtfeld, Rabbi Bruce Warshal, and Dr. Greer Glazer. I'm indebted to them all because in one way or another they helped give birth to this book.

In addition to all of these people, my friends and family members deserve thanks. Without them I wouldn't be able to produce a book, or much of anything for that matter. If I were to mention all of them here, this would be beyond an Academy Awards speech—it would be the entire three hour telecast. I hope they know how much I love them and thank them for everything.

I want to single out my mom and my wife and kids. My mom, Vivian Avivya Mann *z"l*, was a Jewish educator most of her career and she was passionate about her Judaism. She was also passionate about being a Jewish Mother. As a result of these two passions, whenever I posted a column, I could count on feedback from her. Her comments were thoughtful and informed by her deep knowledge of Judaism. On the rare occasion she took issue with something I wrote, her critique was constructive and helpful. She was my greatest fan and her love and support meant the world to me. I am pained that my Mom passed away before this book was finished. Fortunately she was able to see a manuscript of this book and as usual, she was positive and approving. In many ways, the final product is a tribute to her. This book is one way that her teaching, and memories of her, live on as blessings.

I thank my children Josh, Nomi, Shoshana, and Danny for their patience as I've spent so much time traveling or pounding away at the computer. I believe they realize that in my little way, I am trying to make our world a bit better. I thank them for their understanding and love.

To my wife Debbie, I could write an entire book of thank yous. Much of what is good in my life I can attribute to her. As for this book, I simply could not have written it without her. She has helped me with every aspect. First, she takes on far more than her share in our home to give me the time to write and travel. All of my writing is influenced and improved by her insights. Before I would release a column, I sought her thoughts. She was always willing to help with perceptive suggestions. Her help on this book was invaluable as she reviewed draft after draft. She read all of the email I have received and helped cull down thousands to a few hundred. Her knowledge, common sense, kindness, and giving soul have helped me throughout the creation of this book, and indeed on every journey I've taken as an adult. I am grateful to her and feel very lucky to have her as my wife and partner.

So you can see, the help of many made this book possible. Their contributions were invaluable to me and these wonderful people deserve much credit. Of course, any errors or omissions in this book are completely my responsibility as are all of my opinions expressed here.

My final thanks go to the many people who have emailed me and to you, the reader. The writers of these emails have enriched my life. I believe that the readers of their emails will also be enriched. To the readers of this book, I know how busy people are and also how many books are sitting on my bed stand in mid-read. Knowing that your minutes and hours are precious, I appreciate that you are devoting time to this book. I hope you find the rewards worthy. Thank you!

Introduction

Help Me Please...

The email began arriving immediately. People were anonymously pouring their hearts out to me. Daily I'd sit at my computer, reading the unbelievably candid feelings, thoughts, and questions that were being sent to me by strangers. Every day I was startled anew. People were openly sharing extremely personal challenges in their lives and questions about faith, God, spirituality, and religions.

One day, when I logged on to the Internet to hear my PC announce, as usual, "You've got mail!," I saw that I had received an email with an unusual subject line: "From a female Job" (in the Bible, Job was a man whose faith was tested through tragedies).

I clicked on it to open the most staggering email I had ever received. Here is what she wrote to me (as with all the email in this book, I've left most punctuation and grammar unedited):

Subj: From a female Job
Date: 06-03 17:52:08 EDT
From:
To: GilMann@aol.com

Dear Gil:

I am a 49 year old woman. In my short lifetime I have had or continue to have Epilepsy, Lung Problems, Blood Clots, Heart Problems, and six years ago I had a mastectomy of my right breast. My family is fine and we have had our successes. My husband has overcome his own disability to rise in the ranks of his profession while my children do well in school and on their own.

I now face the added crises of a secondary cancer in my lymphic system. I am in 3rd or 4th stage of cancer. I need help but am finding a hard time in believing in prayer the power there of or the reason for it. I am an ethical jew and have found ways to believe in God. That is now tenuous but I am hanging in there. But to pray I cannot and when others say can I say a Prayer for you I have to say yes but remember your prayers are for you not me. I will be fine and I know I will be up and down but I need to resolve my issues
with prayer   Help me please
                        Yael
My hebrew name   shalom

I sat frozen, staring at the screen. Her email was so intimate, honest, and raw. While Yael's email was especially powerful, many of the emails I was receiving left me awed by the people "out there" and that they were contacting me. They so wanted to share experiences and questions with me. How could I best help them? How could I best share these yearnings of "people on the street" with professionals and organizations? How should I harness this energy I had tapped into to achieve the most good?

On the Internet there are many "Ask the Rabbi" and "Ask the Doctor" type sites, yet the people emailing me knew that I was not a rabbi, psychologist, social worker, etc. I discussed my email with a rabbi who worked for an Ask a Rabbi site and he suggested that perhaps people wrote to me precisely because of who I'm not. I do "not" represent a movement, a philosophy, an ideology, or any political or clergy position.

My response has been to try to assist those who contact me by providing information, answers, and other resources. I also encourage writers to further ask their questions—in person—of local professionals and others.

Email and My Life

The email I was receiving was part of a personal evolution that began when I decided to leave the business world. After receiving a degree in journalism, I started my career writing and producing TV news. In the '80s, my wife and I founded a video-based computer training business. To make a long story short, the company grew rapidly, we sold it, and I began to volunteer full time, working primarily in Jewish non-profits. My business and journalism career taught me a great deal about listening and responding to the public, so when volunteering at non-profits, my efforts were usually focused on an aspect of marketing.

I was pleased to be able to contribute my time in this fashion because I believed I could be helpful to these institutions. On top of this, I've always felt passionate about being Jewish. My feelings for Judaism were so strong that in college I considered going to rabbinical school. (I opted not to go, in part because I was not fond of services and did not think they'd let me go through six years of rabbinical training and skip all the services.)

After a few years, my experiences while I was volunteering, combined with my sentiments about Judaism, led me back to writing. In 1996, my first book was published. That book has perhaps the longest title in the history of English literature. It is called:

> *How to Get More Out of Being Jewish Even If:*
> *A. You are not sure you believe in God,*
> *B. You think going to synagogue is a waste of time,*
> *C. You think keeping kosher is stupid,*
> *D. You hated Hebrew school, or*
> *E. All of the above!*

The title may sound flippant, but the book was serious. It was the result of listening to about 150 Jews in focus groups and interviews. In my volunteer work in Jewish non-profit organizations, I was regularly frustrated to see how out of touch those of us who work in these organizations seemed to be with the people we strive to serve — our "customers" so to speak. I wanted to hear these customers and understand them better. So I sought to listen to Jews "on the street" and hear directly from them how they felt about their

3

Judaism, and also, to try to provide them with relevant answers in plain English.

The book was extremely well received. So well, in fact, that it spawned an area of America Online called "Judaism Today: Where Do I Fit?" that followed the themes described in A through E of the book's title. (I should point out that I do not make money from my writing or lecturing.) When the area was launched in 1997, I posted an announcement that I'd be collecting any email I received for possible publication and that I would not reveal the identities of the writers. As I wrote in the first paragraph of this book, I immediately began to receive email from all kinds of people, including, to my surprise, many non-Jews. Eventually, I created my own website called www.BeingJewish.org. The statistics on my website — with its obvious Jewish name — indicate that I have had visitors from more than 100 countries, including, to my amazement, many of the Muslim countries of the Middle East. These visitors from the Middle East have also emailed questions to me.

I was committed to answering every email that came in, which sometimes left me writing until two o'clock in the morning. In the exceptional case of Yael, the female Job, we exchanged many emails, spoke by phone numerous times, and I connected her with professional resources in her community that she came to rely upon. Ultimately, I met her and her husband in their home in Canada. This book is dedicated to her because, by contacting me, she changed my life. Her questions of faith in the face of severe life challenges have inspired and motivated me. I've been so moved by her that I carry her first email with me in my calendar. Thanks to her, I came to truly appreciate that "on the other end" out there in cyberspace are real people who are grappling with significant probing questions and life challenges.

Finger on a Remarkable Pulse

While the extent of the relationship I developed with Yael had no equal, my life has been intertwined with many others who have written. Some who wrote simply wanted to vent, and I thanked them for sharing their thoughts with me. Many wanted to know if

Judaism could offer guidance for a modern-day challenge in their lives. Others had questions about some aspect of Judaism. Some had general faith or religion questions or a desire to know the differences between Judaism and other religions. Often I was able to answer their questions based on my knowledge of Judaism. Other times, to answer their question, I sought expertise from rabbis and Jewish scholars. On a regular basis, I referred people to rabbis, other clergy and professionals, social service agencies, books, organizations, websites, and electronic message or bulletin boards where they could further pursue the matter they had raised.

Many writers thought the issue they had on their mind was unusual or unique. Some of them were right, but more often than not, I found patterns in the email and I could see similar issues raised by many. Frequently, emails ended with the sentiment "Thanks for listening." This phrase, but far more so, the content of these emails, made me realize that I had my finger on a remarkable pulse — a living rhythm of emotions, thoughts, attitudes, and experiences.

I decided that more people needed to see what I was seeing. Individuals needed to see that the issues and questions they often silently kept to themselves were shared by many others. I wanted to champion their voices. Leaders of institutions needed to hear these voices and be more responsive. I also sought to express my conviction that Judaism can and should be relevant.

I began selecting one email per week, which I edited to conceal the writer's identity. I'd then respond publicly in an "Email of the Week" column that appeared online. Here are the titles of some of these columns:

Where Was God on September 11?
Did You Hear the One About the Jew…?
I Am Catholic and Dating a Jewish Guy
Body Piercing, Tattoos, and More!
Why Do Jews Argue So Much?
I Will Not Circumcise My Son!

These columns generated even more email from readers who reacted with opinions, their experiences, and often additional questions.

In 1999, I began to release my column to Jewish newspapers. Many papers began to run the column called *Jewish E-Mail*. Now when I released a column, nearly 200,000 copies of it were being distributed by newspapers across the United States and Canada. A number of websites also began to feature the column. I regularly heard from teachers who told me they were using the columns in their lessons. (By the way, I hereby give teachers and others permission to copy material in this book; please just reference that you found it here.)

Because of my work, I also began to receive many invitations to lecture, and I've spoken in more than 70 cities across North America. To reach even more people, I've decided to publish these columns and some of the additional follow-up email that people sent in reaction to my columns in the form of a book.

My intent in sharing the email in this book is threefold. First, by reading what others have written, I hope you will feel empowered to voice your questions, doubts, issues, and opinions — constructively and in forums on and beyond the Internet. Second, I hope this email helps professionals, institutions, and organizations to better reach, understand, and serve the "people" — some of whose voices may not be heard through conventional channels. Third, I hope the email in this book can help build bridges between Jews and non-Jews, so we better understand our differences and the many thoughts, emotions, and life challenges we all share in common.

Before diving into the email, I need to say a few words about the people who write to me. The only way I can know anything definitive about people who write is if they volunteer information about themselves—which, as you will see, they regularly do. Statistically, there is no way of knowing the breakdown of the people who write to me. Often I can read between the lines to discern patterns, but this is far from scientific. I am able to say that the writers are of all ages, from teens to seniors, and seem to be fairly equally divided between male and female. The nature of a person's comments or questions does not necessarily reveal their background or current type of religious practice or nonpractice.

Although the majority of people who write to me are Jewish, I regularly hear from non-Jews. Non-Jews who write often make a point of telling me they're not Jewish and what religion (if any) they practice. I was concerned that opening myself up on the Internet could lead to anti-Semitic hate email. Happily, over the years, I've received only a handful. In fact, almost all the email I have received has been respectful and positive in tone. They have been a pleasure to read and have reflected to me, a genuine desire to understand.

As for the Jews who write, I hear from every kind. I would like to emphasize that this is **not** a book about "the unaffiliated" or Jews on "the periphery." The Jews who write to me come from all the major Jewish denominations (Orthodox, Reconstructionist, Conservative, and Reform), and I also hear from Jews who are secular, atheists, and do not affiliate with any movement. Some write in part because they're not sure exactly how to define their Jewish identity.

Confidentiality: The Emails in This Book Are ANONYMOUS!

I must make several important comments about protecting the identities of the writers of all the email you will read in this book. I regularly indicate to those who write to me that I might select their email for anonymous publication in a column or book. To further conceal writers' identities, I've changed details in the emails. The names of the cities have been changed, and the writers' names and initials have been removed. If you do see a name in an email, it is a fictitious name. So if you think you recognize someone in this book, that is purely a coincidence. There are three emails in this book where the writers' actual names added special meaning, and I used those writers' names with their permission and noted that the name is authentic.

Here are a few additional editorial comments. Although some emails were edited for brevity's sake, most of the grammar, spelling, capitalization, and punctuation were left as is, to preserve the flavor of the email. This also applies to the subject line which is worth noting as you read. Typical of "email etiquette," much of the writing is often "blurb-like" incomplete sentences or fragments, full of grammatical errors. Whenever Hebrew or Yiddish terms are used, I've provided translations in brackets like these [translation].

A very important point I must make is that this book includes some email responses that may contain incorrect factual information, as well as ideas I personally reject. Their inclusion in this book does not imply my endorsement!

With all this in mind, here are a few examples of emails, first from Jewish writers:

Subj: Why be Jewish
Date: 07-26 00:48:36 EDT
From:
To: GilMann@aol.com

A Catholic woman dating my son told him that he was so fortunate to be a Jew, and shame on him because he didn't appreciate his heritage. She told him to become more spiritual, as he was spending all his time working.. She bought him tefillin [phylacteries — ritual prayer object] for a birthday present. He uses them every day, has become shomer shabbat [an observer of the Jewish Sabbath laws], and is kosher because he is a vegetarian. In May, at age 33, he married under the chuppa [wedding canopy]. And I am the proud mother-in-law of a Russian Jew who appreciates him for everything he is!!!! Imagine, a Catholic made him a better Jew. Thanks for listening

---

Subj: Jewish???
Date: 03-21 21:08:47 EST
From:
To: GilMann@aol.com

Dear Gil:

I was always taught from my mother that I was Jewish... I went to a conservative synagogue in Atlanta for a few years... quit when i was sixteen... (My father was not Jewish.) Here I am 49 years old, married Hispanic, had 5 children, not raised jewish (even though one became a doctor?) I read all of Chaim Potak's books, wanted to seek out jewish community... thank G_d for computers now I can... Don't know why?? I guess blood is thicker than water!!! Send message if you have any thoughts on the matter

[Editorial note: As in this email, you will see in this book that some Jews write the word *God* with a space, underscore, or hyphen between the G and d, because of a tradition to prevent the name of God from being accidentally disposed of or erased.]

Subj: Judaism in a secular world
Date: 08-10 23:33:57 EDT
From:
To: GilMann@aol.com

Dear Gil,

I am a college bound Jewish girl who is nervous about how strong my faith in Judaism is. I have attended Jewish Day school all of my life, but yet I am not sure about my beliefs... in God especially. I know Hebrew to an extent and am aware of the Jewish holidays, prayers, and biblical laws. However I am not sure how I truly want to practice my Judaism. I love the morals and values I have been taught, but I still am confused about how I can find my place in judaism (or my particular way of maintaining my Jewish identity in a secular environment which I have never fully encountered... I am scared). Can you assist me?

Subj: Thank you
Date: 06-15 01:18:18 EDT
From:
To: GilMann@aol.com

Dear Gil:

I was approached today by some Christians who claimed "Jesus was the only way for salvation," and they asked me "What my chances of going to Heaven are?" and I replied "90%." I continued to go on and stated "I believe that I am a good person and enhance humanity with my deeds." I never knew this was part of being Jewish. Both of my parents are Jewish (Although my father states he is an atheist) and I went from being an atheist to agnostic to a believer. I am a social worker and working with substance abusers in the Army, I gained my spirituality because there I realized that there is a force more powerful then myself. I am proud of my Jewish ancestors, but i don't know whether I will be religious. Thank you for putting Judaism in a better perspective for me. Take care.

Subj: why do i want to be jewish?
Date: 07-26 00:57:10 EDT
From:
To: GilMann@aol.com

dear sir

i am a holocaust survivor and i paid my dues for being jewish. I AM JEWISH SIMPLY BECAUSE I WANT TO BE. AFTER THE WAR ,I COULD HAVE LEFT JUDAISM AND GOTTEN LOST IN THE CROWD OF THE WORLD AND I COULD HAVE NOT BE BLAMED, AFTER THE HOLOCAUST EXPERIENCE. HOWEVER I DECIDED TO STAY JEWISH BECAUSE I WANTED TO BE JEWISH.

NETZACH ISRAEL LO YESHAKER
Name (signed in Hebrew)

[This last Hebrew line is from *Samuel I, Chapter 15: Verse 29*. The verse is commonly understood to mean: the Eternal One or the Eternity of Israel is not false.]

That gives you a flavor of the variety of Jews who write to me. When non-Jews write to me, again, I only know if they're not Jewish when they volunteer the information, which, as I said earlier, they often do, as in these typical emails:

Subj: Jesus
Date: 09-30 12:54:31 EDT
From:
To: GilMann@aol.com

Dear Mr. Mann,

I am a christian and have been trying for the past six months to understand why the Jewish people don't believe in Jesus. I've read books, talked with my pastor and others who aren't really sure or have they're own philosophy. I'm hoping you could shed some light on this concept for me. I really appreciate any response you can give. Thank you.

Subj: Judaism
Date: 07-22 21:21:04 EDT
From:
To: GilMann@aol.com

Hi!

I have been recently baptized in Christianity. Throughout the preparation I was never sure if I believed in most of it. I don't believe I'm a real Christian. I have just too much disbelief. There were just so many things I wanted to change about Christianity and where emphasis was put. But here's the problem. I have no idea what to do. I want to learn more about Judaism and maybe convert one day. How would I come about this? Plus I have no idea how I would explain this to my family, friends, etc. especially since in June I was baptized. Thanks for listening. I appreciate it much.

Subj: israel
Date: 09-30 01:27:34 EDT
From:
To: GilMann@aol.com

Dear Gil:

Hi there How Are You
I am visit jewish web site and i get ur e-mail from there
My name is M. i am a Muslim from Jordan
I want to ask u why sharon do this?
did he forget that we are arabs 300 milyon and israel just 5.
i dont mean that we will make a war but he must return to
1967 borders
we accept israel
u know what i am sending u cuz i think that u r a good person
dont forget that we can kick israel out but. but i belive that if this
happend it's not good for all
and i dont know what i can told u but plz reply this e-mail
and if u can fix this problem plz try cuz every one will lose
Initialed

Subj: Conversion and Problems
Date: 05-09 14:22:25 EDT
From:
To: GilMann@aol.com

My greatest desire is to convert to Judaism. Everything I've read, discussed, observed and explored about Judaism touches me in very spiritual, ethical and social ways. It is a way of life which I feel can best demonstrate my belief in God and my desire to improve the human condition.

My "problem" is that I am gay. And the reality of Torah [the Hebrew Bible] and Halacha [Jewish law] on that issue seems insurmountably complicated and complete. How does one resolve such an issue?

I wish you could feel the desperation, loneliness and hopeless-ness that I am feeling about my quest for spiritual nourishment and community. And in my heart I know a vast majority of people in the world, not just Judaism, would be only happy if I was no longer here to be "a problem." Is this how the Jews of Europe felt in WW2? Maybe that is why I feel so drawn to Judaism... the sense of being an outsider, who has so much to offer the world, if only the world could see beyond one simple, private part of who I am. But how can I ask centuries of belief, practice and tradition to bow and change for me? How insignificant I feel.

The Amazing and Mysterious Internet

As you can see I hear from quite a potpourri of people with heartfelt thoughts and questions. Why do they write to me? I believe they do so because I am safely available to them, open to their thoughts, and because they've got something on their mind or something to get off their chest. They're also writing, because they can — thanks to the far-reaching abilities of the amazing and mysterious Internet.

Never in the history of humanity have we had the abilities the Internet gives us to access information and communicate with each other. Further, you can become a one-person broadcaster of your ideas to the world through blogs, podcasts, product reviews, mes-sage boards, and the like. Anyone with access to a computer can participate regardless of sex, age, race, religion, income, education, occupation, interests, appearance, expertise, abilities, or disabilities. And no one need know any of the details about your life unless you choose to divulge the information. For purposes of this book, I've taken all the emails I have received at face value, assuming that the people who have written to me have been truthful.

One aspect of the Internet has special importance for this book: You can be anonymous. Because of the ability to surf incognito, being on the Internet is an activity unlike any other in society. Surfing the Internet is like attending a giant masquerade party, but the experience is even more shrouded and suspenseful; you never know who or what you might discover. No one knows who you are, where you are, or what you are. To add to the adventure, this party goes on 365/24/7 with participants popping in and out at all hours.

Because of all these factors, the Internet gives people unprecedented ability to connect with each other and even create virtual communities. However, I would never suggest that the Internet is a substitute for live, in-person, physical connection and community. The Internet is unique and different.

A Modern-Day Talmud

My mother came up with an insightful observation about the realities of interaction and communication on the Internet. I was showing her some online message boards where people were reacting to things that others and I had written about Judaism. I explained to her that the way an electronic message or bulletin board works is similar to an old-fashioned paper bulletin board. A person posts a comment on some subject (anonymously if they wish). Others then may react by posting a comment of their own. This provokes even more responses as the new comments stimulate even more ideas from other readers. But unlike an old-fashioned bulletin board, on an Internet board, a huge quantity of information can be easily posted and accessed.

After reading a number of postings, my mom said, "This is a modern-day Talmud", (the great collection of Jewish law and commentary). The Talmud's many volumes are a compilation of centuries worth of Jewish sages' teachings. These sages explain law, detail, and nuance in the Bible. The first comments in the Talmud are from the earliest sages. These original comments then generated additional commentary from succeeding scholars who read and debated earlier points. This second commentary then spurred subsequent comments from later sages, and so on. I told my mom that one big difference from the Talmud is that on the Internet, anyone can participate in the dialogue—you need not be a scholar or have any other station in life, other than a workstation connected to the Internet.

In the Talmud, as on the Internet, you quickly learn that there is seldom "one truth" or explanation for anything. Instead there is earnest searching by many people, often in a most personal way. On the negative side, the potential for hateful, dangerous, dishonest, and unhealthy thought and behavior exists on the Internet. On positive side, the Internet is a wondrous place to grow and learn with others or by yourself. Reactions from others can come in "real time" (instantly) or many months or years later.

In summary, the unique characteristics of the Internet have made my interactions with people endlessly intriguing and rewarding. By sharing some of these interactions with you through the pages of this book, my hope is that you will resonate with the answers, questions, issues, and emotions that are expressed. I invite you to email your thoughts to me through my website: www.BeingJewish.org.

How This Book Is Organized: ESP

If I were to summarize all of the questions people—Jews and non-Jews — have submitted to me, I'd reduce them to this: How can Judaism be relevant to a modern person? Or, put differently: Can Judaism help me navigate through my modern life?

For this book, I've selected the columns that generated the liveliest responses. To organize these responses in a way that would be helpful to readers, I decided to borrow something many have told me was helpful from my first book: *How to Get More Out of Being Jewish*.... The book began with a chapter called "What is Judaism Anyway?" I started with that chapter because during interviews and focus groups for that book, I found that few could come up with a crisp answer to the question: What is Judaism?

My experience online has further reinforced my conclusion that most people have difficulty defining Judaism, so I decided to write a column in response to a typical email asking me for a definition.

Little did I know when I wrote and published this column that it would help me organize this book some day:

Is Judaism a Religion or a Race?

Dear Gil:

I have a very simple question, is Judaism a religion or a race? I know it may be a dumb question but I have asked a few Jews I know and they all give me different answers. I am not Jewish, I'm African American, but my great-grandfather is supposedly Jewish. I just want to know if it is possible to have "Jew" in you, like it's possible to have Italian or Indian.

Thank you,
L

Hi L:

Your question is not dumb at all! A lot of people including many Jewish people have a hard time coming up with an answer, as you have already discovered. There is much to say on this subject of WHAT IS JUDAISM ANYWAY? But here, I'll try to give you a brief answer:

My answer is: Judaism is much more than a religion and is NOT a race. I define Judaism as: A way of life.

The Jewish way of life consists of three things that I call E.S.P. E stands for Ethics, S stands for Spirituality and P stands for Peoplehood. I draw them like overlapping Olympic rings as you can see in this graphic.

Judaism = A Way of Life
Consisting of ESP:

In Judaism, each of these circles is considered sacred. The interesting (and confusing thing for many) is that a Jew can live in any one of these circles and never enter the other circles. Plus you can enter the other two circles from any one circle. In addition, the circles overlap so you can simultaneously live Jewishly in two or all three circles.

This can be confusing, but really it is kind of simple. For example, when I say that Judaism is much more than a religion, I mean that even if you do not believe in God you're not disqualified from being a Jew. For example, Hitler sure did not define Jews by their Spirituality! He cared about Peoplehood. In addition, Jews are supposed to behave Ethically whether they enter the Spirituality circle — that is, whether they believe in God or not!

Here I want to say a word about the Peoplehood circle: according to Jewish law, to be considered Jewish by birth, your mother must be Jewish. (Many Jews say either of your parents can be Jewish — but I won't get into that here.)

HOWEVER! Judaism is NOT a race — though our enemies love to call us a race. Any person of any race is welcome to convert to Judaism. if Judaism were a race; you could not convert to become a Jew. Nobody can convert to become another race — but anyone can convert to become Jewish. There are Jews of all races and colors

— for proof, just look at a city street in Israel. I want to make an important point here: Many people (including Jews) think the emphasis on Jews marrying other Jews is repulsive racist thinking. I'd be repulsed too... if Judaism was a race... but it is not. Again, Judaism is a way of life.

The ESP of the Jewish "way of life" is all encompassing. There is no aspect of life that's not included in Ethics, Spirituality, Peoplehood, or a combination of them. There is much more that can be said about the E.S.P. circles of Judaism. In fact, you could write a whole book on the subject. I did! Hope this brief summary helps!

Gil

To reiterate, the reason I think so many people have a difficult time defining Judaism is because a Jew can live Jewishly in any one of the three circles and never touch the other circles. Plus, a Jew can move from circle to circle during their life — or even during a day. At any given moment, a Jew can live in one circle or another or live in a place where the circles overlap.

Here is a story that illustrates what I mean. I was giving a presentation about Jewish Spirituality near Norfolk, Virginia, home of the largest U.S. naval base in the world. A fellow raised his hand and said, "I'd like to share an example of how Jewish Peoplehood and Spirituality happened to me in a most powerful way."

He explained that he had been an Army helicopter pilot for 12 years and had fought in Operation Desert Storm — the Persian Gulf War of 1991. While he was in Saudi Arabia, he was prohibited by military order from outwardly showing that he was Jewish. That meant he could not wear a Star of David, a *mezuzah* [a pendant worn by some Jews or placed on the doorposts of Jewish homes as a sign of Jewish identity] or a *chai* [the Hebrew word for life] pendant. He was even advised to remove the word Jewish from his dog tags!

Anti-Semitism? No. The reasons were to protect the Jewish soldiers should the Iraqis capture them and also because the Saudis were sensitive that non-Muslim soldiers were on Saudi soil defending the holiest sites in Islam: Mecca and Medina. (The latter reason is part of what provoked Osama Bin Laden to terror.)

December rolled around and this soldier received an envelope marked TOP SECRET! The big secret? There was going to be a Chanukah party! The Jewish soldiers in his division and the neighboring division were invited. He described how he gathered in the middle of the Saudi desert about 300 kilometers from anywhere with about a dozen other Jewish soldiers to celebrate Chanukah. Then he hastened to add, "I'm not an observant Jew, I'm not a religious guy, I'm not even sure I could say the blessings over the candles. But when a Jewish chaplain arrived after driving across an empty desert to be with us, lit the menorah candles with us, said the blessing, and then served us potato latkes and gefilte fish, it was one of the most powerful spiritual Jewish experiences of my life… in part because I was there in Saudi Arabia with my fellow Jews."

This is a dramatic example of how Jewish Peoplehood and Spirituality can overlap and occur at the same time. In my experience, most Jews live with an awareness of the Peoplehood circle… a feeling that there are differences between them and their non-Jewish neighbors and that they share things in common with other Jews. Even the most nonpracticing, disconnected Jew feels the Peoplehood circle if an anti-Semite gets on the media and attacks Jews. The response from them or almost any Jew is, "Hey! You are talking about me and *my people* and I don't like what you are saying!" Having a sense of the other two circles—Spirituality and Ethics—is not as obvious for most Jews.

No matter where on the diagram Jews find themselves living, the ultimate goal of Judaism would be for all three of these circles to overlap, one atop the other, at all times and appear as a single ring rather than Olympic rings. When they do, a Jew feels a connection to Jewish Ethics, Jewish Spirituality, and Jewish Peoplehood simultaneously. This is much easier said than done.

This leads me back to this book. I can categorize all of the questions, comments, emotions, and searching that have been emailed to me into one, two, or all three of the following categories:

- **How do I behave? How can I find** *Ethical* **guidance in Judaism...** from an ancient tradition and way of life that could not have anticipated the challenges and complexities of modern life?

- **How and what do I believe? How can I find faith and gain** *Spiritual* **nourishment from Judaism...** in a high-tech world that runs on science and offers many competing spiritual options, from Buddhism to communing with nature?

- **How do I belong? How can I understand and connect to Jewish** *Peoplehood...* in a world where most people are not Jewish?

Behaving, Believing, and Belonging, "the three Bs," are the three components of the Jewish way of life according to the twentieth-century scholar Rabbi Mordecai Kaplan. I call the three components ESP. Traditionally, Judaism has called them Torah, God, and Israel. Whatever you call them, every aspect of Jewish life can fit into one, two, or all three of the circles.

Sex, God, and Christmas

The three major sections of this book therefore are Ethics, Spirituality, and Peoplehood. In each section, the chapters are based on an email someone sent me and a public response I wrote in my syndicated column. As I mentioned earlier, after my columns were published or posted online, they generated follow-up emails from other readers who reacted to the original email or my response.

In this book, then, after each column, you will see a cross-section of the follow-up emails that I received after people read my column. They are a response to my response. Something of a modern day Talmud, as my mother would say, though the writers and I are not rabbis and sages. Again, I invite you to respond as well by emailing me through www.BeingJewish.org.

Sometimes the writers of follow-up emails offered words of support or advice to the original writer, which I often forwarded to the original writer. Other than that, most of these additional emails have never been seen by anyone else before now. At the end of each chapter, I offer some closing thoughts in a section called: Concluding Thoughts to Copy, Cut, Paste and Save.

In the section on Ethics, you will find chapters that deal with behavior — for example, sexual behavior. The Spirituality section has chapters that relate to belief in God and accessing spirituality. The Peoplehood section examines what "belonging" means by exploring such issues as the celebration of Christmas. Of course, sex, God, and Christmas are just a few of the many topics covered under the headings of Ethics, Spirituality, and Peoplehood.

Because the topics of many columns touch more than one of the three circles, they could easily be placed in one section or another. This is not really a problem, though, since Judaism does not make a clear distinction between the circles. In other words, the goal of Judaism would be that Ethics, Spirituality, and Peoplehood should always lead to each other in a kind of endless feedback loop. Put differently, ideally, at all times Jews are supposed to behave ethically, motivated by belief in God and a sense of belonging to the Jewish people.

That's in theory, anyway. In practice, for most Jews, this does not happen very often or at all. Sometimes only one circle is involved, sometimes two (as in the story of the Jewish soldier in Saudi Arabia), and sometimes all three. So as I tried to decide which column belonged in which section of the book, I was faced with an editorial challenge. For example, the column about Jews getting tattoos could appear in both the Peoplehood and the Ethics sections. So I'll tell you up front that many of these editorial decisions are not clear-cut.

But this editorial challenge is similar to the challenge of leading a Jewish life. Life is not easily compartmentalized. Neither are the issues facing a person trying to make the ancient way of life of Judaism relevant to and compatible with the modern world. Many questions that people ask may seem new and indeed they are. Many others deal with the basic human condition and really have been asked in one form or another for thousands of years by Jews and non-Jews. Either way, this book attempts to give voice to the people out there and their questions. At the same time, the book attempts to show Judaism's relevance and ability to answer modern-day questions... asked in a new and most modern of ways: via the Internet.

To Get the Most from Your Reading

I'd like to make one final point before you begin reading the columns and emails I've been describing. Many people are loose when using labels to describe Jews. They use terms such as observant, religious, secular, affiliated, unaffiliated, core, periphery, Reform, Conservative, Reconstructionist, and Orthodox. From my work online, I've come to the conclusion that these labels are misleading, loaded, narrow, and often not helpful. Again, this is not a book about Jews disconnected or unaffiliated from Judaism. Rather, the email shows a hunger expressed by Jews of all kinds, as well as non-Jews, for Judaism to provide understanding, meaning, guidance and relevance.

So whether you are Jewish or not, please read on, with an eye for what you have in common with the people who have written and for how you differ. As I've read the thousands of emails I've received over the years, I've tried not to be judgmental. Instead, I've tried to invest my energies in understanding the writer. In the process, I've learned a great deal about others and myself. I hope the same holds true for you.

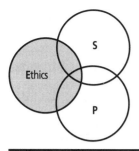

Section I: Ethics

Going online for help when making decisions is routine: deciding about stock or financial questions, researching a medical issue, choosing a hotel in another city, finding the best air fare, doing homework, etc.

But these are nuts-and-bolts issues. Do you look to the Internet to help decide ethically what is right and what is wrong?

In our day to day lives, we're challenged by many ethical questions: how to treat friends, enemies, acquaintances, strangers, employers, employees, customers, parents, children, relatives, animals, the environment, our society, our community, and so on. In grappling with these kinds of issues, we look for ethical guidance from our upbringing, the laws of the land, our religious background, and our personal faith system.

This section is about the phenomenon of people searching for this kind of guidance on the Internet. There are many places on the Internet where one might look — religious websites, chat rooms, "Ask a Rabbi" features, and so on. This section describes situations where someone was struggling with a dilemma, wondering about their options, or torn between choices, and approached me via email to pose a question or share their opinion.

Some writers were torn between a choice offered by the freedom of a western democracy and a differing choice suggested by Judaism — for example, the freedom to tattoo and pierce one's body. Or they may have been confused between different choices offered within Judaism — for example, different intermarriage practices in the various Jewish religious movements. Others may simply have been curious about a given situation and wanted to know what behavior would be ethical according to Judaism—for example, asking about Jewish sexual conduct.

I've found all this probing most intriguing because so much has been said and written about Jews abandoning Judaism. Some of these Jews write off ancient Judaism as having nothing relevant to contribute to a modern world. After all, today, unlike "the olden days" when the ethical guidelines of Judaism were first articulated, women have a different place in society, we have electricity, cars, refrigeration, modern medicine and science, etc. Many conditions of modern life bear little resemblance to the days of old when rabbis and sages promulgated most Jewish law—law that was based on Jewish ethics. Given these changed conditions, is it any wonder that some would contend that Judaism is out of date and out of touch?

My experience writing, lecturing, and communicating online leads me to a different conclusion: many Jews and non-Jews, regardless of their level of faith or religious observance, are interested in knowing what Judaism has to say about modern life situations. The emails in this section are evidence of this. They show that although Jewish ethics may be thousands of years old, many people today still seek guidance from Judaism. These emails are from people who at a minimum want to understand and at a maximum want to incorporate Jewish thinking about ethical behavior into their lives.

These emails speak to the following: How should I behave? How can I find ethical guidance in Judaism... from an ancient tradition and way of life that could not have anticipated the challenges and complexities of modern life? Each chapter in this section is a life situation or challenge that asks these questions in a different form. Here are the chapters in the Ethics section:

Bizarre Jewish Sex?
Can Jews Donate Their Organs?
I Will Not Circumcise My Son!
Body Piercing, Tattoos, and More!
Jews, Blacks, and Prejudice
Are Jewish Teens Immoral Today?
My Rabbi's in Love With Me and I'm Married!
Unknown Things About Rabbis

Chapter 1
Bizarre Jewish Sex?

Dear Gil:

I have been asked by many non-Jewish friends about a practice in which Jewish people have sex through a hole in a sheet. Is this an actual practice with some Jews, or just another example of a false Jewish stereotype?

J

Dear J:

"Sex through a hole in a sheet?" Anybody who would hear something like this about Jews would have to wonder about us!

Judaism's attitude toward sex is between two extremes. Judaism rejects the extreme of "anything goes" and also rejects the opposite extreme that sex is dirty or sinful. Instead Judaism imposes numerous restrictions on sexual relations, but also promotes regular sex between a husband and wife as healthy, worthy of enjoyment and a *mitzvah* (an affirming commandment.)

As for sex through a hole in a sheet, I must confess I had never heard anything like that so I began to investigate. Tracking down information was not easy. Ultimately, I contacted six different rabbis. All six of them said they knew next to nothing about the practice — FYI, four of the rabbis were Orthodox. One of the Orthodox rabbis told me he'd never heard of it.

The other five rabbis told me they had heard some mention of this practice but that is about it. None of the rabbis had ever known anybody who actually practiced "hole in the sheet sex."

Since I was already on the subject, I asked further, what would be the rationale for this kind of sex? None of the rabbis knew. One guessed that it might have something to do with modesty or *tzinyut* since sex in the dark or at night is encouraged by some sources for modesty reasons. Another rabbi thought it might be some form of *negiah* taken to the nth degree. *Negiah* is a part of Jewish tradition that prohibits physical contact between a husband and wife if she is menstruating.

Three of the rabbis told me that in their opinion, this alleged sheet practice would actually be a violation of Jewish law! One told me that Jewish law encourages full contact between a husband and a wife and even grants the wife permission to request full body contact... a sheet in the way would obviously cause a problem!

Just to add a little (more) humor to this mystery, one rabbi told me that he speculated that this rumor may be a result of non-Jews seeing *tzitzit* hanging from the clothesline and assuming it was a sheet with a hole in it. (*Tzitzit* are the undershirt-like garments with fringes on the four corners that many observant Jewish men wear beneath their shirt.)

Rabbi number six I spoke to had the most plausible explanation to me. After racking his brain he called me back to say that perhaps the rumor comes from a little known Jewish divorce law that speaks of a spouse only willing to have sex through a sheet. This is considered so bad that the other partner can cite "the sheet" as grounds for divorce — with no financial remuneration! In other words the law condemns such behavior.

In conclusion, apparently having sex through a sheet is not practiced by Jews and indeed is a false stereotype. I am surprised that you say "many" non-Jews have asked you about this practice since all six of the rabbis barely knew what I was talking about when I asked them. Things in the rumor mill about what we Jews do must be getting pretty slow!

If anybody out there can shed any more light on this subject, I welcome your emails. I suppose now I will receive all kinds of mail with questions and comments on the subject of Judaism and sex. I am sure I won't be bored!

Thanks for writing,

Gil

Email Responses to "Bizarre Jewish Sex?"

Subj: "holy" sheet
Date: 4/28 09:14:03 PM CDT
From:
To: GilMann@aol.com

I had been wondering if this question would be brought up, and sure enough it has. I remember hearing about this so-called "sexual aide for the Orthodox" when I was about 8 or 9 years old — I am now 38! I also have asked many Rabbis — Reform, Conservative and Orthodox about this during the past 30 yrs, and none of them knew of this as being anything more than a rumor either. It's just one of those dreaded "urban legends," but with a Judaic twist!

:)

Subj: Sex through sheets
Date: 5/6/ 9:42:20 PM CDT
From:
To: GilMann@aol.com

I heard somewhere (I don't remember where) that the bogus legend can be traced to the frum [very religious] neighborhoods in Williamsburg earlier this century, where everyone in the tenements hung their laundry on clothes lines outside. New arrivals to the neighborhood would see the Tallis Katan — Arba Kanfos [these are the Tzitzit undergarments referred to in the column] hanging out to dry with their large head hole and strings hanging. Not knowing anything about this traditional garb of the Orthodox, they assumed it was some sort of night clothes and the hole was for sex!

As plausible as the other sources for the rumor.

Initialed

Subj: hole in one
Date: 4/29 6:05:37 PM CDT
From:
To: GilMann@aol.com

The first time I had ever heard of the "hole-in-the-sheet-sex" was when I spent a memorable summer in Crown Heights [home of an Orthodox sect of Judaism, Lubavitch Chasidic Jews]. Need I say more? Actually, I had also heard it from a friend of mine before she got married, we joked about it, and that's what I gave her for a wedding gift... embroidered of course!

My understanding was that it was practiced mostly by Chasidic couples... but not Lubovich, and it had to do with always thinking of something higher, and not to get caught up in the physical appearance, even when copulating. It could have been the way I had interpreted the meaning, but that's all I can offer! I think it was only for the wedding night... but I can't remember.

Subj: (no subject)
Date: 5/9 9:55:30 PM CDT
From:
To: GilMann@aol.com

Dear Gil,

Although not an expert on sex, I do have some info on different religions and cultures. For years people have always asked me about Jews and the sheet. It is not us, however it could be the Mormons. I was a psychotherapist, and years ago I had a client who was raised in the Mormon faith. She recommended a book written by a female member and there is mention of that practice, as well as the fact they wear a religious garment that has openings in various places. I think the book was called "Secret Ceremony." Again, in the middle east it is common for them to hang the sheet out so people can see the blood stain, so people will know the bride was a virgin.

Hope that helps.

Name, LCSW (Licensed, Certified Social Worker)

Subj: Hole in the sheet...
Date: 5/6 7:24:39 PM CDT
From:
To: GilMann@aol.com

I, too, have been asked many times about Jews having sex through a hole in the sheet by my non-Jewish friends. It amazes me everytime I hear it, and all I can do is laugh and emphatically tell them that this is something that I have never heard from any Jew I know, nor is it my practice.

I have talked with Ultra-Orthodox Jewish women who have told me that according to their husbands and Kaballah [Jewish Mysticism], sex is a mitzvah [positive commandment] and is to be enjoyed. I have been told that there are even instructions in the Kaballah for a husband to properly arouse his wife prior to the actual act in order for her to be gratified.

Sincerely, Name

Subj: hole in the sheet
Date: 4/29 6:10:24 PM CDT
From:
To: GilMann@aol.com

Actually I have heard of the practice, but it was about one of the very strict, early, religions here in America. I believe it was one of the Amish, or some such sects, that were beyond our current understanding of modesty between the sexes.

My family background is Pennsylvania Dutch and the verbal traditions of old practices were both rich and varied. How much was truth or fairy tale you could never be sure, a lot depended on who was telling the story.

Subj: hole in the sheet
Date: 4/29 11:17:07 PM CDT
From:
To: GilMann@aol.com

Hi Gil,

I am studying to become a Jew by choice. I heard about "hole in the sheet sex" ages ago, before I became interested in Judaism. At the time I assumed & hoped(!) it was mis-information/rumor. (After all, I rationalized, Dr. Ruth is Jewish!)

I do not even recall where I heard about it, but it WAS linked to tzinut [modesty]... the rumor was that chassidim (specifically women who follow the rules of modest dress) covered themselves even during sex, resorting to a hole in a sheet...

Was SO relieved to know after I began investigating that this is, as you point out, completely contrary to Jewish law.

Name

Subj: Hole in the sheet.
Date: 5/1 11:12:17 PM CDT
From:
To: GilMann@aol.com

Gil,

I am an Orthodox Jew. I have had Jewish friends, other than Orthodox ask me about the "hole in the sheet." Although I am patient in answering I find this "stereotype" to be as obnoxious as all the others including running after money, cheating in business and eating blood on Pesach [Passover]. (Been asked that question by a non-Jewish co-worker).

Name

Subj: Hole in the Sheet Sex
Date: 5/2 12:29:27 AM CDT
From:
To: GilMann@aol.com

Dear Gil,

While I admit I had never heard of this practice in Judaism, I have heard of it before. I saw the practice in a movie Como Agua Para Chocolate (Like Water For Chocolate) which is a spanish movie but has English subtitles. My spanish teacher told me that some old spanish customs had a newly married couple use a hole in the sheet for their first night together. Well just thought you would like to know, adios.

Subj: Hole in the sheet
Date: 5/5 05:10:15 PM CDT
From:
To: GilMann@aol.com

This practice was mentioned in a book by Naomi Ragen. The person who instigated the hole in the sheet sex was an obsessive compulsive, who had been forced into marriage by his parents. The conclusion reached was that he was actually asexual and hated contact with a woman.

This was the first time I had ever encountered anything like this, and it certainly is not common practice among the Jewish people.

Note from Gil: A number of writers sent emails like the one above, so I contacted Naomi Ragen to inquire. Below is her response to me.

Subj: Hole in the sheet
Date: 5/4 11:17:04 PM CDT
From: Naomi Ragen (name used with permission)
To: GilMann@aol.com

Dear Gil,

My, my! Such interest in such a subject. Well, I personally heard of this only when I moved to Jerusalem in 1971. A friend of mine who lived there mentioned it to me as the practice of an ultra-Orthodox Chassidic sect. It certainly was not the norm in any way. And even the ultra-Orthodox deny it exists. However, since there are ultra-Orthodox sects which insist that there be minimum physical contact even during intercourse (because intercourse is a holy act, a mitzvah [fulfillment of a Biblical commandment] for the purpose of procreation and shouldn't be sullied by impure thoughts or deeds), insist on total darkness, and an hour close to midnight, and forbid various kinds of intimate contact, even between husband and wife, I wouldn't be surprised if some of them take it a bit further and interpose a sheet between the couple. But there is no way to verify this. Obviously, a sect so fanatic wouldn't admit any aspect of their personal life.

In my opinion this custom — if it exists at all — is another one of those that creeped into Judaism from the Middle Ages from the non-Jewish world, where sex was held as a sin and necessary evil. Authentic Judaism has always had an earthy, healthy attitude towards marital relations. According to the Rambam [the famous sage Rabbi Moses ben Maimon or Maimonides]: Anything that goes on between a husband and wife is permissible.

Hope this helps,

Naomi Ragen (You might want to check out my book, Jephte's Daughter)

Concluding Thoughts to Copy, Cut, Paste, and Save

As you can see, the email I received about this mystery contained many bits and pieces of clues. The most likely of these is Naomi Ragen's book, but even she acknowledges that her book is based on something she heard but can't document. Amazing how rumors can take on a life of their own.

Armed with the Ragen reference, I approached a Chassidic rabbi and asked him what the story was. Basically, he told me the practice is total nonsense... as did his wife! They told me they have heard this rumor for years and really don't know where it came from.

Of course, this is pretty much what I wrote in my original response — but many readers encouraged me to talk to a Chassidic Jew to find out the "true" story. One of the rabbis I spoke with the first time around was Chassidic. So if you are keeping count, that is two Chassidic rabbis and one Chassidic wife, among others, who have debunked this sheet myth.

So there you have it: Jews having sex through a sheet is a major league rumor!!! The source is perhaps Amish, Spanish, or Jewish. What do they have in common? The syllable "-ish!" This is also the first syllable of the word *ishkabibbel*, which is a good summary of what I have discovered.

The one thing that was clear from all the email I received and the contacts I made is that nobody — I repeat, NOBODY — actually knew of any human of any religion, nationality, or tribe that practiced hole-in-the-sheet sex.

So what can be learned from this "hole" mess? I conclude that we should all endeavor to avoid listening to and passing on stereotypes and rumors. Tempting as it is to speak about others, doing so is not wise, is often destructive, and for good measure, is against Jewish law.

Unintentionally, in my efforts to clear up this mystery, I fear I may have added to the rumor mill. I hope not—I certainly do not want to leave the impression that the Amish, Spanish, Mormons, or anybody else have sex through a hole in a sheet.

A point worth concluding with and reiterating from my original response is the Jewish attitude toward sex. Judaism places restrictions on sexual behavior but definitely does not view sex between married couples as sinful or dirty. On the contrary, Judaism views sex between a husband and wife as positive, healthy, and worthy of enjoyment. I hope this puts this hole-in-the-sheet business to bed—sorry about the pun :) !

Chapter 2
Can Jews Donate Their Organs?

Dear Gil:

I am interested in donating my organs when the time comes but I heard that as part of the Jewish religion we were not allowed. I have been looking everywhere for an answer about Jewish beliefs. Do you have any idea?

P

Dear P:

I must start by wishing you a long and healthy life and that "the time does not come" anytime soon... unless you are talking about donating blood marrow or one of your kidneys! But I am glad you have asked such an important question.

There is a widespread misconception held by many Jews that organ transplantation is prohibited by Jewish law. In a study done in the Toronto Jewish community, the most often cited reason for not signing an organ donation card was that the Jewish religion forbids such an act.

Guess what? They are wrong. There are requirements within Judaism about showing respect to the body after death. Specifically to bury the body as soon as possible and not to mutilate or benefit from the body. But this has not stopped Conservative, Orthodox, Reconstructionist, and Reform rabbis from endorsing the concept of organ transplant. For the most part, the rationale is based on the Jewish law of *pekuach nefesh*... the saving of a life.

The law of *pekuach nefesh* REQUIRES that almost all Jewish law MUST be violated if necessary to save a life! Obviously transplanting an organ can save a life. The main question is when does death of the donor occur, according to Jewish law. The Jewish definition of death "is the absence of spontaneous respiration in patients with no other signs of life." A person who is brain dead and kept alive only by machines fits the Jewish definition of dead.

Two sad but inspiring Jewish donors are Joseph Kroot of Kentucky and Alisa Flatow of New Jersey. I use the present tense because although Joseph and Alisa have passed away, they and their families continue to give in the form of teaching other Jews about organ transplants. Both Joseph and Alisa were young when their lives ended and both of their parents consulted with rabbis before making the decision to donate parts of their children's bodies so that others might benefit and live.

The Kroots have used the loss of their son, their decision, and the fact that six living people benefited from donations from Joseph as an opportunity to teach other Jews about Judaism's positions on organ transplant. On the Internet, they have posted pages in memory of their son with a wealth of information. To read more, on the web, go to: www.transweb.org/reference/articles/religion/shalomarticle.html.

On one such page, they write: "We know that Joseph did not live a long life, but his life was full. He was kind, generous, a little impish, and Jewish. He could not read well, but his corneas are now reading. He didn't find the cure to cancer, but he did follow the Jewish mitzvah of *pekuach nefesh* and 'saved lives.' We are reminded of... the Talmudic saying, 'He, who saves a life, saves the world.' What an honor for our Joseph."

Similarly, the parents of Alisa made the decision to donate organs from her body. In the process, they educated the entire State of Israel and many others elsewhere about Jewish teaching about organ transplantation.

Alisa was an American student studying in Israel when she became the victim of a terrorist attack in 1995. Like Joseph, tissue from Alisa was donated to six people on the transplant waiting list. "People have called it a brave decision, a righteous decision, a courageous decision. To us it was simply the right thing to do at the time," said her father. Their decision had a huge emotional and educational impact on a grieving Israel. Personally, I was also deeply moved especially upon hearing the words of tribute spoken by Prime Minister Yitzchak Rabin six months after her death, when he said "Alisa Flatow's heart beats in Jerusalem."

When a person dies, traditionally, Jews often say *zichrono leevracha* —may their memory be a blessing. To me, the memories of Joseph Kroot *z"l* and Alisa Flatow *z"l* are blessings [*z"l* is an abbreviation for *zichrono leevracha*]. I hope learning about them, their parents, and Judaism's attitude about transplants will motivate you and everyone else who reads these words to talk to your family and then do as I have done: designate yourself as a donor on your driver's license or a donor card. Thanks for writing.

Gil

Email Responses to "Can Jews Donate Their Organs?"

Subj: organ donation
Date: 3/25/1:37:12 PM CST
From:
To: GilMann@aol.com

As a registered nurse working in Transplant Research I applaud your column on the donation of organs. i urge every family to discuss this important subject before it ever becomes an issue, in order to know their loved ones desires. Every day I see the difference a functioning kidney can make in the life of a person with end stage renal disease.

Name, RN, CDE
Transplant Research Coordinator
Name Medical Center

Subj: JEWISH Organ Donation
Date: 3/30 9:17:50 PM CST
From:
To: GilMann@aol.com

In late January of 1996, our daughter returned to this country from her work in Africa to attend a special 30th birthday party for her brother, and our son, Bruce.

She was unable to locate her license and went to the Registry to obtain another. While there, she noted the forms there encouraging people to become organ donors. She returned home with all the information , and when all of our family was together that evening, she said that this was something we should all consider doing, the saving of another person's life .

Little did we know that within a few days, our family would be confronted with having to make this decision. Bruce on February lst, only days before his 30th birthday party, came down with viral meningitis, and in only 1 1/2 days was declared brain dead. When the Dr. asked if we would consider organ donation, as a family, we had already discussed this, and gave our consent immediately, because we knew this is what he would have wanted. To honor our son Bruce, we donated his liver and both kidneys. Our story does not end here, we heard anonymously from all the recipients that their operations were successful. Later we heard that one of the kidney recipients had to go back on dialysis.

However, the young man who received Bruce's liver indicated that he felt so well, that he would like to meet us, to thank us person-ally for giving him back his life, as his condition had been very poor. We arranged to meet, a strange feeling at first for all of us.

We found ourselves telling him that we felt somehow he belonged to us., and he felt the same. He is a fine young man and we are proud that our son Bruce's liver has given him the opportunity to start his own optometry business and to get married. He has vowed to let everyone know the value of organ donation, he has given numerous talks, and soon because he feels so well, he will enter the U.S. Transplant Games.

I thought you would be interested in another story about a young Jewish man's donation of his liver and kidneys which we felt were very much in accordance with Jewish Laws.

The Baron Family of Longmeadow, MA

(Name used with permission. Please note epilogue under "Concluding Thoughts to Copy, Cut, Paste, and Save" at the end of this chapter.)

Subj: Organ transplant
Date: 3/26 9:30:26 PM CST
From:
To: GilMann@aol.com

Dear Gil:

I want to thank you for bringing this important mitzvah [positive commandment] to light for many readers who were previously under the misconception that you dealt with. As a rabbi, I am often explaining to people the very issues you presented.

Todah [thank you],
Rabbi Name
State

Subj: donor
Date: 3/31 7:30:30 AM CST
From:
To: GilMann@aol.com

Dear Gil,

Bravo! As a Jewish RN in a busy Emergency Department, I applaud your discussing this very important topic. I was unaware of the websites you mentioned and I will be browsing them for information I can post in my department to help others decide on this very important issue.

Thank you for putting this topic on the table! I hope many others decide to sign their licenses or donor cards!

Name

Subj: Organ transplant
Date: 3/24 8:40:06 AM CST
From:
To: GilMann@aol.com

Yasher Koach [strength to you]

Thank you for this very important column. It brought a lump to my throat.

Name

PS Perhaps it would be worth noting that while all "denominations" favor organ donation "to save a life," organ donation for research purposes does not directly save a life, and is probably not consistent with Halacha [Jewish law].

Subj: organ transplants
Date: 3/30 8:51:33 PM CST
From:
To: GilMann@aol.com

You are perfectly correct in stating that organ transplantation even to the majority of the Orthodox world is not only permissible but obligatory (there are those like the Agudah [Orthodox organization] which say it is forbidden) however that is not a carte blanc to fill out a state organ donor card. As a hospital chaplain and organ procurement requestor I can tell you that if you follow halacha you can not fill out the state cards because of how they allow harvesting in ways that are not in accordance with Halacha.

Rabbi Name
Director, Pastoral Care and Chaplaincy Services
Hospital Name

Subj: Transplants
Date: 3/31 10:39:05 PM CST
From:
To: GilMann@aol.com

I am Jewish and live in Manchester England and am recipient of liver in transplant last year. I have never had a view on the religious aspect and will ask my own Rabbi and am interested in references on the subject

regards
Name

Subj: Donated Organs and the Death Process
Date: 4/2 2:31:26 PM CDT
From:
To: GilMann@aol.com

Thank you for your advice and clarity.

Shouldn't we leave the natural processes of G*d to happen as it was meant to be? I don't know of any species whose organs are reused after the death of life.

Initialed

Subj: donor
Date: 3/31 10:28:30 AM CST
From:
To: GilMann@aol.com

I have never questioned whether or not i should donate my organs after death. To me this is an inner law of aiding others in any way that I can. I am a devout jew and I understand that there are laws about the body. I see it, however, as the soul is the most important part of the person and that the body is shed when the soul no longer has use for it. Thus if any part of my body can aid in the life journey of another it is my duty to give this gift to help my world family. Thank you for enlightening me on the halachic choices. Now I can inform my family members that didn't believe in my decision.

Name

Concluding Thoughts to Copy, Cut, Paste, and Save

The trauma and blessing of organ donation are difficult to reduce to words, especially for those of us who have not experienced the life-and-death issues transplantation forces families to confront.

I had follow-up exchanges with two of the families mentioned in this chapter after our original contact by email, and I want to end by sharing those stories. The first story involves the family of Joseph Kroot, the 13-year-old whose parents created a website to educate others about Jewish views of organ donation.

One of the places that posted my column was a website based in Israel called www.virtualjerusalem.com. After my column was posted, a woman emailed me and asked if I minded if she translated the column into Spanish. I said, of course she could and just asked if she would send it to me when she finished, because, though I do not speak Spanish, I thought seeing it would be neat. I gave the request no further thought and did not even note where the woman lived.

Some time later, I received an email telling me the column was now translated and I could see it posted on the web. I looked it up and, to my amazement, read my column in Spanish appearing on the website of a synagogue in Costa Rica! I immediately emailed Joseph Kroot's mother in Kentucky and told her that through the miracle of the Internet, from Kentucky to me in Minneapolis to Jerusalem and now Costa Rica, Joseph's life continues to touch lives all over the planet. I find this spiritual.

The second story is about the Baron family of Longmeadow, Massachusetts, whose email is the second response in this chapter. When I was working on this book, I thought publishing their actual names would add an impactful reality that would be important and valuable. They graciously granted me permission to use their names, saying that if publishing their email "can in some way encourage more people to become organ donors, this would make us very happy." Then they told me a remarkable story about the loss of their beloved son Bruce that may indeed encourage others.

As they noted in their email, some time after their son passed away, they had the opportunity to meet the recipient of Bruce's liver—a gentleman of 35, the same age Bruce would have been. The liver he received saved his life, and he was then so physically fit that he planned to enter the Transplant Olympics—an athletic competition for transplant recipients. He telephoned the Barons from the Olympics to tell them that not only did he compete, but he won three gold medals and dedicated one to Bruce, one to Bruce's mother, and one to Bruce's father, saying that he would be grateful forever for the gift of life that they had given him.

As noted in the beginning of this chapter, in Judaism, when describing someone who has passed away, we say, "May their memory be a blessing" (*zichrono leevracha*). Hopefully in this chapter you have seen that organ donation is such a blessing, both spiritually and physically. It is also a fulfillment of one of the highest directives in Judaism—to save human life—even if other

Jewish laws must be violated. If you'd like additional guidance about organ donation and Judaism, Hadassah, the Jewish women's organization, has information. Hadassah has local chapters in many cities around the country. To find the one nearest you, call the national office at 800-664-5646 or go to Hadassah's website: www.hadassah.org.

Chapter 3
I Will Not Circumcise My Son!

Dear Gil:

One topic wasn't covered in your book and I'm curious about your opinion on it. I have a real problem with circumcision and I am not going to circumcise my sons (assuming I have some). Here's why I am against it.

1. I believe in autonomy. I have the right to control my own body. I can have an abortion when I want, have a baby, get plastic surgery, get sterilized, etc., etc., I would be one hell of a hypocrite if I was a staunch supporter of autonomy for myself but then took away my son's autonomy.

2. To quote my Indian ex-boyfriend, "Any religion that says in order to be one of us you have to cut off part of your son's penis is not a religion I want to be a part of."

3. The Bible is fables, written by men (who weren't that educated) so anything in it needs to be taken with a grain of salt.

4. Nowadays, since everyone takes a shower every day and properly cleans themselves, there is no health benefit to a circumcision. 100 years ago when people showered once a year, then sure, it was healthier.

When my son is old enough to understand the ramifications of the situation, then he can make the decision for himself and I'll support it. My current boyfriend (who I will probably marry) agrees with me. I'm curious how you would have responded to this if you were interviewing me for your book.

Thanks

N

Dear N:

Your letter reminded me of a cartoon I once saw that shows Abraham talking to the sky and the caption reads: "Let me get this straight: you want us to cut off a piece of our WHAT?!"

There was a time in my life when I thought of the ritual of a circumcision or *bris* to be barbaric and primitive. I came to this conclusion at the age of 18 when I decided to get a front-row seat at the *bris* of a cousin of mine. I am not sure what possessed me to do this since the sight of blood from a tiny scratch can make me ill. And sure enough, that is what happened to me. In addition, the experience made me seriously question the entire practice.

I have had two boys and I can tell you their circumcisions were extremely emotional and difficult for me to endure and I think were even more so for my wife. And if I had to do it again... I most definitely would!

In my experience, a *bris* appears to trouble most people on some level. The maternal instinct seems to give many women at least some degree of hesitation about a *bris.* Every man I have ever met has more than a few negative thoughts about tinkering with this rather sensitive part of our bodies—your Indian ex-boyfriend and Abraham in the cartoon are good examples. And any man or woman with an ounce of compassion has a strong reaction to the sight and sound of a baby in pain.

Given all of this, why am I in favor of performing a *bris*? Because of a second and more important reaction that I have observed at *bris* after *bris.* I have surmised that those of us assembled who witness a *bris* and hear the baby cry would like to do one of two things— beat up the *mohel* (the guy doing the cuttin'), or cuddle and comfort the baby... and his parents.

We want to protect this baby as if he were ours. And I think that is the whole point: he is ours! He is a member of our community, our people, our extended family. We often speak of a mother bonding with her baby. Through a *bris* I believe as a community, we bond with this child on a most primitive, emotional, tangible, and important level.

Now you mention in your letter that the Bible consists of fables that need to be taken with a grain of salt. I don't have the space here to discuss the validity of the Bible.** Even if I did, nowhere in the Torah is any explanation given beyond a circumcision being a symbol of the covenant between God and the Jewish people (the word *bris* or *brit* means covenant). My response to your point is that a *bris* is the oldest ritual in Judaism. For countless generations, our people have followed this tradition. I wouldn't want to be the person to break this chain.

And while I respect your comments about having autonomy over our bodies and not wanting to be a hypocrite, I am sure glad my parents followed our people's tradition when I was eight days old… an event I blissfully do not remember at all. I sure would not have wanted to be given the privilege and autonomy of deciding for myself when I had a grown man's body! And as an adolescent, I would not want to grapple with the following: "Gee, I don't look like all the other Jewish guys at camp or in the locker room!"

In addition, parents do and must make decisions about their childrens' bodies. For example, you will not ask your child's input about breast-feeding or vaccinations — these too are questionable practices. A *bris* is beyond just a physical decision; it is an emotional and religious decision as well that I believe Jewish parents have a right and obligation to decide for their child.

As to your argument about health benefits, to me this never was, nor is, a Jewish rationale, and besides, in the medical world, the dispute continues as to possible benefits of circumcision.

Related to medical questions, I do want to say a couple more words about the pain. First, babies don't remember (though some dispute this), and many babies today get analgesic to remove pain. And even if this were not true, pain is not necessarily bad. In the case of a *bris*, the babies seem to do fine and I think the temporary pain we feel as a community about a boy's *bris* is healthy.

Or to put this last thought in the words of a cute greeting card: As Jews we celebrate the birth of a baby boy with a circumcision. All future birthdays are celebrated by eating cake!

Hope this has been of help and thanks for writing!

Gil

**PS I have written a couple of columns about believing the Bible.
You can read them on line here:
www.BeingJewish.org/jewishemail/resp1120.html and
www.BeingJewish.org/jewishemail/article46.html

Email Responses to "I Will Not Circumcise My Son!"

Subj: Circumcision
Date: 11/9 6:20:44 PM CST
From:
To: GilMann@aol.com

Dear Gil:

I take issue with your reasoning because the woman who wrote
to you was saying that this tradition is cruel to the baby boy.
Slavery has been a long held tradition. So has anti-Semitism.
Those are chains of tradition that still need breaking in many
parts of the world.

Subj: Circumcision
Date: 10/14 10:55:39 PM CDT
From:
To: GilMann@aol.com

Dear Gil:

Your answer was very appropriate. Unfortunately the author of
the e-mail doesn't understand her religion and is disconnected.

I am pasting an article referring to the medical issues pertaining
to circumcision. It is very interesting to note that the clotting
agent we possess is at its lifelong peak on the 8th day of life and
never reaches that level again. Hmmm, a coincidence? I think not!

Be well,
Name

www.innernet.org.il/article.php?aid=109

Subj: To Bris or Not to Bris.
Date: 10/15 3:18:14 AM CDT
From:
To: GilMann@aol.com

Dear Gil:

As an RN, I have witnessed a few circumcisions in the hospital
— those are the ones I find to be barbaric. They are done in a
procedure room, the infant is strapped down on a hard plastic
board and the techniques they use vary in length of time and
amount of discomfort. They are usually done by the OB/GYN,
occasionally by the pediatrician and almost never by a urologist.
I have participated in corrective surgeries for incomplete or bad
circumcisions — these procedures are the ones that make it to
the urologist.

A bris, however, is a ceremony — beautiful ceremony. It shows
to God and the world you are bringing another Jew into the
world — that you are still committed to being Jewish and
raising your children as Jews (to whatever extent you practice).
Yes, the actual "cutting" is uncomfortable, particularly to the
adult males in the room and to those who can not take the sight
of blood — the question of whether or not there is pain or how
much to the baby is also uncomfortable — but if you find the
'right' Rabbi or Mohel, the ceremony is very moving — the
naming that goes with the Bris is also a connection to our more
recent past — naming for a loved one who is no longer here on
earth, but always close to heart — the Bris is the connection
to our history as Jews — to all of our ancestors

I have had the circumcision conversation with friends and
colleagues who are not Jewish — it's difficult to explain the

importance of the Bris — to really give it a meaning they can understand, but I usually give the definition of the Brit. I also explain how my son was placed on a pillow, draped in cloth and held by my uncle. I then describe the naming ceremony and kind of lighten it with this: "At least in our religion, they get a drop of wine and a blessing."

I agree that looking like other Jewish boys and looking like his father is important

Name

Subj: Circumcision
Date: 10/15 3:50:25 AM CDT
From:
To: GilMann@aol.com

Dear Gil,

I am a retired Urologist 83 years old now. I "went through" Orthodox, Conservative, Reformed to Nonobservant. Notwithstanding this, I strongly and openly identify myself as a Jew. I was in active practice for 43 years.

The arguments pro and con circumcision are in the "abstract " as far as I am concerned, because of what I observed during that very active span:

1. Only uncircumcised men, or those men who, for various reasons, had circumcision done late in life, develop Cancer of the penis.

2. If you were to actually see a case, it would repel you, it is that horrible.

3. If you could be party to the mutilating and ineffective treatment, you would be horrified.

4. If you could witness the frustration, fear, consternation and revulsion the wife experiences during the course of her husband's affliction, you might well change your mind about circumcision.

Circumcision, if nothing else, insures that your sons will not be subject to such risks.

Incidentally, I have two grown sons, each of whom had a Brith Melah [another way in Hebrew to say circumcision]. I had been so appalled at the horrible results I had on occasion seen done by both Mohels and Physicians (which I was called upon to surgically revise), that I circumcised each of them myself.

I endorse ritual circumcision, if only as insurance!

Name, MD,
City, State

Subj: re: email of the week
Date: 10/15 7:48:51 AM CDT
From:
To: GilMann@aol.com

Hi,

I agree with the woman who chose not to circumcise her sons. I believe strongly in Jewish ritual and community. I am currently applying to Rabbinic school. However, I believe that it is essential to focus on the spirit of ritual and not just the letter of it. There are many other rituals in Torah that we have adapted or let go of. Some things like ritual sacrifice and circumcision seem to be antiquated.

I know many circumcised men who never give a second thought to the covenant between God and the Jewish people. Their behavior and their choices do not honor it. To me, this is far more important than the state of their penis. I believe that circumcision should be a choice. It is unfortunate that parents often value ritual over spirit.

Name

Subj: Bris
Date: 10/17 3:38:51 PM CDT
From:
To: GilMann@aol.com

I am a Reform Jew, and truly believe that not all man-written traditions apply to our lives today, but this one is a "mark" to be worn with pride and reverence to all those who came before us and especially of all those to come.

Subj: Bris
Date: 10/15 3:54:23 PM CDT
From:
To: GilMann@aol.com

Gil: I have to agree with the reader who contends that the raison de etre for the bris is no longer valid, due to the vast differences in sanitary practices then and now. Having been a "sondiker" [the honorary job at a Bris to give the baby a pacifier usually dipped in wine] for my grandson, he not only fought with all of his puny strength, but turned blue and passed out. I see no reason for it now, except for the Orthodox who's robotic answer is always, "It says in the bible —" Enough already!

Name

Subj: Bris
Date: 10/15 12:13:33 PM CDT
From:
To: GilMann@aol.com

Dear Gil,

It saddened me to read the letter of the week. Unfortunately it did not shock me. I am saddened that so many of our people think that the Torah is just fables written by some old uneducated men. What a tragedy that this woman has been denied the treasure of our Torah which was given to us by G-D

This topic is of special interest to me because, G-D willing we will be having a bris on Sun morn 10/17 for our 2nd son, 3rd child.

G-D bless you.
Name

Subj: Bris question
Date: 10/15 10:27:22 AM CDT
From:
To: GilMann@aol.com

Your questioner might, by application of logic develop a series of reasons to discontinue any aspect of Jewish observance. If that were an acceptable approach, and we accepted absolute democracy on all issues, I think that any of us can see we would pretty soon have so many acceptable interpretations of the traditions that we would have no common base. That would quickly lead to the end of the Jewish people.

Therefore, if the person is truly interested in being Jewish, thereby implying an interest in Jewish continuity, they should seriously reconsider the concept of unlimited individual autonomy regarding halachic [Jewish law] issues. I don't mean to imply that we don't change things, because we do, but that there is an accepted process that usually includes discourse amongst knowledgeable leaders of our community.

Name

Subj: to bris or not
Date: 10/15 2:56:14 AM CDT
From:
To: GilMann@aol.com

I've known several adult male converts to Judaism who needed more than just the pinprick of blood to satisfy the circumcision requirement. I would much rather shudder with the concept of the pain at 8 days, then to walk as gingerly as they had to for somewhat longer than three days. Having attended a fairly large number of them now, I know that with the current numbing gels that are available, the parents feel far more pain than the child. There have been a few without any outcry at all — or if there was, it was because the pacifier slipped, and not because of the cut.

Also, the mother is not commanded to do this. The father is. Predating the Oedipus complex concept by thousands of years, one subconscious reassurance for father -son relationships is that any of us "could" have pulled an Akeidah [the sacrifice of Isaac in the Bible] trick. Instead we bring our son into the covenant.

Subj: circumcision
Date: 10/26 12:24 AM CST
From:
To: GilMann@aol.com

hello

i'm a 40 jewish mother of 3 children... 1girl and 2 boys...

i just wanted to say that though i am jewish i did not circumcise my boys... i could not give them any pain that was not necessary. my God loves you no matter what... circumcised or not !!

and as far as being different... there are more and more people choosing not to circumcise!!!

i have made my decision and am truly at peace with it... and my sons are still jewish...

thanks for reading

Name

Subj: "Bris" of course
Date: 10/26/99 7:53 AM CST
From:
To: Gil Mann@aol.com

Dear Gil:

How many more "traditions" are we, as Jews going to break from?

You should also mention a recent study concerning the rise of Cancer of the cervix in jewish women... The conclusion being in the "sexual revolution" more jewish women had multiple sexual partners and not all were circumsized... leading to theory when jewish women had sex with circumsized jewish (or non) males that the incidence of this cancer was very low if it existed at all... Gives us food for thought on several levels doesn't it?

Name
City, State

Subj: circumcision
Date: 10/27 10:44 PM CST
From:
To: GilMann@aol.com

I saw the article about the women who did not want to circumcise her son. Though she has a right to her own decision, she is taking away from her sons life. As a Jew it is part of our culture and traditions and if and hopefully he wants to continue being Jewish and marry a Jewish woman he cannot marry her in the Jewish law. He cannot be called to the Torah either. reason for this is. That is what makes him part of the Jewish religion when a boy is 8 days old. Besides studies have shone that it is healthier and cleaner for a boy when he becomes a man... Also the sex is better.

I am now pregnant with my first child. And if it is a boy I WILL have him circumcised along with a bris. I think it is important to continue the Jewish traditions and if we don't who will. You are going to let Hitler win after almost 50 years. We have to marry Jewish and raise our children Jewish and let them continue the religion as Abraham set forth 5760 years ago. (OK with some modernism to it.)

Signed a very concerned Jew who worries about the continuation of Judaism.

Subj: To Bris or not to Bris
Date: 10/30 11:46 AM CST
From:
To: GilMann@aol.com

I am a Jewish female in an interfaith marriage. Recently, June in fact, I gave birth to a happy bouncy baby boy. To have a Bris was never a question in my mind. It is a covenant between GOD and the Jews and I would not want to break the chain.

My husband was very concerned and unsure of the Bris. He agreed to circumcise his son but, was concerned about the Bris — a party celebrating cutting a piece of his son.

Our son's Bris brought together members of my family that had not spoken in 5 years. It was a beautiful, meaningful ceremony. The mohel, Dr. Name, was wonderful. The ceremony included pieces of the bible and written verses from the heart. Aaron's family had the opportunity to write letters to Aaron about future hopes.

The emotions involved in the Bris — the family letters, etc. — overshadowed the main reason, the circumcision. If I had another son would I Bris? Absolutely!

Subj: To Have Or Not to Have a Bris
Date: 11/11 3:16 PM CST
From:
To: GilMann@aol.com

I was sad after reading the letter from the woman regarding not having a Bris for her not yet conceived child.

By having a non Jewish boyfriend she prepares herself for the eventual disassociation with traditional Judaism. First goes the Bris, then the Shul [synagogue], then the education. The people of the Bible had a very deep connection spiritually with Hashem [God, literally meaning The Name]. They believed in the importance of a family religion, Torah study, and the sanctity of Prayer and Mitzvoth [commandments]. These principles are what allowed us to survive.

Let us be honest. Reject the "core" of our belief and you are left with the "peel." I pray that G-d will sway her marriage choice to a committed Jew and that she waits to have children until she has committed to raising a Jewish child in a spiritually rich home.

Subj: Circumcision
Date: 12/9 6:55:44 PM CST
From:
To: GilMann@aol.com

I was concerned about the response that today sanitation precludes the need for circumcision as a health issue. For some reason, my mind goes back to Viet Nam, where men had to go weeks, maybe months without proper hygiene and suffered for it, especially their feet. Perhaps, so long as there are wars... there should be circumcision.

Subj: circumcision
Date: 12/3 8:57:16 PM CST
From:
To: GilMann@aol.com

dear Gil, There seems to me to be a strong relationship between body piercing, tattooing and circumcision. They have been used for tribal distinction for untold ages. Biblical Hebrew men had many rules of dress (fringed garments) and how wear their hair (not shave the corners of the beard) besides the circumcision to make them unique. This may have served as a deterrent to desertion because it was so in eradicable. Interestingly, the females, although they were chattel were not "branded."

Subj: Circumcision
Date: 11/12 7:37:34 AM CST
From:
To: GilMann@aol.com

As I rapidly approach the age of 60 next month, I humbly thank my life long Catholic father and mother (may they rest in peace) for having had me circumcised prior to bringing me home from the hospital. My parents raised me to be a free thinker and allowed me to search for a religion I could fully accept and live my life by. Over the years, I went from Catholic to Baptist, to Lutheran, and finally to Mormonism. Alas, there was none that didn't have any flaws or other things that I could not accept. Then I began to research Judaism after having witnessed the persecution of a well educated and experienced applicant for a teaching position in a local college. Now, after studying for 17 years, learning to read and write Hebrew and understanding the Hebrew in the Siddur [prayerbook] I am converting and having a Bar Mitzvah soon. I have to have only a token bris at the age of 60, but if necessary I would have the whole thing if that were what it took to be found worthy of being adopted into the tribe of Abraham.

Subj: Circumcision
Date: 11/24 8:55:37 PM CST
From:
To: GilMann@aol.com

I once asked a rabbi why is this procedure for binding ourselves to G-d performed on this spot of the body? He said that the site of the procedure is on the organ through which tremendous joy enters our lives and is also the place where the sperm comes out in order to create new life. My own thought is that this organ can be used for very good purposes and for very evil purposes. That by binding our baby boys to G-d through this ceremony/ surgery and by explaining to them as they grow up both poten-tials for this organ, that they will choose to use it properly.

Concluding Thoughts to Copy, Cut, Paste, and Save

This subject of circumcision generated as much or more mail than any subject I have written about over the years. What to make of this? I've tried to understand this strong response ever since.

Why did this topic catch your interest? Maybe that is part of the answer.

There is more than one reason, but here is the main conclusion I've reached: all of the attention is due to the area of the body we're discussing. Fifty percent of the world (the males) takes this subject VERY personally. Circumcised or not, it takes very little for guys to think of this part of our anatomy. The notion of cutting or hurting this sensitive organ will make most any man cringe and definitely gets our attention. Then there is the other fifty percent of the world — who usually have at least some interest in this appendage. In addition, most women cringe as well at the thought of their baby enduring any physical pain.

I've read explanations that Jews were asked to make circumcision a sign of their covenant with God precisely because we are especially mindful of this part of the human physique. In addition, the penis is a critical and tangible element in the reproductive cycle. What would be a more obvious place to mark that Jews, from generation to generation, should have a unique relationship with God?

Rabbi Yitz Greenberg explains that circumcision is an unavoidable reminder to Jewish men that they have a commitment to behave in holy ways prescribed by God in the Bible. Circumcision prevents Jews from hiding from that duty by posing as "ordinary" people.

What about Jewish women, you may be wondering? First, there is the traditional Jewish explanation that women do not need this outward physical "reminder" because they are naturally more holy than men. This theme is elaborated on in the chapter called "Why Does Judaism Discriminate Against Women?"

But beyond that, in modern times, an equivalent ceremony has become commonplace for Jewish baby girls. The ceremony is called a baby naming and does not involve placing any physical mark on the girls. The ceremony varies from family to family but generally includes many of the blessings commonly recited at a *bris* that welcome the child into the people Israel and speak of the parents' gratitude and responsibility for their new baby girl.

Some argue that this should be good enough for the boys as well. Some go even further and argue in strong terms that circumcision is mutilation. I don't share these views and see circumcision as a sacred ritual that has been a part of my people from day one. Personally, I find meaning and value in the rite of circumcision on many levels, not the least of which is spiritual (and this chapter could have been in the Spirituality section of this book — or the Peoplehood section, too, for that matter).

I'm a fairly flexible and open-minded guy when it comes to Jewish thinking and practice. Ceasing circumcision, though, crosses a line for me that I don't feel comfortable violating. However, you can see from the variety of opinions expressed in this chapter that not everyone shares my thinking. These diverse opinions give you a hint of the challenges facing Judaism in this modern age. These challenges go far beyond circumcision. Today, everyone seems to have opinions about Judaism and Jewish practice, as you will see as you read on…

Chapter 4
Body Piercing, Tattoos, and More!

Dear Gil:

I have a facial piercing and my rabbi believes it should not be allowed. I need to know some things about the Biblical point of view on piercing. All the things I have found have to do with ear piercing and not facial (because it wasn't an issue) so doesn't that make the facial piercing issue depend on how you interpret the Torah?

L

Dear L:

You are asking a very pointed question (pun intended) about facial piercing and the Bible. The answer to your question would also apply to the other "bod mod" or body modifications that have become popular today.

These modifications run the gamut from piercing on every part of the human body (and I do mean EVERY part) to tattoos and procedures that radically modify the human body — like branding skin with hot metal and surgeries that split people's tongues. Yes, people do this! *TIME* magazine even ran an article called "Ah, the whiff of burning flesh! What to do when a tattoo seems too tame!"

If you are looking strictly at the Bible for guidance, you will not find a tremendous amount of information. The Torah does specifically prohibit tattoos. Commentaries explain that this has to do with avoiding pagan practices. I once heard that partially to spite this prohibition, the Nazis made a point of tattooing Jews in the concentration camps.

The Bible also mentions, but does not prohibit earrings and believe it or not — nose rings. (Isaac's wife Rebecca is given a gift of a nose ring.) But you would be hard pressed to find much about other body piercing and certainly nothing about branding or tongue splitting.

As for those practices, we can draw some guidance from a statement in the Torah that prohibits gashing or wounding oneself. Of course, one might make the argument that an ear piercing is wounding oneself and yet ear and nose piercing appears to be allowed in the Bible. So what would be wrong with any other modifications to the body—cosmetic surgery or anything else a person desires?

Here we need to look to our rabbis for direction. Their guidance seems contingent on the answer to the question "What is the purpose of the modification?" Are you defacing the body or are you doing something that adds beauty? Are you doing something that increases a person's self-esteem? Are you doing something that is part of mainstream culture (i.e., earrings, which are allowed) or for its shock value to the others who see you? Are you doing something just to fit in?

As you might guess, our rabbis seem more inclined to approve of beauty and improved self-esteem motivations and frown upon shock value or just trying to fit in. Though one could argue that customs of looking beautiful in a society and trying to fit in are the same. Obviously making some of these decisions is not simple. The decisions are influenced by fundamental teachings in Judaism.

One teaching is the value of modesty. A second teaching is the Jewish attitude about the body. The human body deserves dignity, says our tradition, since it is not our possession. Our bodies should not be viewed as objects we own but rather as creations of God, not to be desecrated. Finally, there is a strong emphasis in Judaism that says Jews should not adopt all the behavior of our non-Jewish neighbors. (This last teaching is one of the rationales given for the dietary laws of keeping kosher.)

So where does this leave you? First, it puts you in a position to have a more intelligent discussion with your rabbi about why he or she objects to your facial piercing. Perhaps more importantly, you now know some of the questions that Judaism would ask of you.

Ultimately the questions are: Why do you want to modify your body? Are you doing something that will be a credit to you and that you can feel proud of? How does your image of God play into your decisions?

Only you can decide for sure, but as you seek answers, I encourage you to ask your rabbi and others... and I thank you for asking me.

Gil

Email Responses to "Body Piercing, Tattoos, and More!"

Subj: Tattoos, Body Piercing etc.
Date: 11/27 6:13:37 AM CST
From:
To: GilMann@aol.com

Dear Gil: This email perked my interest. You see, I have a 20 year old who one day came home from college with an arm band tattoo. Thank goodness that he is very artistic and drew out what he wanted and even I must say it is nice. He put it on his arm where it can't be seen if he rolls a shirt up. He listened to what I had to say about doing it before he had it done. He specifically asked me to ask my Rabbi about it. I applaud him because he did his homework before jumping into something that is so permanent. A lot of these kids do not think of the repercussions of the things that they do. Even though we are suppose to judge people on their intellect and what they have inside... it is still a visual world where first looks count.

Name :-)

Subj: Body Piercings
Date: 11/20 5:57:53 PM CST
From:
To: GilMann@aol.com

My mother sent me the URL for your published reply about body piercing. I'm not quite sure what her exact motive was (being a Jewish Mother, she definitely had one!) but I am grateful for the explanation in your letter anyhow.

I am a well-pierced 90s chick. Have my ears pierced, though I rarely wear earrings — and when I do, they are small, simple silver hoops. I do have my nose pierced. I got it done in Israel because I thought it would suit my nose. As a theatre student,

I often get teased by the faculty at my school about the piercing, but I have a special stud that is practically invisible on-stage and on-camera. One of the reasons I have kept it for so long (five years) is because I feel in some way I am paying tribute to the often forgotten women of the Bible. In some ways, though this may sound like a stretch, my nose ring makes me feel more Jewish.

The last time I was in Israel, I got both of my nipples pierced. I don't know what possessed me to tell my parents; they were not impressed, to say the least. My parents have always had a laissez-faire attitude about my body and my clothes, perhaps because I have never dressed too outrageously. Never dyed my hair, or wore leather dog collars. I think they even like the nose ring, though they'd probably never admit it. But the nipple rings just seems gross to most adults — and most people my age as well. They actually are beautiful, though only my closest friends have seen them. And they are only for me. I think one of the reasons people get so creeped out by nipple rings and some of the other body piercings is that they are often associated with sex and sexuality. I can't deny that I knew the stigma attached to piercings like nipple rings when I had them done. However, I had very important reasons for getting them done

I spent the whole of last year in Israel, studying there. I lived for a year with three other students. Let me say, first of all, that there is no way to describe an experience like the one I had in words, especially in a short letter. I will, however, try to sum up how this experience led me to the nipple rings. First of all, my closest friend and roommate, (woman's name removed) had nipple rings. Two of her best friends had nipple rings. These two friends spent almost every Shabbat at our apartment (an escape from the dormitories) throughout the year. Needless to say, with a bunch of girls running around every Shabbat, I saw a lot of nipple piercings. At first I was shocked and disgusted, then curious, then openly interested. I was teased over and over that I would want to get my nipples done too by the end of the year.

As the end of my incredible year drew near, I began to think about what the year had meant for me. What had I accomplished. I don't think I even knew why I had really gone in the first place, until I got ready to leave. I thought about my apartment, and my roommates. Four girls, all very strong-minded, opinionated, intelligent, and active — always active. One was a Feminist, Peace Now supporter. One was Conservative! (To us liberals, she seemed like a radical...) she interned for a right-wing Israeli political party — was very much against giving land for peace. One was a Hippie Party gal/bookworm. Then there's me. Just a big mesh of things. But the environment in our apartment was unbelievable. With four extremely different opinions, the scene could have been treacherous. It wasn't; it was the most open environment I have ever lived in: intellectually, emotionally, and physically. I have never felt so comfortable living any other place in my life. The year before, living in Columbus, two of my three roommates had been Rural-Ohio-Small-Town-Christian-Prudes. I never left my room without being fully dressed. In Israel, our apartment was entirely physically open. We walked around dressed (or undressed) for comfort. I became extremely comfortable with my own body — really for the first time. As I was thinking about all of these things, I decided that one way to commemorate all of this would be to get my nipples pierced. I wanted to have a physical reminder — something I would see every day — of my accomplishments and experiences in Israel. I wanted to remind myself how far I'd come, and have a symbol of that with me always so I would never go back to feeling uncomfortable or ashamed of my body. So far, five months later, it has worked.

I think that one of the reasons Jews have such a big problem with body piercings is that Jews have big problems with bodies in general. All the modesty laws, the puritanism of our religion, has distanced us from the reality of our physical selves. I think it's ironic that Jews, who have all these customs and practices to make our every day activities, and even mere physical human functions, ritualistic and holy and a tribute to God, are uncomfortable, even ashamed, of skin, physicality, and, yes, sensuality and sexuality.

I would love to hear your response. Don't know how much of this makes sense but let me know if you need clarification. Thank you for specifying in the published letter that piercings are really a personal decision.

Sincerely, Name

Subj: Body Piercing
Date: 11/18 8:12:03 PM CST
From:
To: GilMann@aol.com

Dear Gil,

I am a 15 year old with many piercings. Currently, I have five. Two in each ear lobe and one in the upper cartilage of one of my ears. Being a teenager, it is probably assumed that I am rebellious and only want to fit in. That, however, is not the case. I am a strongly opinionated individual. I am not rebellious, either. If you were to ask my classmates, they would tell you that I am a quiet, reserved individual. According to my teachers, I am what every teacher wishes for. However, my rabbis have different opinions. They are both disgusted with my piercings. I used to baby-sit for both of their children, and after my fifth piercing, they stopped asking me to baby-sit. I approached both of them and they told me that they didn't approve of my piercings and it was a bad influence on their children. They expressed their disgust to me about my piercings. They think that I'm piercing myself to fit in. That is far from the truth. I am piercing myself as a way of expressing myself and my creativity. It's a way of showing people who I am. And I like the piercings — they make me happy. They make me feel like me! I currently decided to get two more holes — one in each ear. My rabbis heard and told me that if I did this, they would not allow me into their synagogue. I am hurt. Why should I be punished for being myself? And why do rabbis have the authority to do that? I mean, it's not like I'm dressing like a slut to their place of worship! I don't understand why I am being punished for having different views and beliefs than those of my rabbis. They don't ban Christians from their synagogue because they have different beliefs, so why am I being banned? And for crying out loud, it's only my ears! It's not like I've pierced my eyebrows, my tongue, my lips, or any other obscene body part. To make things even more interesting, it's a Reform synagogue.

Should rabbis be allowed to prohibit you from entering their place of worship because of how many holes are in your ears?

I am frustrated and upset about this issue. Please advise me, and other teenagers in my place, what to do.

Most sincerely,
Name

Subj: circumcision
Date: 12/3/ 8:57:16 PM CST
From:
To: GilMann@aol.com

dear Gil, There seems to me to be a strong relationship between body piercing, tattooing and circumcision. They have been used for tribal distinction for untold ages. Biblical Hebrew men had many rules of dress (fringed garments) and how wear their hair (not shave the corners of the beard) besides the circumcision to make them unique. This may have served as a deterrent to desertion because it was so in eradicable. Interestingly, the females, although they were property were not "branded"

Subj: RE: Tatoos and body piercing
Date: 11/20 8:44:07 PM CST
From:
To: GilMann@aol.com

Could you e-mail me perhaps a copy of that e-mail answer on the subject above? I'm interested since I don't believe in piercings

and defacing ones body with tatoos and have an ongoing difference of opinion with a friend on this very subject.

Thanking you in advance, I remain,
Respectfully yours,
Name

Subj: Piercing, etc.
Date: 11/19 6:46:31 PM CST
From:
To: GilMann@aol.com

Hi there,

I just read your piercing column (pun intended) and am stuck in an
uncomfortable position. I never knew that tattoos were specifically
prohibited in the Torah, and I always figured they were sort of like
not naming babies after the living — prohibited by tradition more
than anything concrete. I have two tattoos, and I wanted to know
if it is true that I cannot be buried in a Jewish cemetery and what
other censure I might face as a result of my modification. It seems
to me that hair bleaching, nose jobs, etc. are much worse than
tattoos because they either serve to deny one's physical Judaic
heritage or deny one's age, both of which I consider true gifts. I
also believe a tattoo is much more about beautifying than any of
those procedures. So where do I stand?

Thanks,
Name

Concluding Thoughts to Copy, Cut, Paste, and Save

The popularity of tattoos and piercing are a perfect example of the intersection of a modern world, Judaism, and the Internet. How can a person incorporate an ancient tradition like Judaism with the 21st century?

To explore this question, I've used this chapter a number of times when I teach teens. The chapter offers many lessons that make for lively discussions. This topic challenges us about our personal identities, our religious identities, our bodies, society, fitting in, what is good or bad, ethical or unethical, what is obedience or rebelliousness, and ultimately how we each make choices.

In these classes, and even more so in the email that people send me, I'm constantly struck that Judaism's "opinion" on these challenges intrigues so many people. I'm even more impressed that "what Judaism has to say" matters to non-Jews and Jews who do not appear to be observant of Jewish law or ritual.

From this, I maintain that Judaism most definitely can be relevant in our modern lives. What is critical, however, is finding ways to make Judaism accessible. Clearly, the Internet is one way.

The rest of the chapters in this book will continue to demonstrate these issues. Reading all of this material has led me to many conclusions about making Judaism relevant and accessible. As you'll see, the conclusion to this book is devoted to this subject.

In the meantime, read on and you will see many more examples that have led me to my conclusions.

PS: If you're dying (this pun intended too) to know the answer to the question posed in the last email about whether having tattoos will prevent a person from being buried in a Jewish cemetery, I consulted with several rabbis to find an answer. Even though Jewish law prohibits tattoos and/or many piercings, the rabbis all had the same opinion that body adornments would probably not be an obstacle to burial in a Jewish cemetery.

Below is my response to the writer:

Shalom Debbie!

I'm not a rabbi so I can't give you a legal reading. I suggest you ask your rabbi. I would guess that non-Orthodox rabbis would not have a serious problem with your tattoos (of course I don't know what your tattoos say or how big they are)—but there is only one way to find out for sure: ask. Personally I wouldn't worry so much about your tattoos. I'd spend the same effort on trying to be a good person and treating others ethically. I suspect most rabbis would agree with me.

Thanks for writing!

Gil

Chapter 5
Jews, Blacks, and Prejudice

Dear Gil:

I remember when there was a sense of community between Black and Jewish people. A camaraderie that doesn't seem to exist anymore. Are any of your readers working to change this? I'd love to hear from others.

P

Dear Gil:

I am African-American, 48 and I am and have always been a friend of Israel and the Jewish people. My mother worked as credit manager for a furniture chain that was Jewish-owned and they gave her a chance to make good, long before equal opportunity employment.

What I don't like is the schism that is steadily growing between the Black and Jewish communities. Our two cultures that have suffered similar histories — slavery and its degradations, and the Holocaust and its cruelties give us more in common than anything else.

I will always be a supporter of the Jewish people and I know that with the Love of God we, as a people, will advance together. Live in Perfect Peace,

K

Dear P and K:

In 1968, when I was in fifth grade, I had a white teacher who was a hero and ahead of her time. My teacher, Ms. Helland, marched and fought for civil rights in the South in the sixties and had her life threatened. She taught us of the evils of racial discrimination and developed a curriculum that I remember vividly to this day of amazing contributions made to America and the world by Black people (years before there was a Black History Month in our country). I will never forget her anguish when Martin Luther King was assassinated that year.

The lessons she taught about prejudice and discrimination resonated especially strongly with me because I knew my family had suffered because of hatred. Both of my parents lost large numbers of their families in the Holocaust.

With this as a personal backdrop, I view as tragic the strain in the relationship between Jewish and Black people in recent years. I have read all the claims and counterclaims by Jews and African-Americans on all sides of the various disputes. Yes, I have seen data showing anti-Semitism amongst African-Americans. I have also personally heard on many occasions Jews speaking racist words against Blacks. While both behaviors are pathetic and immoral, I want to believe that most Blacks and Jews would like to get along.

I agree with your comment that we have much in common. We, who as minorities have suffered from persecution, must work together. We used to do this a lot. Many people don't realize that in 1909, Jews were amongst the founders of the NAACP (including two rabbis). A year later, Jews also helped form the Urban League.

During the civil rights movements of the sixties Jews participated in large numbers, contributing money, marching in the South, even giving their lives. Martin Luther King himself wrote "It would be impossible to record the contribution that the Jewish people have made toward the Negro's struggle for freedom — it has been so great."

But today, Blacks and Jews don't seem to work together as we did in the sixties. As a reader of this column you may be thinking "I am just one person, what can I do?" I have one timely suggestion that relates to the current controversy about the Confederate flag flying above the capital in South Carolina. The NAACP and others have called for this flag to be removed as it is a symbol of slavery and bigotry toward Blacks.

As a Jew, I empathize with this protest. Imagine if the Nazi flag was flying proudly from a city hall in a German town or for that matter from any government building anywhere in the world. Would Jews not protest loudly and clearly?

Well, we Jews should be loudly and clearly protesting now in solidarity with African-Americans. I am not motivated by the politics of this issue. I am moved by a sense of ethical obligation to speak out as a Jew. The Torah tells us repeatedly to remember Egypt and what being an oppressed minority feels like.

So readers, I encourage you to speak up. Email or copy this column and send it to others, write letters to the editor, and ask your rabbis to do so as well. Contact your local Jewish Community Relations Council and ask them to issue a statement. Ask teachers in your religious schools to teach children about this flag controversy and why Jews should care and speak up. Do something!

These efforts may be a small step in improving relations between our two peoples, but it is a step. As the Talmud says, "You are not obligated to complete the work but neither are you free to ignore the work." I hope you will speak up!

Gil

Email Responses to "Jews, Blacks, and Prejudice"

Subj: Jews and Blacks
Date: 1/28 1:36:06 AM CST
From:
To: GilMann@aol.com

Dear Gil,

A professor of mine once said, "America used to be the world's Melting Pot, where everyone came and eventually merged into the American culture. In this century, America has become the world's Ice Cube Tray, where each group is being herded into its own cold little compartment. This is political, and is being implemented by people who know "divide and conquer" is the way to destroy a people."

In the past few decades, it seems as though — every time there is a warming of black/white relationship — a fear/hate campaign is instigated (from where, I don't know) that starts everyone looking at each other differently, and the good relationships cool and disappear.

I believe that the only answer is to refuse to stay in my own "cube." That is, I wander out into other peoples' cultural, ethnic, and religious contexts — always as a Jew, but as an interested and loving observer, and participant, if allowed. And I speak out for treating others the way I want to be treated — which is what you suggested.

If everyone did these two things, as much as they were able in their particular life's pattern, I believe that the people who want to "divide and conquer" would be at least set back. And the people who want to be HUMAN and let everyone else be HUMAN would be encouraged to do even more.

Subj: racism
Date: 1/28 11:25:06 AM CST
From:
To: GilMann@aol.com

Dear Gil:

I don't think the schism is new. In 1969, I was a senior in high school. I took an Afro-American history class as an elective. Half the class was black the other half white Jews. (My high school was smack in the middle of the Jewish ghetto, but there was a lot of bussing, cause of massive overcrowding in all the high schools in my city.) As we learned, we also discussed what we were learning. One day, one of the Jews said that he could under- stand what the blacks were feeling about whatever we were talk- ing about, because the circumstances were similar to what the Jews had gone through. The black kids in class were apoplectic. How dare we compare, we have never suffered like they have. All of the white kids were kind of confused, we were in that class because we wanted to learn and understand the black experience. It was an elective, we didn't have to be there-we wanted to. I don't think we should get into a fight over who has suffered more but I get upset when I, as a Jew am called an oppressor of blacks. I do speak up, contribute to black causes, institutions, etc., will boycott S. Carolina, but to be truthful (politically incorrect or not) The black cause may lose my support if I continue to get called names or putdowns because I am Jewish.

Subj: Blacks and Jews
Date: 1/28 3:27:12 PM CST
From:
To: GilMann@aol.com

Sorry, but this issue seems so outdated to me. The "African American community" and the "Jewish community" isn't where the action is today. Anyone who lives and works in urban America, and I suspect in suburban America too, comes into contact with plenty of people of other races, creeds, colors and national origins. People under 30 are downright uncomfortable if the crowd they're in is too homogenous — at least my kids are.

For those of either group who don't know any of the other group, do some carefully chosen volunteering. When you form personal relationships with the full range of people who live in the United States today, you stop spending time bemoaning what the out of touch leaders are or are not doing.

Name

Subj: Blacks and Jews
Date: 1/29 9:54:33 AM CST
From:
To: GilMann@aol.com

It will take more than the wisdom of the sages to resolve the issue
raised by the black writer. Jews by nature and teachings have
been non violent in their personal and community relationships
and shy away from confrontation. Tradition teaches us to accept
all people as children of G-D and to open our hearts and homes
to those in need. Difficult to do when one has a concern for
personal safety. The designation 'African American' appears to
seek exclusivity, us against you. Conversly, we are Americans of
Jewish persuasion, not 'Jewish Americans'. Jews continue to be
the scapegoat of the black leadership leading the black populace
to the conclusion that we have been/are the oppressors. This is
not a win/win situation.

Subj: Blacks, Jews, and Prejudice
Date: 1/30/ 1:17:16 PM CST
From:
To: GilMann@aol.com

Dear Gil,

It truly is a shame that two groups who share so much pain in
their histories caused by slavery, prejudice, and hate cannot
come together to strengthen the fight against bigotry.

We can point fingers in so many directions as to the cause of
our separation. However, I believe one of the major causes is a
lack of strong leadership on both sides. Years ago both rabbi's
and black preachers stood together to fight oppression and
prejudice. Today, there are leaders on both sides who actually
spout hate, racism, separatism, and lies. Louis Farrakhan
comes quickly to mind. Of course there exist many leaders

today that still fight for acceptance and against hate. It appears that they are fighting far to quietly and thus are allowing those blinded by hate to shine in the limelight. Our leaders must stand up and shout that prejudice and hate are against our doctrines!

Instead of a focus on the positive aspects of one another, we find a preoccupation on the negative. As individuals, we can decide to make an effort to accept one another as equals. But beliefs, attitudes, and actions often flow down from the leaders of the day and until our leaders are willing to consistently condemn racism and pledge to work together, their followers will not be inclined to change.

Sincerely,
Name

Subj: Response
Date: 2/5 9:21:54 PM CST
From:
To: GilMann@aol.com

Hi,

As an African American Jew by Choice, I read your letter with a heavy heart. The divide between African Americans and Jews seems to be widening. I don't think it is as large as the media has portrayed it (not every African American person listens to Farrakhan — and his ilk) but there is some distance there.

I do know that some African American people are jealous of the strides that Jews have made and their sense of community and they feel that Jews are not there for them like they were in the sixties. To me, the things that Jews have had to overcome around the world can serve as motivation to African Americans that, we too, can achieve despite odds against us.

I wish I knew what to do. The commonality of experiences shared by African Americans and Jews is one of the things that made me embrace Judaism. I have no solution to this rift but I wish things were different. If there were ever two groups that could learn from each other, Jews and African Americans are the ones who would benefit the most.

Thanks for the article. Maybe someone else will have the answer.

Please encourage Jews not to give up on African Americans and to know that there are people out there who want things to be different.

Subj: Blacks & Jews
Date: 2/9 7:50:12 PM CST
From:
To: GilMann@aol.com

Sad to say, the strife between blacks and Jews in America today is all to evident. It is almost as unforgivable (from the Jewish perspective) as strife amongst Jews.

However, the source of this strife is apparently well documented. Julius Lester [a Jewish African American] was a scholar in residence at our shul [synagogue] for a Shabbat that focused on the problem. He is uniquely qualified to speak on the subject and his remarks and responses to questions were frank, interesting and enlightening.

In short, he indicated that the black community of today does not see itself as ever having had a "suffering" experience that might be considered to be common with the Jewish people. We are just another group of whitey "haves" trying to either take away something from them or horn in on their experience. Makes you almost wonder what the contributions of Jews to black equality was all about.

Name

Concluding Thoughts to Copy, Cut, Paste, and Save

Will people ever get past their prejudice? What happened to the bond that once existed between Blacks and Jews? After reading the email in this chapter, you could end up feeling that the answers to these questions are two hopeless "no's." Lest you leave this chapter depressed, I end with the following column that I wrote based on an uplifting email I received from a Black teenager. It contains sentiments and suggestions that are definitely worthy of copying, saving, and using in our lives.

Inspired by a Black Teen

Dear Gil:

I am a 16 year old African American and I just wanted you to know that there are a lot of Blacks that support the Jews. One of my goals in life is to strengthen a positive relationship between Jews and Blacks. I'm currently taking the Holocaust class at my school and I'm looking forward to learning more about Jewish history outside of school. I really want to become involved, so please, tell me anything that would help and if it is possible for me to work for one of the organizations this summer, or at least help out a little bit.

B

B Shalom!

How refreshing and uplifting to read your email! So much so that I wanted to share it and my response in the hope that all my readers will be inspired to act. Your email took on even more significance as I began to research an answer to your question. I came upon this sad statistic: In 1999, approximately 10% of all hate crime incidences occurred in schools or colleges according to the Anti-Defamation League (ADL).

We regularly hear discouraging data like this and of Black/Jewish tension but good news and good people like you are seldom publicized. This week will be an exception.

Before I answer your question, I want to state my unscientific opinion that I believe most Jews view past injustice against African Americans with disgust and think discrimination is just plain wrong. I have written in the past about Jewish activism in the civil rights movement. Examples are ample, but here is one: Jews were amongst the founders of the NAACP!

Far less monumental are examples likes this email that someone sent me: "[10 years ago at a Jewish retreat,] one woman, in her late 40s told the group that she became a Jew because of her involved work in the Civil Rights movement. She said that one day she looked around and realized that she was the only white person there who wasn't Jewish, and she vowed to learn more about such a religion."

Her email and yours lead me to believe that there are many good people out there who are prepared to roll up their sleeves to improve race relations. I am hopeful that many of them will pursue the leads I am now going to offer you.

I found a number of programs to bring Black and Jewish teens together to learn, grow, and work together. In a number of cities, a program called Operation Understanding exists. This program selects about a dozen African-American and a dozen Jewish teens who meet monthly for study and dialogue. The programs vary from city to city, but some of them even include travel to civil rights sites in the U.S. and trips to Israel and Africa. Their website is www.operationunderstanding.org.

Next are a couple of similar programs named after the late Texas Congressman Mickey Leland, an African-American who was a great friend of Israel. He died in 1989 in a plane crash in Ethiopia. If you search the Internet on his name you will find what is currently available.

Next, here are two websites you should check. They are not specifically for teens, but on one, I found an internship program for college students.

www.partnersagainsthate.org — Click on "Promising Programs" and look up your state.

www.rac.org — This address is part of Religious Action Center of Reform Judaism in Washington, DC. Search on the words Jew Black and you will find resources programs there to bring Jews and Blacks together.

Finally, I suggest you look up the local chapter of the ADL or the Jewish Community Relations Council. Tell them you'd be interested to work with them as a volunteer or maybe even as an intern. If you have any problem locating them, get back to me.

Your email was a day brightener. I hope teens and adults in the many cities where my column is read will be inspired by your lead and follow up on the contacts I have offered to you. Thanks for writing!

Gil

Chapter 6
Are Jewish Teens Immoral Today?

Dear Readers:

People constantly contact me to ask about the relevance of Judaism to modern life. This week, I received an email from a teacher that addresses this question in such a compelling and disturbing way that I decided to add little comment to allow room for his words...

Dear Gil:

I teach the 9th grade course on Jewish Ethics & Values at my synagogue. We live in interesting times, ethically speaking. Just look at the newspaper. On any given day there are stories about cloning, abortion, debates over the right to die, atrocities of war, mischief in the White House, etc. The world is getting more and more complicated. How do we decide what's right and what's wrong? How do we help our children become moral individuals?

These are not idle questions. My Sunday school students and I have been talking about stories that have been in the news recently. One concerned a Virginia man who turned himself into the authorities for a crime he had committed nineteen years ago. It seems that he had discovered God in that time. After discussing the matter with his wife, he decided he couldn't in good conscience provide spiritual council to others, including his own children, knowing that he was living a lie himself. I asked my class whether this man did the right thing in turning himself in. More than half said no. The man would have done better devoting himself to good works, they said; nothing would be accomplished by owning up to what he did. Indeed, the prosecutor in charge of the case has said he is wrestling with the very same issues. The parents of the young woman the man murdered, however, see no ambiguity in the matter.

Another case concerned a teenager, a student at Berkeley, who idly stood by and watched as a friend abused and murdered a seven-year-old girl. (The details are actually much more grisly than I make it sound.) The parents of the dead child have demanded that the student be expelled from the university. University officials said that reprehensible as the young man's inaction might have been, he broke no laws and thus there are no grounds for expulsion. I asked my class what they thought. Again, half said the boy should not be removed from the school. He should have intervened, they said, but he did not break the law. He earned his place at the university by his good grades, they said, and he should thus be permitted to stay.

The class discussions were much more complicated than these summaries suggest, of course. What troubled me about the students' responses to both cases, but particularly the second one, is the lack of any sense of moral obligation, any sense that there might be standards that transcend what is legal. According to German law at the time, what the Nazis did was perfectly legal. No one today, however, would argue that it was right. The same is true for slavery in America 135 years ago.

Are my students morally defective? Absolutely not. They care deeply about right and wrong, and they'd be rightly insulted by any who would suggest otherwise. The problem is, the world out there is not giving them — indeed, and it probably cannot give them — the tools they need to make meaningful moral distinctions. They are well versed on what is legal and what is scientifically possible and what is fashionable, but standards of morality seem to be falling through the cracks. Those standards can only come from the home and their religious heritage. I'm talking about teaching our children that there are ethical dimensions to everyday life that law and custom can't address.

When my class discussion moved from questions of law to questions of personal accountability and integrity, the students began to see both of the cases above in a different light. I reminded them that college applications ask about things like community service and the like because they want to know something of an applicant's character. Didn't the bystander's refusal to intervene say something about his character? Then I quoted from the Talmud, where it says that a person who can prevent another from sinning but does not, shares in the sins of that person. Which society would they rather live in, I asked, one in which decisions about whether to help people in distress are judged on what is or isn't legal, or one in which people are simply expected to help? This time the answer was unanimous.

J

Dear J:

Your students, indeed all of us, are lucky you are their teacher. Does Judaism have anything to offer a modern person living in a modern world? Your classes and teachings answer that question with a loud and resounding YES!

So are Jewish teens immoral today? I'd like to offer this question to my readers. What say you, readers? Email in your comments to GilMann@aol.com. Thank you!

Gil

Email Responses to "Are Jewish Teens Immoral Today?"

Subj: Are Jewish Teens Immoral?
Date: 7/23 4:00:46 PM CDT
From:
To: GilMann@aol.com

I don't think these teenagers are "immoral." They are just uneducated in morality concepts. They are probably only repeating back what they have learned from the popular culture. The sad fact is that the public schools do not teach morality to students, so the only place where students will learn morality is in the home or in their religious school programs.

Name

Subj: Re: Immoral teenagers
Date: 7/23 7:54:33 PM CDT
From:
To: GilMann@aol.com

Dear Gil,

I read with interest the letter from the 9th grade Ethics teacher of a class in a Jewish Sunday School. As a 22-year veteran teacher in the public high schools in New Jersey, I'm afraid that I have to agree that kids today are sadly lacking in morals. The few Jewish kids I encounter in my school do seem to have higher standards, but perhaps this is wishful thinking on my part — I have no proof. The kids at my synagogue definitely have higher standards!

In our weekly classroom discussions of ethics and morals (I teach English and music, but always work these topics in!), I find that most students feel that if one doesn't get caught, one has done nothing wrong! Yet, I receive at least one private note every week from one student or another who agrees with the ethical position I have taken, but who felt uncomfortable dissenting with the majority in class.

A specific example involves purchasing an item and receiving back extra change. The question is whether to return the extra change. When I tell the class that I always return the money, as one voice they hoot and holler that I'm foolish. Yet, after drawing a verbal picture of a mom and pop store, saving for the family, etc., I convince almost all of them that the money belongs to the storekeepers, not me.

Our kids want and need moral guidance. They need someone to tell them right from wrong directly — without so many gray areas. I previously stated that I teach music and English; that's not exactly true. I teach children. I teach them what they need to learn in order to grow up to be decent, honest, contributing citizens of this country. And that's not easy to do when over half of my students come from homes where English is not the primary language, and 65% of them are on one form or another of public assistance.

Thanks for listening,
Name

Subj: Are teens immoral today?
Date: 7/21 5:59:55 PM CDT
From:
To: GilMann@aol.com

Dear Gil,

I am the mother of a 16 and almost 21 year old. Both children are considered "good" kids — that is, they have never been in serious trouble, work hard in school, get good grades, and are high achievers in their fields of expertise. (My daughter is a 5 time national dance champion, my son is a pianist who is distinguishing himself in many ways).

What I have seen as their main difficulty is making lasting friendships because they are too "good." My son lost his whole group of friends last year because of drug usage (he refuses). He is slowly rebuilding a network of friends. My daughter, we recently found out, experimented with drugs in high school for a short time. Thankfully she discontinued this, although she does go out with friends to bars and has one or two drinks. The problem? All their friends think they are weird — too straight.

Many parents today have not taken the time to talk to their children about rules and respect. How do you expect the children to think and act otherwise if they do not have strong parental role models?

Name

Subj: immoral teens?
Date: 7/22/ 3:09:50 PM CDT
From:
To: GilMann@aol.com

How do Jewish teens compare morally to other teens?

Jewish and non-Jewish ideally learn similar basic morality. What differences there are between (American) Jewish teens and non-Jewish teens are becoming less succinct.

As my 23 year old answered the question, "Jewish teens don't give a damn about religion anymore." My 15 yr old daughter answers: "I can't do something because I'm Jewish," so for her, she feels her Judaism shapes her morality at least at this point. My 16 yr. old son however, seems to go along with the "crowd," so if they think it is cool to steal, then that is what they do, even though they know it is morally wrong, and even if it takes getting caught (as was the case with my daughter) to learn the lesson. Morality issues such as, Marijuana use, underage drinking and smoking, premarital teen age sex, interfaith dating, disrespect for parents, teachers, elders, and the law, etc. seem to be prevalent in all walks of teenage life

How do Jewish teens compare morally to teens of yesterday?

Society [used to be] much more conservative. Pregnant teens were often isolated from their peers; it was morally unacceptable to do certain things in public. I went to a private girl's high school. There were 80 in my graduating class, twelve were Jewish. I heard a rumor many years after graduation that most of the class had had sexual relationships before they graduated. My personal opinion is (and I don't know for sure) that the Jewish girls were probably still virgins. Anyway, it certainly was not out in the open who had sex and who didn't. There was much less teen violence in the news. Drugs were not an issue. Teen discussions often centered around what was right and wrong. Schools demanded respect and dress codes.

How do Jewish teens compare morally to adults?

My 19 year old daughter told me last year that she did not plan to have just one sexual partner and she did not plan to wait until she got married to have sex. This is not in my moral code. My 16 year old thinks there is nothing wrong with wearing a tongue ring, even though I see it as disgusting and morally suggestive as well morally unhealthy. I'm sure adults today did some pretty stupid things as teens, but what they did was not as open as it is today and hurting our parents was a consideration.

Subj: Moral guideposts
Date: 7/24 9:15:02 AM CDT
From:
To: GilMann@aol.com

This is the unfortunate but natural result of the "moral relativism" that has invaded our entire secular educational sector, from kindergarten to university. Hopefully, somewhere, we will begin to accept the premise that certain actions are absolutely right and others absolutely wrong. I applaud that teacher for attempting to wrestle with these matters in class.

Name

Subj: Conscience and Morality to Today's Teens
Date: 7/24 1:27:26 AM CDT
From:
To: GilMann@aol.com

WOW! Now there's a loaded subject. As the mother of two teenage boys I can't begin to tell you how many arguments I've had with both of them, a 19 yr old and a 16 yr old, on good vs. evil and all the shades of grey in between. They have both been in situations when they have been called on to either stand aside and allow something objectionable to occur or step in and risk injury to their persons or reputations. Both these young men have been in their share of fights for what they considered worth fighting for, but which seemed questionable to me. Reinforcing their positive motives is an ongoing job, as any parent should know. Plus, we ourselves must be willing to be examples of what we teach. That's where the real learning exists.

Concluding Thoughts to Copy, Cut, Paste, and Save

Frankly, I don't know if teens or Jewish teens are more or less moral today than teens of prior generations. On the one hand, I suspect they are less moral — and I base that purely on the steady diet of violence and disdain for the value of human life that today is a standard part of recreation and "entertainment" (movies, TV, computer games, etc.). I just can't believe that this relentless bloody bombardment is harmless to a child's moral development or to society in general.

I think many would agree with the following: "Children now love luxury; they have bad manners, contempt for authority; they show disrespect for elders and love chatter in place of exercise. Children are now tyrants, not the servants of their households. They no longer rise when elders enter the room. They contradict their parents, chatter before company, gobble food… and tyrannize their teachers." Sound like a good description of teens today? Surprise: those words are thousands of years old, from Socrates! So, on the other hand, I am not convinced that teens are less moral today than they ever were.

The one thing I do feel confident saying is that kids and teens are heavily influenced by what they see their parents do morally and immorally. In fact, if you pause for a second, I'll bet you can quickly think of something you remember seeing your parents do when you were growing up, that struck you as particularly moral or immoral behavior.

When parents are dishonest, take advantage of others, gossip, or treat people poorly, they are really teaching their kids that if you can get away with the behavior, why not? The opposite is also true. Modeling moral behavior will greatly increase the odds that a child will emulate upstanding behavior.

But how do you determine what is moral behavior? I strongly believe that Judaism can and should help guide moral decision-making (although I don't mean to suggest that I agree with every Jewish teaching or that Judaism is the only source for moral guidance). A time-honored tradition in Judaism is to examine and debate situations in life with learned people and with each other and seek the solution that will make a person moral or a *mensch* [a decent and worthy person]. This has been done for centuries in Judaism and continues today.

I'll end with four concrete suggestions that I humbly believe would make the world a better place if everyone pursued them:

1. Get the book *It's a Mitzvah!* by Rabbi Bradley Shavit Artson. This book has many practical and relevant teachings from Judaism about living morally, from feeding the hungry to preserving the earth.

2. Visit the website: www.ziv.org. The Ziv Tzedakah Fund has joined with the Giraffe Project to develop an outstanding curriculum about people who stick their necks out to do good. Search their site for this curriculum, which is in use all over the country. Do what you can to get it into a school near you!

3. Talk to your child or a child you are related to about where you give your charity, why, and how you decide how much to give away. This, of course, is but one of countless moral issues you can discuss. My experience in teaching teens is that a situation or question properly posed will easily stimulate discussion. Properly nurtured and respectfully argued, these debates are more than healthy… I think they are necessary if we are to have teens and ultimately adults who will behave morally.

4. Heed the advice of Robert Fulghum (the author of the famous essay: *All I Really Need to Know I Learned in Kindergarten*) when he said: "Don't worry that your children never listen to you; worry that they are always watching you!"

Chapter 7
My Rabbi's in Love with Me and I'm Married!

Dear Gil:

Please have patience as this is hard for me to write or discuss and I feel I'll burst if I don't share this with someone who can help me.

Since I was young, I have been an active member of my synagogue — volunteering and attending often. It is like home to me — at least, it used to be. We have had many rabbis during this period — our current rabbi has been here 6 years and the board and congregation are pleased with him.

I'll cut to the chase: my rabbi has fallen in love with me! THE FEELINGS ARE NOT MUTUAL! We are both married... to other people! In my case, I am and have always been happily married to a wonderful husband. Both of our spouses know of the rabbi's feelings for me, but no one else knows. The rabbi has done counseling to deal with the problem.

But this has not stopped his affections for me. He regularly sent me emails — until I blocked them and he continues to send me cards and gifts. To avoid him, we have even joined another synagogue which saddens us greatly and denies me "my shul" where I grew up.

My belief in my religion has not been shaken. But I don't feel I have a spiritual leader and that creates a terrible void within me. This rabbi has been through several family deaths with us and we could not have asked for anyone better.

Where do I find peace with this situation? What do I do? How do I live with this? I would be interested in the responses from your readers. I think a lot of people would find a story like this hard to believe. I know I would if I weren't living it. Why would a rabbi do this? Why could he not control his feelings? I know a rabbi is just a man like all others but are we holding him to a higher standard than we would anyone else? Thank you for your thoughts and consideration.

P

Dear P:

What a difficult problem! I think you answered at least one of your questions when you said the rabbi is just a man. In this case, a man with a problem that severely impacts his leadership. Judaism teaches that leaders can be flawed—even great leaders: Moses and King David are classic examples of this. King David had a serious lust problem, too!

I think the reason Judaism shows us flaws in our heroes and leaders is to teach us that all of us have the potential to act in Divine ways or like an animal—even our leaders. In other words, our leaders are only human—they are not God.

Perhaps a positive way for you to view this unpleasant situation is that since rabbis are only human like us, we are equally entitled to speak to, pray to, or work on behalf of God. Unlike many religions, Jews do not need an intermediary between God and us.

Your situation shows that each of us is capable of great good and great wrong… even our rabbis. The great good that you are capable of achieving is finding a way to ignore, accept, or even forgive this problem/flaw your rabbi has… difficult as it is, and I do appreciate the difficulty.

"Wonderful," you may be thinking, "a theology lesson and I am still stuck with my problem!"

I'll end with two more concrete ideas. First, I think you should communicate to your rabbi that if he does not stop sending you gifts, emails, cards, etc., you will share what you have received with the rabbinical association he belongs to. Perhaps you should anyway, since he sounds like he could use help. Further, his behavior may be bordering on illegal and you may wish to speak with an attorney.

Secondly, I am asking my readers for advice. Your problem, though rare, is far from unknown—I know of two Jewish clergy who had affairs with congregants. So readers: please email me your advice on how you would handle both the rabbi and the problem of being forced to change synagogues. I will write a follow-up column if enough good advice comes in. As always, I will alter any email I publish if necessary to protect confidences. Thank you.

Gil

Email Responses to
"My Rabbi's in Love with Me and I'm Married!"

Subj: boundaries
Date: 5/26 8:32:59 AM CDT
From:
To: GilMann@aol.com

Dear Gil,

I had a relationship with my rabbi that lost its boundaries. The rabbi was single, I am not. We shared many interests in common and thought of each other as "soul mates" in many respects. We ate meals out together, went to conferences, on outings, always unaccompanied. Never did the physical boundaries cross, but it was an ever-present issue, the tension was fierce. I fell in love and it was horrible.

In my determination to keep the rabbi's friendship and closeness, my relationship with my wife deteriorated. In fact, I think this relationship with the rabbi was a way of getting needs for attention, appreciation, etc. that were not at the time being fulfilled by my wife.

After a few years of this excruciating situation, I finally got the strength to end the relationship. It has taken an act of God and will to move on. My marriage has recovered and is now strong again, but I feel terrible still for having put my wife through that pain.

To this day, the rabbi has never apologized or acknowledged any impropriety. I think it takes two to tango, and I have asked for forgiveness and made amends as best I could to all involved. If she had acknowledged what was going on at the time, it could have been out in the open and dealt with. Instead, perhaps because of fear for her career, she refused to say anything at all other than that.

So, now the woman who wrote you can know she is not alone. If you have never been in this situation, it seems the answers are so clear. When you yourself have been there, or are there, it is anything but clear. I prayed, created, read books, studied Torah, prayed some more, sought counseling and spoke to a very few close friends. It took a loooong process to get the strength to sever the relationship. It was the hardest, but likely the wisest, decision I have ever made.

B'shalom [in peace],
Initialed

Subj: re: my rabbi is in love with me
Date: 5/10 5:46 PM CDT
From:
To: GilMann@aol.com

This woman has so far handled this in a very civil and adult manner so as to protect herself — but she has (understandably) done nothing yet to protect others who might become targets of his obsession. This Rabbi has clearly violated a boundary and poses an emotional threat to others. The support of his Board and Congregation would probably wither abruptly if he were exposed. A responsible, effective, influential Temple "elder" needs to be involved as a "confronter" to get this Rabbi into a very practical and effective therapist or program. Today it is her; who was it yesterday? and who will it be tomorrow?

Unfortunately as a physician and as a temple board member I have been close to situations of physicians, psychologists and even a Rabbi involved in these horrible situations. It would be very desirable to "save" this Rabbi from the inevitable professional destruction caused by his behavior but it is essential to protect others first.

Initialed

Subj: re: my rabbi is in love with me
Date: 5/11 8:49:10 PM CDT
From:
To: GilMann@aol.com

Gil,

Unfortunately, this situation is far more common than you would believe... and it is not limited to rabbis, but any person (generally a man) in a position of intimate power over another. There have been many, many books written on this subject (clergy who fall in love with parishioners, therapists who cross the line with people who seek counseling, doctors who seduce the spouses of dying patients, etc). I have personally dealt with an experience of this nature and found it devastating — my trust was destroyed, and while I could move on to another synagogue, another therapist, another doctor, I never again trusted in the way I had before.
I believe that, sadly, you will be inundated with responses from women who have been in similar situations.

Name

Subj: RABBI IN LOVE
Date: 5/18 1:47:10 AM CDT
From:
To: GilMann@aol.com

Dear Gil,

A similar story happened to me with a catholic priest.

At that time I wasn't married but I felt for his sake and mine it will be better not to pass by the church which was on my way to work any longer. But I had to face the fact that it was pleasant to have such a considerate man on my way to work. It took me a lot of forgiveness and understanding of his distress (as he was distress too) for things to get back into the right place and as a matter of fact we didn't cross each other on the street any longer.

Years later meeting again by accident, he told me how distressed he was and how that made him think about his role of clergyman and man as a whole, (as you know the catholic priest cannot marry). In his case to be faithful to his religion he left the clergy to marry.

All my best wishes,
Initialed

Subj: email of the week
Date: 5/11 10:06:05 PM CDT
From:
To: GilMann@aol.com

Dear Gil,

Being a Rabbi is sacred. It is essential to be trustworthy. He is not in love with her. It has nothing to do with her or he would treat her in a loving way and honor her feelings and her marriage. He does not sound emotionally evolved enough to be a Rabbi. He is not a spiritual leader. She is enabling his behavior by keeping it a secret. She needs to take responsibility for herself and hold him accountable!

Name

Subj: re: rabbi lust problem
Date: 5/12 3:44:25 AM CDT
From:
To: GilMann@aol.com

Dear Gil,

Here's another suggestion: social workers do what are called interventions. Possibly a get together with a social worker, the rabbi in question, his wife, the victimized couple. Maybe face to face, when the rabbi sees "P" sitting with her husband and is confronted by them and the rabbi's own wife, maybe then it'll hit home.

Also, someone should ask did "P" do anything even remotely or naively provocative to lead this rabbi on. What made him hone in on her in the first place? Does he think he's still getting vibes from her? If she finds out what is going on in his head, maybe she can stop whatever he thinks she is doing. Getting into the mind of an obsessed person can maybe help understand where he is coming from to get him help.

Last, but not least, his synagogue's board of directors should be told about this... in case they want to send him packing and choose a different rabbi.

Also, tell "P" just because this rabbi helped her family during difficult times, she shouldn't feel connected to his leadership abilities anymore. Maybe it was during this time of vulnerability that he got it into his head that there was a spark. He has crossed the line... taken advantage of her, and I would be afraid this might happen again with other synagogue members.

If she likes her original synagogue, let her go back, and get rid of this bad apple. He is no longer able to be a suitable leader. Tell "P" not to be a victim here and be forced to run away from her synagogue. She needs to stand tall, take action, and purge her community of this pariah.

Sincerely, Name

Subj: OH VEY!
Date: 5/12 2:29:11 PM CDT
From:
To: GilMann@aol.com

JUST DON"T CALL IT LOVE

It's not love, it's obsession bordering on addiction

Subj: response to email about the Rabbi being in love with a married woman
Date: 5/12 6:22:11 PM CDT
From:
To: GilMann@aol.com

I'll cut to the chase. I think that the rabbi has overstepped boundaries, to say the least. His behavior is inappropriate and leans towards harassment, if it isn't already. This lady should definitely report him to the rabbinical board or whatever authority is deemed appropriate.

What I don't understand upon reading her email to you is that she says both her spouse and his [wife] are aware of his amorous advances. Why haven't they done anything about this? I can't believe the rebbitizin [rabbi's wife] is standing by watching her husband making a jackass out of himself.

The only conclusion is that this is nothing new to her and that her husband has done this in other congregations. What about the writer's husband. Why hasn't he taken any action, short of beating the guy up, of course. Is he a wimp?

Why should she and her husband be forced to abandon her temple which she loves just to avoid this idiot? Sounds like a soap opera to me. It does remind me of that case in new Jersey, where a rabbi is being accused of hiring a hit man to kill his wife. He also had had affairs with members of his congregation. Another winner, right?

Sincerely,
Name

Subj: Rabbi's in love with me
Date: 5/12 7:30:45 PM CDT
From:
To: GilMann@aol.com

Gil,

I am a psychiatrist, and as such have dealt with multiple cases of 'clergy abuse.' It doesn't sound as though any actual physical violations have occurred, but boundary violations have and continue to occur. This woman must let someone who is in a position to address this issue with the Rabbi know what is going on.

I am concerned that there may be other individuals who have been approached by this Rabbi. This is often a pattern of behavior, and not an isolated incident. This woman may need supportive counseling and professional help to realize that she is not alone and she did nothing to cause this.

Yes, the Torah tells us of our leaders and their faults, but I hope that we will help our leaders and others when there is help available to deal with these faults. And in some cases the 'faults' may in fact be illnesses that need medical treatment.

Regards,
Name

Subj: My Rabbi's in love with me and I'M MARRIED!!!
Date: 5/13 10:49:36 AM CDT
From:
To: GilMann@aol.com

I need to be up front with you from the start. I am not Jewish but am a Christian who is interested in learning more of Judaism. I believe that the same type of problem appears in all religions because we all fall short of G-d's glorious ideal.

To be honest I don't believe that the Rabbi is really in love with you and I say that because if he truly had love in his heart he would be exhibiting a different type of behavior. Their can be no doubt on the law in this matter so the Rabbi is doing as all of us do and indulging in his own selfish needs and desires.

I would advise putting the matter in the open. Sin flourishes when it is hidden and needs to [be] put in the light and dealt with. Telling the Rabbi that this is not love but is lust and that it is sin is what needs to happen.

Subj: Mix Baby
Date: 5/26 8:51:41 AM CDT
From:
To: GilMann@aol.com

Dear Gil,

My mother had an affair with our Rabbi. I am the result. My mother was married with two children already from her supposedly happy husband and I was never explained the circumstances of this relationship she had for a brief time. I can say it has been extremely confusing for me. It was difficult growing up with the fact that our Rabbi somehow dropped out of his own marriage and had this affair and then poof! everything went back to normal on both sides.

I can say that I really never had any contact w/my biological father. I will say though just before my Mom's passing, I was told that the relationship she had with our Rabbi was true love and it was the first time she had a choice in her life. This left me terribly confused.

My only recommendation to any married women who might encounter such circumstances is, think and think clearly who can be affected in this circle. You must look deeper then personal needs, desires and flattery. Being a Rabbi is the center of a community and the weight of all consciousness.

Sincerely,
Initialed

Subj: Romantic Rabbi
Date: 5/15 12:23:49 AM CDT
From:
To: GilMann@aol.com

Dear Gil:

Judaism is a religion that is most concerned with actions. Your writer asks, "Why could he not control his feelings?" Most people cannot control their feelings, the Jewish question would be "Why did he take inappropriate actions based upon his feelings?" The fact that he fell in love with her is not different from when a therapist has feelings of counter-transference. However, a therapist acting professionally, will deal with his feelings without the client ever being aware of his issue. The same should be true for the rabbi. He should have dealt with his issue without making them her problem.

P also asks "are we holding him to a higher standard than we would anyone else?" I think that the answer should be no, but I would argue that his behavior would be unacceptable from any professional who works with and impacts people's lives. Rabbis should strive to live lives that are examples of moral and ethical behavior for their congregants to follow. They should do this not to live up to a higher standard, but rather to lead others to live the way that we all ought to be behaving.

P is still left facing the decision of remaining in a new congregation to avoid this rabbi vs. returning to her old congregation and dealing with him. There is no right or wrong here, it depends upon how she feels. Either way she ought to report him to his rabbinical organization. His behavior should not be allowed to continue unchecked. It sounds like she could benefit from counseling for this issue herself.

Saddened in State Name,
Rabbi Name

Concluding Thoughts to Copy, Cut, Paste, and Save

With all the news of sexual impropriety and the clergy, and what you have read in this chapter, you might have the incorrect impression that the problems described here are the norm for rabbis. Lest you have that misperception, I direct your attention to the next chapter. I'll include some final thoughts for both chapters there. This next chapter, in my experience, is much closer to the norm for rabbis and is as uplifting as this chapter is upsetting.

Chapter 8
Unknown Things About Rabbis

Dear Gil,

Recently, I found out how my rabbi cares, in ways most people don't see. I thought I'd share this with you, maybe to help others realize that their own rabbis probably do the same, with no recognition. Our rabbi is very kind and caring... most people do not see everything he does, that is the wonderful things he does. This story, is one I just heard. It is only one person, but think of how many other times he's done this. And no one knows.

Our synagogue is having a campaign to raise money, to build a religious school, enlarge our social hall, and do many other things to improve our temple. I am on the campaign, and have been given the job to ask congregants for money. I was given one woman's name

I called her and set up a lunch date. The morning of our lunch date, I thought it was stupid to drive 45 minutes to this woman's house, just to ask for money. Little did I know her heart was to come pouring out...

I knew that her husband had died recently, just 12 days after her son's Bar Mitzvah. But, I did not know much else about her.

She told me this story how before her husband passed away she had become seriously ill, and almost died. While in the hospital, our rabbi went way out of his way to visit her every evening. She recovered, and bounced back to her normal self. Three months later, her sister was diagnosed with cancer. When her sister died, she had to fly out to the funeral. My rabbi said he needed to go with her, and paid for himself, the woman, and her husband, to travel and stay there.

Then, two months later, her husband was diagnosed with cancer and died a month later. Between all of this, she had a Bar Mitzvah going on. My rabbi made all the arrangements for the service and party, and pitched in a little, from his own pocket.

When her husband died, my rabbi drove 45 minutes to her for shiva [the traditional prayer quorum for the 7 days of mourning], and

45 minutes back. He gave up time with his own family, to be with their family.

Now, one year later, she is preparing for a Bat Mitzvah. She has very little money, and will be unable to throw a party. My rabbi again, stepped in, and is planning their party. He is paying for the whole shebang, and is going the extra mile to make it wonderful. The touching part is that he is planning it from Israel, and will not even be able to attend. He feels that their family needs a party. He is also a little low on cash, but he insisted on doing this.

My point of the story is that no one from our congregation knows this story. It is all unknown to the world. If this is one of the things he's done for one family, that is not known… think of how many other things he does that no one sees.

Thank you for taking the time to read my letter. I hope it makes people realize that just because you don't see it, doesn't mean it's not happening.

Sincerely,
C.

Dear C.

I cried when I read your letter. So often people write to me to tell me of their problems with Judaism and Jewish Institutions. I have heard many complaints about rabbis and in all candor, have some of my own.

But almost every rabbi I have ever met is truly a nice person who is trying the best they can to further Judaism and to help people. Your letter is a most remarkable example.

I was so moved by your letter that I plan to use it as a response of the week… perhaps this week. Of course I will change details to conceal your rabbi's identity. *Tzaddik* [righteous person] that he appears to be, I suspect he would want to remain anonymous.

Still like you, I think others would benefit from reading of your rabbi's selfless dedication to a member of his congregation. The confidential nature of a rabbi's job requires him or her to keep their acts of kindness and assistance to themselves. But I agree with you, this rabbi—and I believe countless others—regularly perform acts of *gemilut hasadim* [acts of loving kindness] and no one ever knows… Now many do.

Thanks for writing!

Gil

Email Responses to "Unknown Things About Rabbis"

Subj: Judaism Today
Date: 2/58 9:17:21 PM CST
From:
To: GilMann@aol.com

Dear Gil,

I am writing this to let you know that the Synagogue does help if you are in a financial crisis. I know from first hand experience. My husband and I had just gotten a divorce. Money was very tight or nonexistent for me. I would never have gone to ask for charity, but I felt bad about not being able to afford tickets for the High Holiday Services. I called the Rabbi to ask if there was some way I could attend and pay off the cost of the tickets. My Rabbi said, I have a seat for you and your daughter. He would pay for it from the Rabbi's Discretionary Fund. I have always been grateful, and make sure that when I give to the Synagogue I always give to the Rabbi's Discretionary Fund so that he can continue to help others that he feels need it, without the embarrassment of going before the temple board and asking for a handout.

Subj: another great rabbi
Date: 2/5 9:46:20 PM CST
From:
To: GilMann@aol.com

i read this past week's posting and wanted to share with you
some chesed [kindness] from my own rabbi. when i moved here,
i was a young single mother with 2 children, the oldest of whom
is a paraplegic. i moved here for health reasons, and was able
to make the move only because i have a good name in chinuch
[education] and the local Hebrew school here hired me as soon
as they saw my resume. the rabbi meets with everyone who
moves into the community. rotten as it may sound, i figured
he was going to hit me for synagogue membership dues, an
appeal, or something. he knew nothing about me and my family
or finances yet. but the first words out of his mouth, besides
welcoming me, were, 'what can i, and what can the community,
do for you?' i was so shocked! i had not come across that
before, except of course sort of from the Lubavitcher rebbe z"l
[abbreviation for zichrono livracha — may his memory be a
blessing], who gave whatever he had to anyone. when i
explained my situation to the rabbi, he got the chesed [kindness
or social action] committee to organize some relief hours for me
with women from the community volunteering time to stay with
my daughter for a bit now and then. a year later, my other child
was badly hurt in an accident out of town. i called the rabbi to
say misheberach [a prayer for healing] for her, and he asked me
how long i would be away. when i explained that i couldn't go
because i had no money for the flight nor could i afford to miss
work, he personally gave me money to go and assured me i
would not lose pay while i stayed with my injured son. and he
took care of it. i hope u got pleasure from this, and if are
interested, i will tell you the community where i am, where the
rabbi always emphasizes chesed in word and deed.

Subj: Rabbi's Kindness
Date: 2/6 8:45:12 AM CST
From:
To: GilMann@aol.com

That was a very touching letter about the rabbi's generosity. You are correct that we too often find fault.

I am day school teacher and came to know that one of my students' parents had to declare bankruptcy. I called this child's rabbi and explained that the mother was embarrassed that they could not pay the fees. Without a second's hesitation, he told me to send him the bill. The school had a check within the week.

Even as I write this, though, one kindness is overshadowed by many other opposite experiences and horror stories. Our recently "ousted" rabbi who was supposedly such good friends with one couple (having spent an entire Israel mission with them.) Yet, four months later when they lost a beloved relative, he would only do the funeral for a fee now that he was no longer with the temple.

Another friend whose wife died shortly after the high holidays and the rabbi would not officiate at the funeral until their new pledge for the year had been paid.

It does go both ways!!

Shabbat Shalom
Initialed

Subj: Response of the week
Date: 2/7 4:25:17 PM CST
From:
To: GilMann@aol.com

Hi…

The posting on "Good things about Rabbi's — or was it unknown things? was a welcome break from the more commonly talked about "bad" things like charging so much for membership, even more for High Holy Days, and so on.

I wish sometimes we would hear more of the "good" and less of the "bad." There are plenty of wrong things encountered each day, much better to hear of the good things so we know there is a reason for it all and gain new strength to keep plowing through all the wrong things.

Shalom,
Name

Subj: Rabbinic role models
Date: 10/30 2:24:20 PM CST
From:
To: GilMann@aol.com

I am also a rabbi, and I have a family. This story troubles me. It seems as if we are saying that the only way to be a truly caring rabbi is to give up one's family to serve the congregation. I make hospital visits, and I try to see my congregants who are hospitalized at least two or three times a week — but I would not leave my family every evening to go to the hospital.

I use my discretionary funds for tzedakah [charity] purposes — but I would never take thousands of dollars away from my own family to pay for plane tickets and B'nai Mitzvah parties for a congregant.

My job often takes me away from my family — going to shiva minyanim, [a prayer quorum for mourning] for example. But there are times that I don't go to a shiva minyan, and send the cantor or someone else to lead the service, because I need to be with my family.

There may be reasonable explanations for some of the things that trouble me — perhaps the rabbi was using discretionary funds, but the woman did not know. Perhaps the rabbi does not give tzedakah money to UJC [United Jewish Communities formerly known as UJA] or other organizations, and the thousands of dollars he spent on this family constitute his tzedakah for the year. Perhaps this rabbi only went to one or two shiva calls and did not spend every evening away from his family.

But without knowing more details, I would never hold this story up as a model for other rabbis. It appears to be a model of how a rabbi can burn himself out and destroy his family. A rabbi is supposed to be a teacher and exemplar of Jewish behavior, including shalom bayit [the Jewish commandment to maintain peace in one's home]. How can this rabbi teach commitment to family when he puts his job ahead of his family?

Similarly, there have been several movies in the past couple years (Dangerous Minds, The Principal) that portray amazing stories of how teachers or principals can turn around troubled schools, classes, or students. The problem with such stories is that their message is that in order to be a great teacher, one needs to put one's life at risk and/or devote one's entire life, 24 hours a day, to the school. These teachers and principals have no family life — there would be no time.

These are not stories that portray realistic role models for our behavior, yet we look at the characters and turn them into heroes. A true Jewish hero is one which we can emulate, not one whose behavior is ultimately self-destructive.

This rabbi did wonderful things, but at what cost. Should he really be held up as a role model? Is it possible to find a rabbi who does amazing acts of gemilut hasadim [loving kindness] but also spends most evenings, as well as regular days off, at home with his family? Can a rabbi be a tzaddik [righteous person] without impoverishing his or her family?

L'shalom,
Rabbi Initialed

Concluding Thoughts to Copy, Cut, Paste, and Save

The previous chapter, this chapter, and the final email from a rabbi all lead me to the same conclusion: rabbis are people. Like all people, they have strengths and weaknesses and they have lives to lead that are both private and public.

Unlike the ancient Jewish priests of biblical days and the clergy in many other religions, a rabbi is not thought to have any kind of superhuman connection to God. So (as I responded to P in the prior chapter), Jews do not need a rabbi to pray and are empowered to communicate directly with God without the need for anyone to serve as an intermediary. Rabbis are not considered divine, nor are they vested with special powers relative to God (although there have been legendary rare rabbis who were so spiritually and ethically deep that they have been revered as holy).

Judaism has traditionally emphasized the "humanity" of rabbis. Rabbis are encouraged to marry, have children, and lead "normal" lives like their "flock," although their behavior is expected to be above reproach and even pious. Some of the most famous rabbinic sages in history had other professions (such as Maimonides, who was a physician) and were rabbis "on the side." The traditional role of the rabbi was to teach; in fact, the word rabbi means "my teacher." The role often included interpreting and judging Jewish law. Over time, especially in modern times, the role of the rabbi has become a full-time vocation and more closely resembles clergy of other religions.

As I have read email over the years from Jewish writers, I have seen two contradictory and consequently unrealistic expectations of rabbis. I would describe the contradiction this way: Jews place rabbis on a pedestal, and expect them to provide wisdom and guidance and be a role model from "on high." But when the rabbi's teaching, sermon, or directive is not to the congregation's liking, the congregants complain, "Who appointed you God?"

To me, this contradiction is a result of having two incompatible expectations:

1. The traditional notion that rabbis are "of the people," and

2. A more modern (and non-Jewish) notion that clergy have a unique relationship with God that is difficult or impossible for the layperson to attain.

On top of this, our society has become more and more business oriented, and the synagogues, schools, and other institutions that employ rabbis have grown to be complex organizations. So many Jews now have expectations of a rabbi that are virtually impossible for one person to achieve.

"The" rabbi is often expected to be a great orator, administrator, fundraiser, social worker, counselor, confidant, teacher, and more. In addition they must perform these duties with constituents of all ages, have a sense of humor, be personable one-on-one yet have a commanding presence at weddings, funerals, or when leading services or teaching a class. They should be visionaries and strategic thinkers as well as experts in day-to-day issues and matters of Jewish law. Just for good measure, their spouse had better be gracious, hospitable, and nicely dressed. If the rabbi is well liked, he or she is supposed to maintain his or her health, vim, vigor, and work ethic until old age. The frosting on this entire cake is that they are expected to lead their lives as impeccable role models of Jewish religious observance and ethical living for a "reasonable" salary.

Can you imagine corporate shareholders expecting a fraction of this list from the highly respected and compensated CEOs of the world's largest companies? Of course not, because only the rarest of humans could possibly meet these standards. I would suggest that Jews adjust their expectations of rabbis and be a bit more realistic about a human's capabilities.

What is reality? Again, I say rabbis are people. Like all people, rabbis are not perfect; they have flaws and make mistakes. I'd also reiterate that most of the rabbis I have met are kind souls who have within them a special calling to further Judaism and care for others. Most work tirelessly, and the only time they are truly "off work" is when they are on vacation out of town where nobody knows who they are. Even then, some rabbis extend themselves for people back home or sometimes for a stranger they encounter. Most of the rabbis I have met are very capable and intelligent people. Some are very modest and some have the kind of large ego that often comes with exceptional abilities.

Generally, and allowing for definite exceptions, I've found rabbis to be exemplary people trying to do good. Do I ever criticize a rabbi? Yes, but I try to be fair. I believe a realistic expectation for rabbis is that they live up to the meaning of their title and be our teachers of how Judaism can and should guide our lives.

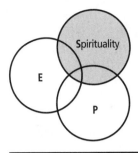

Section II: Spirituality

"I'm not sure I believe in God..."

The number of times people have expressed this sentiment to me is beyond counting. When expressed by a Jewish person, I often perceive guilt or misgivings. After all, what kind of Jew could make such a statement? Didn't the Jews bring the concept of one God to the world? Or as some have said to me, "If there really is a God, am I going to someday pay a big price for my shaky or nonexistent faith?"

Many people secretly harbor these and other kinds of doubts and questions about God but wouldn't dare speak openly about their doubts and questions — this is much too intimate.

I've found this reserved behavior strange given the offerings in the media today. Turn on the tube or radio at almost any hour and you will hear some of the most unusual sexual practices anyone could imagine openly described and even bragged about by practitioners. These kinds of discussions are not intimate anymore, but ask someone "Do you believe in God?" — now that's an intimate question!

On the Internet, however, all the rules are different. Because of the safety of anonymity, we're emboldened to bare our souls more freely, and I've received all kinds of email related to God, faith, and issues of spirituality. While this email quietly conveys the writers' innermost thoughts, it is part of a louder trend in society: the search for spirituality. For evidence of this, go to any major bookstore in any mall and look at the number of the selections about spirituality. The media has even coined the term *seekers* to describe the throngs of people looking for faith and spirituality.

Traditionally, Judaism has not emphasized searching for spirituality. Behavior has been stressed over belief, and this is reflected in the huge body of Jewish law about how to behave and the educational thrust on understanding these laws. By behaving according to Jewish law, Jews are supposed to elevate themselves in holiness and in this way access God. God is even quoted in the Talmud (the revered collection of Jewish law and commentary) as saying, "If only they (my people) would leave me and obey my Torah (laws and teachings)."

Notwithstanding, many today are looking for spirituality and answers about God. This section examines some of the questions posed by these people. Their questions can be placed into three categories:

1. Does God exist?
2. How does God operate? Or, What are God's ways?
3. How can I find God?

God's Existence and God's Ways

These two categories are interconnected. For example, questions about God's existence are often tied to questions about how God operates or the ways or nature of God — for example, How can there be a God when there is so much evil and pain in the world? Where was God on 9-11? Why does God allow children and good people to suffer? The tragedy, horror, magnitude, and shock of the Holocaust lurks close to the surface of many of these questions.

Finding God

Questions about the existence and nature of God are also tied to questions about having faith, finding God, or accessing spirituality. In general, people ask: If there is a God, how can I find inspiration, guidance, and comfort from God?

This is asked in two ways. One approach focuses on Jewish ways of finding God: questions about Jewish prayer, synagogues, services, rabbis, and so on. The other approach focuses on accessing God through sources and religions other than Judaism.

Why are we looking so hard? I think because we realize how tiny we are and because the challenges of life are so large. In spite of great human accomplishment and knowledge (described to me by one person as the "religion of science") or, ironically, as a result of these achievements, we realize our understanding of the world is very small. This is combined with our questions about how to make sense of the difficulties life presents and, ultimately, the fact that we all face death.

Collectively, the emails in this chapter ask how and what do I believe? How can I find faith and gain spiritual nourishment from Judaism... in a high-tech world that runs on science and offers many competing spiritual options from Buddhism to communing with nature? Each chapter in this section asks these questions in one form or another. Here are the chapters in the Spirituality section:

I Am Very Angry at God!
Can a Jew Pray in Christ's Name?
Do Orthodox Jews or Reborn Christians Know "the" Truth?
Will Jews Burn in Hell?
Why Does Judaism Discriminate Against Women?

Chapter 9
I Am Very Angry at God!

Dear Gil:

I have always had rock-solid belief the Lord will protect and defend me. When my son died at 8 years of age, I admit, I did waver a bit. But, through all that, I still trusted and believed even though I got mighty angry at G-d. I "wrestled" but good.

Two years ago my beloved husband, David, died after a long and painful illness. Yes, the Yarhzeit [observance of the anniversary of a death] comforts but... I miss him so terribly and I still cry for him.

But now, I have a new challenge. My wonderful sister is dying of cancer. She's in pain, she's so scared. I am VERY angry at G-d. VERY angry. How can I stop this anger I am feeling? My child, my husband and now my sister. The pain is incredible and I don't know how to get around it. I "talk" to G-d, I pray and I "wrestle." But, I just cannot stop the anger. Do you have some wisdom to share that might ease the anger, and truth be told, some doubt I feel creeping into my heart?

I have grown weary of what seem like the usual clichés and platitudes. I am sorry to take all of your time like I have. I deeply appreciate whatever you might have to offer.

L

L Shalom!

As I read your letter I thought — What's wrong with being angry? Who could blame you after the painful losses you described? I think something might be amiss if you were not angry. You might feel a little better if you gave yourself permission to be angry. I asked a friend of mine who is battling cancer about what you asked me. She told me, "Moses was sometimes angry with God. At times, I too have been angry with God... It's OK, she (God) can take it."

Moving from anger to pain, I'd like to offer you a Chassidic saying that you might find comforting: "Who ever said that one must pray with a whole heart? Perhaps it is preferable to pray with a broken heart." (Rabbi Uri of Strelisk)

Your heart sounds understandably broken as you struggle with God. Two resources that could offer you some guidance as you struggle are Harold Kushner's book *When Bad Things Happen to Good People* and the National Center for Jewish Healing at 212–399–2320. They have both provided help to countless hurting people.

Locally, I suggest you seek out a Jewish healing prayer service (or talk to a rabbi about creating one). Here is a prayer from one such service (the Center for Healing can send you others). This prayer (I am sorry, I don't know the author) touched me — perhaps you too will find it meaningful:

> "Each of us enters this sanctuary with a different need. Some hearts are full of gratitude and joy: They are overflowing with the happiness of love and the joy of life; they are eager to confront the day, to make the world more fair; they are recovering from illness or have escaped misfortune. And we rejoice with them.

> "Some hearts ache with sorrow: Disappointments weigh heavily upon them and they have tasted despair: families have been broken; loved ones lie on a bed of pain; death has taken those whom they cherished. May our presence and sympathy bring them comfort.

> "Some hearts are embittered: They have sought answers in vain; ideals are mocked and betrayed; life has lost its meaning and value. May the knowledge that we too are searching, restore their hope and give them courage to believe that not all is emptiness.

> "Some spirits hunger: They long for friendship; they crave understanding; they yearn for warmth. May we in common need and striving, gain strength from one another, as we share our joys, lighten each other's burdens and pray for the welfare of community."

A main point of this prayer and Jewish healing services is that you should not struggle alone. I do not understand God's ways or why there is so much pain in this world, but I do see that God gave us others. Just as life can be so wonderful we must share it with others, life also hands us difficulties that are far too painful to endure alone. Especially at such times, we need help with our answerless questions and constructive outlets for our dark thoughts and emotions. So don't struggle alone. Share what is on your mind with family, friends, rabbis, professionals, and others.

Please continue to reach out as you have to me. Together with others, I hope you are able to find the comfort you seek and deserve. Stay in touch!

Gil

Email Responses to "I Am Very Angry at God!"

Subj: re Angry with God
Date: 2/10/ 7:04:47 PM CST
From:
To: GilMann@aol.com

It is my hope that you find comfort in knowing that there are others who are strangers who truly care about your anguish.
I have had many personal struggles within our family, I have no answers as to why. I only know what has worked for me.
Memories that are cherished of good times, humor, live for the beauty of each day and find something good in it, if only the smell of a flower, the sun casting warmth, the laugh of a loved one. For me (it may seem trite, or not enough to others) I would have rather had the pain of losing someone then to never have them in my life at all. So I rejoice in their life even though my heart aches in losing them. Enjoy each day as a gift that your sister has left. Try to read to her, make it meaningful, look at old albums and share happy childhood memories.

In Friendship and hope for you and peace in your heart.
Name

Subj: anger and the journey
Date: 2/18/ 9:34 AM CST
From:
To: GilMann@aol.com

I applaud the willingness to talk about a subject few of us will, and that is anger with G-d. In a faith which creates a foundation upon which we draw, there are times when that very same faith leaves us blank and unsure.

I myself am a survivor of cancer. Throughout my treatment, I didn't want to be angry, thinking it was wrong or demonstrated my lack of faith. Oddly enough, while the radiation treatments caused physical problems, the real threats to my survival were taking place in my heart. But I just wouldn't let myself see the pain and frustration, the anger and the fear.

I grew well and went on to pursue a graduate degree in theology in order to help answer the nagging questions. But still I ran, I hid from my own heart. I wanted to know Adonai's [God's] place for me and that I was loved, but I wouldn't allow myself to look, to seek, to cry, to feel the anger.

Now, I find myself facing a new disease. I am trying hard to maintain a positive attitude. But finally, I have had to give heed to what has been locked inside for so long. I have finally looked up and asked, even screamed, "Why me?! Am I that awful?! What have I done wrong?!"

Granted, no life-changing answer ever came, but in its place, a growing freedom to be in dialogue with the Most High. To tell G-d in my prayers just how I feel, what frightens me, what I need, and yes, to openly talk about the pain. True, this doesn't promise an answer or some magical means to take away the anger, but, what it does give birth to, is a direct honesty with the Giver of Life. It may sound strange, but G-d can take it, so, give it back, in large portions!

We've been given music to celebrate, laughter to feel the dance of the earth, and in part, voices to pause, reflect, and yes, share our emotions from joy to anger with the One who has given us this life. As long as there is air in our lungs, and a thought rolling over in our minds, we owe it to those we love, ourselves, and to the Eternal, to take an honest role in our feelings, up to, and including all that angers. May the journey offer you peace!!

Name

Subj: Re: Don't blame God... He is your only hope
Date: 2/18/ 12:00 AM CST
From:
To: GilMann@aol.com

It is not fair, in my view, to state that God preserves anyone's life over other's because He might deem them "worth" it. God does not choose who lives and who dies based on merit. How else would you explain the deaths of millions of innocent Jews during the holocaust or any other wars?

Subj: Re: Poor Woman
Date: 2/17/ 8:44:17 PM CDT
From:
To: GilMann@aol.com

Dear Gil:

I suppose it is natural for that poor woman to be angry at God for the misfortunes that befell her family, but the anger is misplaced. God does not "take" people or make them suffer. While I have no answers for the woman in the article, I can only offer the example of my wife.

In 1956, my wife and her family lost their home and everything they owned when the Russians invaded Hungary. One of her brothers and one of her sisters were seized and never heard from again. In 1958, four of her relatives died attempting to flee their homeland. In 1962 my wife's first husband died tragically of cancer. In 1966 her Father died. In 1968 her mother died. In 1969 her sister died in a tragic car crash. My wife has lived constantly with the death of those closest to her. She does not blame God nor is she angry. She accepts that which she cannot change and does not blame God or anyone else for her situation. The one exception is that she is fiercely anti-communist, and who could blame her? (I think her admiration of me is enhanced by the fact that I bombed North Korea during the war.) Far from being angry, my wife acknowledges that God (the God of Abraham) sent me to her to be her husband and raise her children as my own. It is the wrong question to ask "What is the meaning of life?" God commands us to ask "What meaning will I create for MY life?"

My heart goes out to the woman who has lost so much, but perhaps by only looking at the negative she is failing to see the whole picture. My words may not bring her any comfort or solace, no words can, I think. We cannot choose the situations that confront us in our lives, but we can choose our attitudes towards those situations. In any case, my sincerest condolences, sympathies, and prayers go out to her.

Name

Subj: Re: I am very angry with G-D
Date: 2/18/ 2:15 PM CST
From:
To: GilMann@aol.com

Dear Gil,

Since I believe nothing happens by chance, I had just finished reading a commentary on the Parasha [weekly Torah portion] of the week when I turned on my PC and read the email from the woman who said she is very angry with G-D.

I liked what you wrote and just wanted to add something I read in the commentary, "The Chofetz Chayim [a famous sage] teaches that G-d does not make impossible demands upon us. Every person is obligated to do only that which he or she can. As King Solomon said in Mishlei [Proverbs] 9:10, "All that you find within your ability to do, act upon it... " which is to say, only that which is within your ability. We must do only that which has been placed upon us."

I don't know if she will gain any comfort at all, but I believe it confirms what you said about her right to be angry.

Thank you,

Subj: Re: I am very Angry!
Date: 2/25/ 8:24 AM CST
From:
To: GilMann@aol.com

I am able to identify with the writer's losses and feelings. My mother (who lived with us) died five years ago and my husband's third yartzheit [anniversary of death] is today. My sister and her husband have each had serious illnesses — hospitalization & surgery — this winter. I have returned to attending synagogue services and functions on a regular basis and have found it helpful for me.

I keep Kushner's book at my bedside and have sent it to many friends in their time of need. I also have found great help from the meditation tapes (also at my bedside) and books of Dr. Bernie Siegel. She might want to share Dr. Bernie's books with her sister. His original work was with cancer patients, but he has since broadened his scope.

I have found great help in a local support group for grief and loss. The writer might want to check with local hospices and synagogues for such groups. They might not, in the case of hospice, be solely Jewish groups, but they will certainly at some point touch on G-d and her feelings of anger.

As you mentioned, anger is a normal part of grieving. Questioning is a part of life — of growing and learning and finding peace if not total understanding. And it all takes time.

May we all find that peace of spirit as we travel this journey called life.

Subj: Angry at G-d
Date: 2/27/:19 PM CST
From:
To: GilMann@aol.com

First, I want to say that my heart goes out to this woman for the pain and suffering she has to endure. Secondly, it would be helpful if I and anyone else who so wishes would pray for her sister. Perhaps you could print her name so "mishuberras" [prayers for healing] could be said. Then, I want to say that I speak from several positions — I am a human being, a psychologist and a speaker — who speaks on self esteem.

Your anger is real and genuine and it needs to be expressed and recognized. The recommendation to be involved in community is a very good one — for it is only with others that our feelings can be acknowledged, accepted, and then, hopefully, the harmful ones, released.

Why is anger harmful? Because it doesn't hurt in any way, or actually affect in any way, the being against whom it is being directed. It does, however, very much hurt the one who is harboring it.

However, when I can step back for a moment and ask myself "would I rather that the entire possibility of the situation never have happened?" I usually answer "no." In other words, if asked, would you rather have not had a son at all, or, if possible, to be grateful for what I'm sure were a wonderful and gratifying 8 years with this precious gift that had to be taken away?, what would you say? It is so hard when we are focusing on the loss to try to remember the joy we felt by the "having" but that is what keeps me going.

There is no reason that we can understand why one person's life seems so overwrought with tragedy while other seem to get away "scott free."

I hope that one day, you will be able to see beauty and hope in life again, that the pain will be diminished and you will be able to remember and appreciate that the precious gifts that were taken away were yours to enjoy for whatever time you had them. In the meantime, recognize that you have every reason and right to be damned angry and resentful, that your sister is fortunate to have someone around now who can love, care, and support her during her illness and remember that there are many people who are caring for you and with you right now and who will pray for both your sister's recovery and your strength to care for her and to go on.

I do, yet, believe in Hashem [God, literally meaning The Name] and I pray to Him to be with you during this time and forever.

Subj: Re: Angry at G-d
Date: 2/28/ 6:42 AM CST
From:
To: GilMann@aol.com

There actually is a reason that some suffer tragedy and others seem not to and that is that events in the universe occur entirely at random. The universe is therefore indifferent to good or evil. This is difficult to accept but is probably healthier than hating God.

Name

"We must question the story logic of having an all-knowing all-powerful God, who creates faulty humans and then blames them for his own mistakes." Gene Roddenberry

---

Subj: (no subject)
Date: 2/10/ 8:52:53 PM CST
From:
To: GilMann@aol.com

Coming home from work tonight, I was praying for some sign that God could hear me, The prayer that you quoted from the Jewish Healing Service made me feel not so alone and I thank you for it. I can certainly empathize with the woman that wrote to you. My heart and prayers go out to her.

Subj: anger at God
Date: 2/10/ 10:47:38 PM CST
From:
To: GilMann@aol.com

Paraphrasing Tolstoy — all happiness is the same, but everybody's pain is unique to them.

I have found that at least for me, time does not ease the pain, it merely makes it less debilitating. The God that I believe in is in the fact that I do wake up and continue living each day despite, during, and maybe because of tragedy. Judaism has always been quite clear that the grief must be experienced, especially in cases where grief is presumed appropriate. Part of grief is anger. Anger at the world for turning when yours has stopped, anger at the sun for shining, and anger at God for "letting" these things happen.

Until the pain is livable, words remain just words. Background and meaningless, except for the meaning our fevered senses attach to the bits and pieces that reconnect us to the world, our souls and God.

Name

Subj: In Response to why does G-d hate me
Date: 2/13/ 11:56:19 AM CDT
From:
To: GilMann@aol.com

This woman is doubting G-d's existence or G-d's will because she doesn't trust that Hashem really does know what's best, or that Hashem really does love her. Me, I choose to assume I don't have the whole picture. Yes, she is in pain. And sometimes life is pain. Sometimes choosing to trust G-d is hard. But for me, I cannot afford the arrogance of doubting that my life is according to G-d's will, or that Hashem does know what's best, however hard it may be in the middle.

It is arrogance to doubt G-d? Why do we comfort people when they decide they know better than G-d that something is bad or not right? Why do we not tell them that whatever G-d gives us to deal with, G-d also gives us the strength to deal with (and yes, not alone). It's not that I don't sympathize with the pain, but I think we are asking and answering the wrong questions. Not 'why is G-d doing this?', but 'what is G-d giving me to help me get through this?' and 'what can I learn from this that will bring me closer to Hashem?'

When asked why did so and so die? my only answer is the complementary question why did I live? And when both questions are asked together the only possible answer is that we can't know G-d's will, except, sometimes, in hindsight.

L'Shalom
Name

Subj: Angry at Gd
Date: 2/10/ 7:53:22 PM CST
From:
To: GilMann@aol.com

Gil

I was deeply moved by the sorrow and despair of Ms. "L." I, too had very painful days that stretched into years. I lost just about everything. In the midst of my despair, I almost lost my faith. Ms. "L" must feel very lonely and singled out by life. Pain has the ability to make you feel isolated regardless of how many people are around you. Indeed, pain teaches you that there is an existential aloneness that you cannot escape. Nobody, no matter how close they are to you, can possibly unburden the intensity of the pain. But faith can help us see strength and love within ourselves.

Judaism teaches us about the glorious gifts that we are given by God. We are given the ability to make choices, to love, to hope, to dream, and to endure. Judaism also teaches us about life's constant transformation. Our essence, I believe, transforms itself into life-giving energy when our physical being dies. Like other forms of energy, it never gets destroyed. Life's transformation is what we must look for when our hearts ache intensely. Ms. "L" will not be able to touch or see the physical beings of those she loves who have died. But they are part of the universe now, a part of life that she can see and touch. Whereever there is a manifestation of life, there is a manifestation of God... and that's where our loved ones go. She has been given the gift of choice. God is waiting for her to decide which way to go. God provides strength as we walk.

Name

Subj: To the Lady in Pain from Loss of her family members
Date: 2/10/ 11:37:51 PM CST
From:
To: GilMann@aol.com

Hi, Gil

I feel so much for this lady. My foster mother is not Jewish, but she has a prayer group and she teaches prayer to several groups in her retirement complex. I will ask that they pray for this lady.

Now, I think she needs to contact a grief support group for herself. There is also a cancer support group for women. I will try to find out the exact name of it.

I have been watching Oprah Winfrey's show. Today she had Gary Zukav on again. He is not pushing a religion nor does he pretend to be a psychologist, but he has some very helpful ideas in his book called "The Seat of the Soul." This lady needs, REALLY NEEDS, to take some quiet time for herself. I agree that it is not wrong to be angry with G-d; however, as Gary says, we are put here for a reason, and our life's work is to heal the problems we were born with. "When you are in the throes of your agony, that is your holy place," and the starting place of your healing. I agree that the healing group is also a good place for her to go, or to start one, if there is none in her town. Maybe it is her life's work to do, that to provide a quiet, loving, healing place for others and in so doing find peace and healing for herself. He says, "You cannot have control over what happens to you. You can control only how you respond to it and use what you learn from it."

Name

Concluding Thoughts to Copy, Cut, Paste, and Save

As I reviewed this section and gave thought to a conclusion, I was most conscious of the original writer's comment that she had "grown weary of what seem like the usual clichés and platitudes."

Out of desperation and awkwardness, these are the kinds of words that seem to stumble from our mouths when we communicate with a person enduring pain or grief. I have heard horror stories of "words of comfort" that have been offered with the intention of helping, that, in reality, were insensitive and instead compounded the person's suffering. This is why Judaism teaches that upon visiting the house of a mourner, we should say very little. Rather, we should show our support by our presence, giving mourners the option to speak if they wish. Listening can be the most compassionate thing to offer at such times.

One could say that some of the comments from the emails in this chapter would be unhelpful. Still, I include them because there is another Jewish lesson in all the emails in this chapter. Judaism places a huge emphasis on the importance of community. At no time is community more important than during crisis and loss. I was personally moved by the cyber-community that responded to this woman's plight.

I forwarded many emails to her. Not long after, she wrote back to me. Here is an excerpt of what she wrote:

> "I have been feeling pretty good lately. My attitude has improved greatly and my friends comment on it frequently… I appreciate your forwarding on the responses to my original letter to you. I never expected such a range and depth of reactions. Most enlightening."

A friend of mine who was the rabbi of a huge congregation once told me that working with so many families over the years taught him that anyone who lives long enough will experience some tragedy in their life. When life slams us to the pavement, we are left dazed, wounded, and groping for answers. Why must we endure such pain? What role does God play? Where is God at these times? As I said earlier, I do not pretend to know. But I do know, confirmed by the emails I have received, like those in this chapter, that we need each other and that we have a tremendous capacity to heal and to help though our acts of kindness. Could this be God? Are these kinds acts part of the Divine spark in each of us?

Whether or not this idea is consistent with your image of God, perhaps the most important lesson that can be drawn from this chapter is that even a small act of kindness can go a long way—like sending a compassionate email to a stranger in pain.

Chapter 10
Can a Jew Pray in Christ's Name?

Dear Gil:

I am Jewish and work at a Catholic Hospital. It is a wonderful job that I enjoy. The only thing that reminds me that I am working in this environment is the fact that the building is adorned in a Christian manner (i.e., crucifixes in the rooms) and most large meetings are preceded with a prayer.

The prayers, ad libbed by a staff member in attendance, generally are not religious in nature ("please look after the people in this room," "help us to follow our mission," etc.). They do, however, begin with "Heavenly Father" and end with "In Christ's Name We Pray."

During these prayer times, I do not bow my head, close my eyes nor say "Amen" as do the rest in attendance. I do, however, remain quiet, eyes focused forward. My question: Am I being rude to my co-workers by ignoring their observance? Is there a better way to behave without dishonoring my own upbringing? I've always wondered...

B

Dear B:

A difficult situation you are describing, made all the more difficult by two opposite responses that I will offer you.

I checked with a rabbi who told me that according to *halacha*, or Jewish law, Jews are not supposed to participate in worship of religions other than ours.

He then told me a remarkable story about the Chief Rabbi of Mexico, who was visiting Iran after the Ayatollah Khomeini took power. At a public meeting with the Ayatollah, as a part of a Muslim prayer session, all got down on their knees and bowed to Allah... all but the Rabbi that is.

He was worried about his behavior, but felt he had no choice. His worry was warranted. When the prayer was over, he was taken out by Iranian soldiers. He was then brought to the Ayatollah, who asked through an interpreter why he refused to bow. The Rabbi responded that he was prohibited by his Jewish faith.

The Ayatollah responded, "You are a man I can trust. You will not do things just to please others." The Rabbi then asked for intervention on behalf of Iranian Jews and was granted some form of help.

Notwithstanding *halacha* and this inspirational story, I have found myself in situations such as those you are describing, and usually my response has been to bow my head out of courtesy and say nothing.

An equivalent might be if a non-Jew visiting a synagogue remained seated when the rest of the Jewish congregation stood for prayer… like when the Torah Ark is opened. Or if a non-Jew would refuse to wear a *kipah* or *yarmulke* [head covering traditionally worn during prayer as a sign of respect to God above] in a synagogue where Jews wear them. These rituals, like bowing one's head, are signs of respect to God. But if your beliefs make bowing your head difficult or impossible, you might think of bowing your head out of courtesy to your non-Jewish colleagues.

Surely some would disagree with me and I understand that, since I have not felt 100% comfortable bowing during Christian prayer. Sometimes, a way I can feel more comfortable bowing is if I silently offer a prayer to "my" God. (After all, we bow our heads during our *Alenu* prayer.)

Where does this leave you? One solution would be to respectfully approach those reciting the prayers if you feel you can—given that the hospital is Catholic and they are entitled to their beliefs. Explain politely and gently that you would like to participate and that you don't mean to offend, but your religious beliefs and laws would require the prayer's wording be more generic about God without references to Jesus. If they say this is not possible or you feel making the request is inappropriate, then you can decide how or if you will participate per the arguments above.

I hope that this helps you to find a way to show respect toward your colleagues and perhaps even add your Jewish voice to theirs, so you too can pray for the guidance, wisdom, and compassion to heal the sick and comfort those in pain.

Gil

Email Responses to "Can a Jew Pray in Christ's Name?"

Subj: Re: Can a Jew pray in Christ's name?
Date: 2/26/ 9:53:32 PM CDT
From:
To: GilMann@aol.com

Dear Gil:

I don't believe that her coworkers will be offended by her not participating in their prayers, but I do believe that it is wrong for her to ask them to change the way they choose to pray in order to accommodate her method of prayer. She must realize that she has chosen to place herself in a distinctly catholic environment and they have a right to pray as a group as they see fit. They also must realize that she is not catholic and she, as an individual, also has a right to pray in the manner in which she believes. Personally, if I was a patient there, I would welcome both methods of prayer. In my opinion, two lines to God are better than one!

Name

Subj: E-mail of the week response
Date: 2/24/ 11:35:17 PM CDT
From:
To: GilMann@aol.com

An equivalent might be if a non-Jew visiting a synagogue, remained seated when the rest of the Jewish congregation stood for prayer... like when the Torah Ark is opened. I beg to differ with you. They are clearly not the same issue. Standing for the Torah, which is not contrary to the non Jew's religion, is being courteous. Prayer in the name of false G-d's is blasphemous (and a violation of Jewish law) and has dire consequences in our belief system.

But, if your beliefs make bowing your head difficult or impossible, you might think of bowing your head out of courtesy to your non-Jewish colleagues.

My suggestion would be to either keep your head up and say nothing or better yet, if you know the pattern and timing of the meeting, enter the room discreetly after they finish their prayer service. If anyone notices and asks, politely explain the issue.

Subj: E- Mail of the week
Date: 2/25/ 7:01:04 AM CDT
From:
To: GilMann@aol.com

Dear Gil:

I was in much the same position as the woman in the Catholic Hospital. When I was in Army Boot camp it fell to lay leaders to give an evening prayer. The one chosen to do it was the son of a Christian preacher. Of course the prayer ended in Christ's name. Upon hearing this I broke the circle and walked back to my bunk. Of 60 people, I was the only (to my knowledge) Jew. As soon as I could, I approached the lay leader and told him it was necessary for the prayer to be nondenominational for me to take part in it. He was genuinely helpful and we spent some time looking through the bible to find psalms that fit everyone's needs.

I have never been one to go quietly along with the masses and I strongly feel that the woman at the Hospital should voice her feelings to the administration. No one should ever be forced to feel that they must go along, especially at their place of employment. If it is necessary there are laws to protect her rights. Staff meetings are not prayer meetings.

Just had to chime in with my 2 cents.

Name

Subj: "In Christ's name we pray... "
Date: 2/25/ 2:47:13 PM CDT
From:
To: GilMann@aol.com

Dear Mr. Mann;

I would like to express my concern for "B" in the above referenced email question. I hope she realizes that she may never feel comfortable, and, in all likelihood, it will not change. She should feel good about herself for not compromising her principles nor her faith. She should also feel good about herself for caring about being respectful of others faith. If more people were like her, this would be a much more compassionate place.

Sincerely,
Name

Subj: Christian Prayers
Date: 2/25/ 5:31:36 PM CDT
From:
To: GilMann@aol.com

I have been in this situation, and it was one of the things that prompted me to become the host committee chair for an international engineering conference. I got tired of all the good ole boys from Auburn and Georgia Tech getting up to the podium at lunch asking all of us to give Baptist or Presbyterian or Methodist thanks in the name of Jesus Christ. After many years of sitting at a banquet table with a couple of software developers from India, my Israeli robotics expert friends, and a Chinese professor from Oregon State, I was determined that when I got up in front of the group, everybody would be able to pray along with me. I got to try out my non-denominational blessing at a regional conference in St. Louis. It worked well.

Unfortunately there is still the parochial mentality that assumes that "everybody goes to my church." It should not take being a minority to recognize that most people don't know your religion or practices. But, the employee of the Catholic hospital should expect to find Catholic prayer and feel free to stand or sit quietly until it is over.

Name

Subj: Bowing your head to Christ...
Date: 2/26/ 2:47:52 AM CDT
From:
To: GilMann@aol.com

Gil,

Coming from a midsize city where the Jewish community is quite small, I can speak well of this issue.

I have never, nor will I ever, bow my head in prayer for anything having to do with Christ. When I have gone to non-Jewish ceremonies, it has mostly been on invitation (baptisms, weddings) or funerals. Not that I am any kind of egomaniacal person but I truly feel that my presence alone shows the respect I give to the situation regardless of whether I sit, stand, bow my head, or otherwise when everyone else does.

On the other hand, I would give the same respect to those non-Jews who would come to my shul and want to be present for a ceremony or service. Should they choose to sit, stand, or bow their head with me is not of issue but rather that they are present to share the simcha [happy event].

The bottom line for me has to do with what is in one's heart. How can I expect my non-Jewish friends to understand my reverence for the Torah or, in kind, how can I possibly understand the depth of their reverence for Christ? And is it really mandatory that we do understand each other in this way? I say no but rather that we should respect the differences.

Sincerely,
Name

Subj: Can a Jew pray in Christ's name?
Date: 2/26/ 12:18:45 PM CDT
From:
To: GilMann@aol.com

I have been faced with a similar problem in my work situation. However, unlike the person working in a Catholic hospital, I work in a public school system in an urban area. We do not have prayers in the school, of course, but whenever there is a retirement dinner, someone always makes a prayer. I always hope that they will not add the words In Jesus' name we pray, but they always do.

No one seems to notice anything wrong being that we are workers in a public school system, and I don't want to make waves by saying anything. This is maybe just a once a year occurrence. However, I have chosen to look forward and remain silent during the prayer. There is only one other Jewish teacher in my school and I notice that she does the same.

When and if I have a retirement dinner, I will certainly request that they refrain from such a prayer.

Subj: Jewish Prayer in Christian Setting
Date: 2/29/ 12:26:23 AM CDT
From:
To: GilMann@aol.com

This woman's dilemma reminds me of the time that my then 14 year old son was on a soccer team with Mormon kids. They did a short prayer before each game, and a different child was chosen to do the prayer each game. My son had not volunteered to lead all season, and the coach picked him anyway during a game. My son recited the Kiddush in Hebrew which left all of the kids' parents asking us to translate. Of course, we did so literally, [the Kiddush literally praises God for creating the fruit of the vine] not wanting to tell the Mormon, teetotaling parents that our son had just blessed the wine!

Of course, we asked him afterwards, why he did not say a prayer of thanks instead. He replied simply, "I like wine!"

P.S. We have taught our children to be respectful, as we would want others to be respectful of our rights. We do not bow and we silently substitute Hashem [God, literally meaning The Name] for their names for G-d.

Subj: Praying in Jesus' name
Date: 2/26/ 5:00:57 PM CDT
From:
To: GilMann@aol.com

Gil,

I work with a born again Christian, and he likes to say grace in Jesus' name when we go out to lunch. I am not offended and take it as an opportunity to remember G-d during my day. I think we often get hung up on "form " in our religion. We need to remember the 11th commandment more, Love thy neighbor as thyself!

Regards, Name

Subj: CAN A JEW PRAY IN CHRIST'S NAME?
Date: 2/27/00 1:07:28 AM CDT
From:
To: GilMann@aol.com

Dear Gil,

I was born Protestant and converted to Judaism. I am now President of my Jewish Community Center.

In this situation, I think that the hospital worker has two choices — either to conduct him/herself with respect and dignity, or to leave the room momentarily. I vote for the quiet dignity. I see nothing wrong with bowing the head or closing the eyes. I would say a silent Jewish prayer at that moment, for healing of the sick. I would not say "amen" when Jesus is named, though. In other settings, I would look for dignified opportunities to mention my own religious practices.

This is an employee voluntarily working at a Roman Catholic institution, and I think that it would be outrageous and ridiculous to ask that those people utter a generic or non-denominational prayer. In a secular or public context, I would agree that request should be made, but not in a Catholic hospital. I also don't see how this person thinks the prayers are "not religious in nature" when they are praying, "Heavenly Father, help us follow our mission, in Christ's name we pray." Sounds pretty religious to me, and entirely appropriate for that group of people in that setting.

Shalom,
Name

Subj: Praying "In Jesus' Name"
Date: 2/27/ 8:37:05 PM CDT
From:
To: GilMann@aol.com

Are you out of your mind? If you were among heathens, would you also take part in their human sacrifices? Or ritual cannibalism — taking in some dead Jew's body and blood? That's essentially what you are doing when you are taking part in specifically Christian worship.

If you have to be there, simply stand eyes ahead and say nothing. That way you don't offend them and you don't offend G-d.

Name

Subj: Re: Can a Jew Pray in Christ's Name
Date: 3/2/ 10:02:17 AM CST
From:
To: GilMann@aol.com

Dear Gil,

While I work in a Community Hospital, I do work among people of varying faiths. I have gone to funerals, weddings, confirmations, etc, in different churches and synagogues.

I stand when everyone stands and sit when everyone sits or kneels. I do this out of respect for those whose home I am in. (Their house of worship.) I bow my head during "thanks" when I am in someone's home for dinner and that is their ritual or custom. I usually offer my own silent prayer of thanks, and have at times been asked to offer my own, aloud in my hosts home.

I listen to the services of others and can usually find a generic message, sans Christ or Allah — just of humanity and daily living. When prayers are read or offered, I will usually offer my own, silently. I have said Mazel Tov [congratulations] at friends Christian Weddings, Baptisms, etc.

In order to live in this Melting Pot, I believe understanding each others customs and beliefs is the only way to stop Hatred and Bigotry and support tolerance, respect and friendship.

Name

Concluding Thoughts to Copy, Cut, Paste, and Save

Everyone seems to have strong opinions on this subject. Yet if you find yourself in the awkward positions described by these emails, what to do?

Sandi Berman emailed to tell me that she regularly found herself in this position as her professional association always opened meetings with a prayer. Her solution was simple and wonderful. She published a booklet of possible prayers for meetings that could be recited comfortably by people of any religion. Even the mayor of Houston has used the booklet!

She wrote her own prayers and also borrowed from:

Union Home Book of Prayer
Gates of Prayer
Language of Judaism
On the Doorposts of Your Home
Kabbalat Shabbat service

Here is an example of a prayer from Sandi's booklet:

We pray for the friends and family gathered here today and ask that you help those who are not yet able to find the happiness of freedom. Give strength to those of us who are restoring the land.

Teach us all, wherever we live, to grow in knowledge and to love each other. We pray for all peoples and ask that you help the hungry to find food for their bodies and food for their minds. Teach all of Your children to do to others the kindness they would like done to themselves.

The booklet is now in its second printing, and Sandi is donating any profits to charity. If you'd like a copy, write to: siberwriter@aol.com or send a check for $4.00 payable to:

Sandi Berman
Post Office Box 270471
Houston, TX 77277–0471

As I reviewed Sandi's booklet and read and reread this chapter, I was struck by the irony of how our common desire to seek spiritual help from God often divides us. With this on my mind, I wrote a little prayer of my own. Prayer is a personal affair, but as this chapter describes, we often pray publicly. So feeling a bit vulnerable, I'll end by sharing my personal prayer. I am not sure God will be moved by my words, but perhaps others will be.

Together

I understand that drop by drop…
water carves canyons,
over millions of years.
Why are our lives so short?

I understand that stars are huge,
and unreachable.
Why are we so tiny?

I wish we knew more,
I wish we could do more,
I wish we lived with less pain.

Help us to wish together,
Ask our questions together,
And find answers,
And understanding,
Together.

Chapter 11
Do Orthodox Jews or Reborn Christians Know "the" Truth?

Dear Gil:

Attacks by Orthodox Jews on non-Orthodox Jews offend me because I don't believe anyone has a monopoly on "Truth."

I work with a Hindu woman who teaches children about human values and ethics. She told me she explains to them about different religions by likening it to a trip to Chicago from Indianapolis. This is something even the smallest child in her class can comprehend. I can take I–65 to Chicago; you can take Rte 52; someone else may take I–74 into Illinois and go north from there. No matter what route they travel, the point is that they arrive at the same place—a concept of God that functions for each of them. I like the analogy. It's simple, but also rather elegant in its way.

L

Dear L:

I agree with your comment, "I don't believe anyone has a monopoly on 'Truth.'" At the same time, I can also find a way to respect religious people who believe they do know the truth.

As opposed to your analogy about highways, I think the analogy many religious people would use is that they know with certainty that the world is round and it drives them crazy that so many unenlightened people believe and behave as if the world is flat. Some of these religious people even think that "a flat world view" is dangerous and they are just trying to help others avoid the danger.

I learned this lesson in eighth grade when Sue, the girl who sat behind me in Social Studies, became a very religious born-again Christian. There were few Jews in my school, but she knew I was Jewish and almost daily told me about her newfound and unshakable faith. One day before class she told me that she was praying specifically for me.

At first, I was shocked and offended. "What? Why?" I asked. She explained with certainty and concern that X number of Jews would be saved when Jesus returns — despite the fact that we do not believe in Jesus. She was fervently praying that I be one of the fortunate Jews who is saved. I was astounded, but no longer offended. She was praying because she cared about me.

I don't remember a thing I learned that year from my teacher (I don't even remember the teacher's name, I do remember my classmate's first and last names), but from that short exchange with her, I learned a couple of Social Studies lessons that have stayed with me to this day. One lesson was that people view the world in incredibly differently ways. Truth to her was certainly not truth to me and vice versa. We may all be on different highways to God — to use your Hindu friend's analogy — but we sure see both the highway and the destination (God) differently!

Lesson two was that in spite of these differences, it pays to listen and understand each other. We may not agree, but we can learn to respect each other… especially each other's intentions.

I once studied with an Ultra-Orthodox rabbi in Israel. That experience furthered my appreciation of lesson two. The rabbi told me he does not hate Reform Jews. On the contrary, he cares deeply for them and is therefore driven to teach and help them understand Judaism for their betterment, for the betterment of the Jewish people, and for the betterment of the world. Because, in his view of truth, if all Jews practiced Judaism as he did, the era of the Messiah and peace would be upon us.

I think it would be quite the day when my reborn Christian classmate and this Ultra-Orthodox rabbi would agree on the "truth," even though they were both were 100% positive that they knew the "correct" truth. That alone says something about the elusive "truth" and the highway to get there. I could not agree with either one of their fundamentalist viewing of "the" truth or their highways.

However, I was able to respect them both because I believe their intentions were loving. By no means do I believe that all religious fundamentalists have good intentions and I am always wary of anyone who claims they know the Truth, the Way, or "the" anything. Still, before I get offended, I try to understand such people and their intentions. Because even though I do not believe anyone has a monopoly on truth — including me — I do believe, as these two examples taught me, that I can learn something from almost anyone or situation.

Thanks for writing!

Gil

Email Responses to "Do Orthodox Jews or Reborn Christians Know 'the' Truth?"

Subj: Do Orthodox Jews or Reborn Christians Know the Truth?
Date: 1/7 3:35:38 PM CST
From:
To: GilMann@aol.com

Dear Gil:

I am a middle aged woman who is studying Judaism because I feel that I am drawn to become a convert.

I have seen many a reborn Christian in action. And even with all of their certainty that their view of Christ and the Truth is the only view, their actions unfortunately leave much to be desired. Like you, I have tried to understand the person and the motives before running for my life from those that would save me. I have tried so hard to reconcile my life to the Christian beliefs that I have been exposed to, only to find that they do not on their own, support a legacy of love and compassion. From my viewpoint, the Christians who truly live their lives in a "Christ-like" fashion are few and far between indeed. It seems to me, that the message that Jesus of Nazareth tried to get across, was one of compassion, love, humility and service. NOT hatred, oppression or violence. Sometimes it seems, where faith takes over, the brain takes flight!

And so, I find that it is much easier for me to speak with God directly, using the tools and resources available to make my own decisions about how best to serve him, and leave Jesus to the Christians. God will surely reward the just and punish the unjust. I just hope my life will be an example of justness, love and compassion, which to me, is the picture I have of God Himself.

Thank you for your column.

Sincerely,
Name

Subj: Truth?
Date: 1/12 1:59:41 PM CST
From:
To: GilMann@aol.com

Gil,

I wrote a lesson about Truth a couple of years ago. Many claim to have it. Few realize what it really is. I know that the every day Christian does not have it, at least not all of it. When they say that they have the "truth" they are mistaken, for they do not honor the Sabbath, nor do they celebrate the feast rehearsals. The Truth is the Word of God, the Torah, Prophets, and the Writings. "Thy Word is Truth," as David so aptly put it. The Truth equals the commandments, all of them; the statutes, the judgments, the precepts, the whole law. To have that "truth" you would have to adhere to it, be in obedience to it, walk in it. We are to do it/truth, and hear it/truth. We are to share it/truth with others. Truth is light/knowledge, without truth you will be in darkness/no knowledge.

That is my take on truth.

Shalom, Name

Subj: Truer Truth
Date: 1/22 11:04:19 PM CST
From:
To: GilMann@aol.com

Here's how I handled this kind of situation. I was on maternity leave, and so was home to those nice, earnest Jehovah's Witness proselytizers. It was a diversion to have a conversation about the Bible instead of spit up, so I continued to chat with them from time to time (showing them Jewish Publication Society translations, etc.) They must have thought I was a hot prospect, because one day a delegation showed up and asked me "Do you know what God wants you to do?" I smiled and said, "Absolutely. God wants me to be a Jew, and God wants you to be a Jehovah's Witness and ring my doorbell." That was their last visit.

Concluding Thoughts to Copy, Cut, Paste, and Save

Often a column I post evokes an email from a reader that is worthy of becoming a column of its own. Once in a while, the original column becomes the parent of two follow-up columns.

The latter happened in the case of this chapter's column, which gave birth to two follow-up columns. One is called: "My Truth Is Truer Than Your Truth... Buzz Off!" and I'll conclude this chapter with that column. The other column is called "Will Jews Burn in Hell?" and is the subject of the next chapter.

Both of these columns were responses to questions about how to answer fundamentalists. Really, they speak to the larger issue of spiritual identity that many Jews struggle with as a minority in society and the world.

You will be able to see this spirituality identity issue in the column that follows. Read on to see a different aspect of this identity explored further in the next chapter.

My Truth Is Truer Than Your Truth... Buzz Off!

Dear Gil,

I was disappointed that your column did not offer the type of response I was looking for. How about providing a few brief, direct and to-the-point (yet polite and non-offensive) buzz-off lines that can be used by those of us who do not appreciate unsolicited lecturing about "The Truth." It would be great to have a small arsenal of appropriate replies ready for self-defense when we are attacked by those holier-than-thou types (of any religion). You know who they are: the ones who refuse to respect other people's rights to their own beliefs, but instead feel compelled to criticize others for not believing as they do.

Truthfully,
P

Dear P:

To tell you the truth :), I have yet to find the need for such lines. I just don't find I'm harassed to the point of needing to get people off my back.

Of course, a person looking for a fight can always find one and maybe I have yet to have a problem because my personality is basically non-combative... Minnesota Nice we call it in the Midwest. So to me, a "non-offensive buzz-off line" is something of an oxymoron.

This does not mean I won't stand up for what I believe in. But in my life, I've found I can get more accomplished with honey than vinegar... and it is a lot more pleasant for me too. This, then, is what I say...

Rather than telling a person to buzz off, I find I can easily avoid folks who might be after me with their version of "the" truth with comments like, "Sorry, I don't have time" or "I'm not interested," "No thanks," etc.

If I actually do have the time, I usually am interested to find out more about the way the person thinks and how they got to that place. Perhaps this is because my career nowadays is listening to people speak about their religion. So I like to ask questions about a person's background and try to understand how a person who knows "the" truth got to be so certain of their way of life.

Often, I must say I cannot fathom the person's thinking or some-times what seems more appropriate to me is their "lack of thinking" — some of these folks seem brainwashed to me. But who knows... certainly not me, and I don't get upset. I remain curious about their thinking and I wonder what kind of person they are.

There are four kinds of students according to the Jewish volume, Ethics of the Fathers (*Pirke Avot*).

The sponge that soaks up everything.
The funnel takes in at one ear and lets out at the other.
The strainer lets the wine pass and retains the waste.
The sifter holds back the coarse and collects the fine flour.

I like this analogy, and regardless of what kind of person I am listening to, I seek to be like the sifter. So I'm interested to hear from others — even those who claim to know the truth — in an attempt to glean knowledge from them. They are usually more than eager to teach!

In addition, I've yet to meet a person with such strong convictions who came to their convictions quickly. So I have found a certain tolerance (not always) from such firm believers to allow others to find their way to the truth.

I suppose if I encountered a person who did not have this tolerance or patience, my response might be something like "You are lucky that you have found such clarity in your life. I am still searching and I need more time and need to do my searching on my own terms with my own teachers."

If the conversation deteriorated, I think I would have to end with a comment to the effect of "I think you and I will just have to agree to disagree because we are not going to convince each other of our point of view."

Apropos of this subject is a quote I found from Chassidic Rabbi Mendel of Kotzk, who warned his students: "Be sure to take care of your own soul and of another person's body, not of your own body and another person's soul." I think all of us — especially anyone who claims to know "the" truth — can find much to reflect upon in Rabbi Mendel's advice.

Perhaps these responses may have disappointed you further because I did not supply you with any good zingers or buzz-off lines. Don't get me wrong, I do enjoy hearing or reading them — as a joke, but I'm not the type to use them.

And so, even though I'd never say the following to a person, I'll leave you with a political bumper sticker I read once that speaks to the issue of religious fundamentalists who think they know the truth: "If you want a country run by religion, move to Iran!"

Gil

P.S. Since writing the column above, I found another appropriate bumper sticker: "God is too big to fit inside one religion." What I like about this one is the nudge to all — from the right to the left — to be opened minded about "the" truth we each think we know.

Chapter 12
Will Jews Burn in Hell?

Dear Gil:

How do you answer fundamentalists (especially Christians) who maintain that if you do not believe in their theology, bad things will happen to you after you die (i.e., if you don't accept "Jesus," you will burn in "hell"). The same goes for fundamentalist Muslims — if you don't accept "Allah" the way fundamentalist Muslims do — bad things will happen to you after you die. Many cults are very similar to this ideology.

I have a difficult time "respecting" individuals who believe this way. This form of having "the Truth" is a form of religious racism, and is VERY close to the Nazi ideology of superiority. These fundamentalists (Jewish, Christian, Muslim, etc.) are no more than "religious Nazis..." with a heavy "superiority" complex. It is the fringes of those fundamentalists that commit acts of violence. E.g.: Christians who murder doctors just because of the kind of surgeries they do, Jews who murder Arabs just because of who they are, Muslims who murder Americans just because of their nationality, etc. Nazis that murdered Jews just because of who we were. Do you see the similarity in "superiority" belief and the action that can and has followed?

I don't have a problem with being a devout religious person. I have a problem when that leads to feelings of superiority, intolerance, and ultimately violence!

In peace,
E

Dear E:

My answers to your question are twofold. First, I usually don't respond to these kinds of fundamentalists and I don't worry about their line of reasoning because if they are right, I and a few other billion of God's children are in big trouble. I just don't buy the argument. Rather than waste energy on it, I try to be a good person.

On rare occasions, I have replied by asking how could God forsake so many billion of his/her children? The one time I actually asked this, I had a very fruitful and interesting discussion. Maybe because the other person—a very religious Christian—was a great lover of Jews and Judaism and was not pushing his beliefs on me. These are also reasons I was willing to ask him in the first place.

While I was at it, I also asked him how a decent person who lives a life of goodness, kindness, and generosity, but did not believe in God or accept Jesus, could be destined to Hell. His answer was that in his opinion, this person was walking in God's ways whether they realized it or not and would have a positive fate in the next world. His answers gave me insight into his faith and world view, and I am glad I posed my questions to him.

Now switching to the realm of violent fringe religious extremists, I have a second response that is completely different. These are not people to be ignored with a shrug of a shoulder [as we learned on 9-11; see my comments at the end of this chapter], nor would I engage in a theological debate with them. These people are dangerous and must be watched carefully — by appropriate law enforcement and watchdog organizations. If you encounter such folks, you immediately should contact your local police, FBI, and ADL or Federation.

I want to comment quickly about two more points in your email. First, as you noted, all religions including Jews have fundamentalists who take their beliefs to the point of violence. (Remember Baruch Goldstein and the 29 Muslims he gunned down?) What perhaps distinguishes us is how quickly, completely, and resoundingly Jewish leadership condemns such extremism when it occurs. In addition, thank God, there are extremely few Jews of this ilk.

I also wanted to respond to your use of the term *Nazi*. While I see your point, I think the words "Nazi" and "Holocaust" are thrown around much too easily, including your reference to violent religious extremists. As you noted, they tend to be fringe groups, small in number and members, unlike the Nazis of World War II.

As for the nonviolent vast majority, if you really feel you must respond to a fundamentalist, I suggest you do so with respectful questioning. This will increase the odds that both of you will walk away from your encounter minus feelings of superiority and intolerance.

Thanks for writing!

Gil

Email Responses to "Will Jews Burn in Hell?"

Subj: Just a note...
Date: 6/19/91:34:03 PM CDT
From:
To: GilMann@aol.com

Dear Mr. Mann,

The recent e-mail you printed about Jews burning in hell troubled me. I know that there are radical fundamentalist groups out there and quite a bit of anti-Semitism also but please know that there are many people who admire Jewish people and their religion. Right now, as an agnostic, I am not really sure what I believe in but I do know that if I ever do proclaim to be anything it will probably be Jewish. I was brought up Catholic and was always told if I did not believe in Jesus I would burn in hell. That is a real powerful statement to a confused child. Throughout my adolescence I was curious about Judaism but never pursued it because of fear I now am ashamed to admit. But I did not know any better at the time. Now that I am in my 30s I am able to see Judaism for what it truly is, a blessing. Anyway before delaying you any further thank you for taking the time to read this and know that there are people who are not Jews who love and respect your religion and I do hope to become part of it someday.

Sincerely,
Name

Subj: Will Jews go to hell
Date: 6/23 5:51:39 PM CDT
From:
To: GilMann@aol.com

GilMann,

I want to share with you my experience as a "Born Again Jew." I was raised in the Jewish faith and in the Synagogue. I went to Temple as often as my grandfather, (zada) would take me. I understood not a word as it was all in Hebrew but I knew there was something there I wanted and I needed. I knew there I could feel love between people and God. There were mostly men of course but I did not care. My reasons were personal as are all our reasons for searching for God.

When I became an adult I decided to search even deeper for myself. I began to ask questions of the people around me at work. They each had their own beliefs and none of them were Jewish. One of my co-workers bought me my first Bible and I read it for myself. I had never heard about Jesus Christ but as I read my curiosity grew. In time I began to attend church and seek for more answers.

In time I began to understand that no matter how good a person I was I could not earn eternal life. I saw that God loved me and had a way for me to attain eternal life and peace and joy while I was on earth. I accepted Jesus Christ as my personal Savior in 1997. Later I became a licensed pastor and director of a ministry for homeless men.

All my Jewish family has accepted me but far more importantly they accepted Jesus as their Savior. Acts 16:31 promises us this will happen. If you believe Jesus is able and you must remember Jesus was a Jew. We can be in Christ Jesus and still hold on to our Jewishness as the Old Testament makes up 39 of the books of the Bible. Therefore the New and Old Testaments are important to God and are complete when together.

May Each of You Find Him,
Initialed

Subj: Well who knows the time maybe near...
Date: 6/19 4:45:33 PM CDT
From:
To: GilMann@aol.com

I am a christian, and I believe in Jesus Christ. The Christ that was crucified for us two thousand years ago. I guess you can say I am a radical from what I believe and know to be true and real. I believe Jesus was raised from the dead. I believe I was saved 5 years ago. I wasn't expecting to be saved...

We are all sinners and need a savior, that's what christians should teach and point out and make it simple. For by Grace are you saved, not by works. Works would be a form of cash payment to God from us to get to heaven. And no can buy love just as no one can buy their way to Heaven. It is the "Gift of God" free salvation through Jesus Christ. Easier and cheaper HUH?...

This might shock you. But I hope that it my give you peace with God. Peace with others. The bible has this verse. It states that If you are not FOR CHRIST, THEN YOU ARE ANTICHRIST...

Well that's what I have to say and I think that's enough. I hope and pray that God richly blesses you. May the God who is able to do all things abundantly, Love you, keep you safe, and bless you.

One of God's messenger's right?

Subj: Jews in Hell
Date: 6/25 10:03:39 AM CDT
From:
To: GilMann@aol.com

Gil: This came from one of my Internet buddies. It seems to address your topic. I thought you might like it,

Name

From an actual question given for mid-term Chemistry Exam at University of Washington:

Question: Is Hell exothermic (radiates heat) or endothermic (absorbs heat); Support your answer with a proof.

Most of the students wrote proofs of their beliefs using Boyle's Law (gas cools when it expands and heats up when it is compressed), or some variant.

One student (named Mark) however, wrote the following:

First, we need to know how the mass of Hell is changing in time. So, we need to know the rate that souls are moving into Hell and the rate they are leaving. I think that we can safely assume that once a soul gets to Hell, it will not leave. Therefore, no souls are leaving.

As for how many souls are entering Hell, let's look at the different religions that exist in the world today. Some of these religions state that if you are not a member of their religion, you will go to Hell.

Since there are more than one of these religions and since people do not belong to more than one religion, we can project that all people and all souls go to Hell. With birth and death rates as they are, we can expect the number of souls in Hell to increase exponentially.

Now, we look at the rate of change of the volume in Hell because Boyle's Law states that in order for the temperature and pressure in Hell to stay the same, the volume of Hell has to expand as souls are added. This gives two possibilities:

(1) If Hell is expanding at a slower rate than the rate at which souls enter Hell, then the temperature and pressure in Hell will increase until all Hell breaks loose.

(2) Of course, if Hell is expanding at a rate faster than the increase of souls in Hell, then the temperature and pressure will drop until Hell freezes over.

So, which is it?

If we accept the postulate given to me by Theresa during my Freshman year, "It will be a cold day in Hell before I sleep with you," and take into account the fact that I still have not succeeded in having sexual relations with her, then (2) cannot be true, and so Hell is exothermic.

The student got the only A.

The real question is: Did Mark get the A, or did Mark get the girl.

Concluding Thoughts to Copy, Cut, Paste, and Save

While this last email is humorous, this topic can be deadly serious. For centuries disputes about who knows "the" truth has led to violence. This bloodshed continues to this day. This column was published before 9-11 and I am sure that tragic event would have spurred on a lot of email. For 9-11 was a most horrific example of what religious fanaticism can unleash in the name of the truth. Further, these followers of Islam believed that their murder of non-Muslims in a holy war was not only just, but that they would be rewarded in Heaven for their killing!

Well before that terrible day, I had been wary of theology that spoke with certainty about Hell, damnation, Heaven, and salvation. This is largely because of my Jewish upbringing. When saying this, I refer to three things. First, debate about finding the truth is the *modus operandi* of Judaism. (One example of many is that in rabbinical school, students traditionally have learned with a partner to question and challenge each other.) Secondly, the history of the Jewish people shows the suffering that can result when others assert they know "the" truth. Finally, for most Jews, matters of Hell and Heaven are not a major thrust of their Judaism or their Jewish education.

To underscore this final point, you may have noted that most of the email in this chapter is from Christians. This is because I received little email from Jews on this topic. Why?

I believe Christians wrote because a large part of a Christian's identity and theology involves salvation through Christ and conversely on damnation in Hell for non-believers. This is a basic of Christian theology, so logically this topic would concern Christians. As a rule, I found the emails were sent in with concern for Jews who do not believe in Christ and face an unpleasant future in Hell. One such writer had a respectful email exchange with me, which he concluded by writing that he had at least "done his duty" in trying to convince me to accept Jesus. His final line, which I found touching, was, "Regardless of which of us is right... I pray God may bless each of us for our faithfulness to His ministry."

As for the Jewish response or lack thereof, I believe Jewish readers do not get very agitated by this topic because as I noted, in Judaism, little time is spent learning about life after death; even less time is expended about going to Hell — though Judaism definitely has teachings and beliefs about the subject. Still, Hell is simply not a significant part of Jewish theology for most Jews. For example, I've personally never heard a rabbi speak about Hell. Rather the emphasis in Judaism is on how we behave in and improve this world — regardless of our faith in God.

This difference between Judaism and Christianity has been most apparent to me at funerals. I have been struck both by how little is said at Jewish funerals about the world to come (vs. describing what the deceased did while alive) and how much is said at Christian funerals about the deceased now being with Jesus.

In keeping with the themes of the last two chapters, I am not going to get into who has the correct version of truth. I would like to point out, however, that often in society, we hear of Judeo-Christian ethics — the implication being that ethics of Judaism and Christianity are the same. While the two religions have many shared ethics, they also have significantly different worldviews and consequently some significantly different ideas about the truth.

In contrast to the violence the world has experienced in the name of religious truth, there are many civil ways to assert our understanding of truth. The Internet and some of the email you read here are prime examples.

To further explore how these views can shape your understanding of truth, regardless of any religion you do or do not practice, a good website to visit is: www.beliefnet.com.

As you do so, keep in mind the following saying — the author I don't know, but the sentiment appeals to me — "I love people who seek the truth. I have a hard time with people who claim to know the truth."

Chapter 13
Why Does Judaism Discriminate Against Women?

Dear Gil:

Why are women 2nd class citizens in our religion? I am referring to praying in the synagogue and not being allowed to read from the Torah. I read that it relates to women being inferior and not having the knowledge of a man. This creates turmoil inside of me. How can I embrace my faith when I read that women are unclean? Women are the ones that bring life into the world. How did we get such a bad deal?

D

Dear D:

You'll probably enjoy this ditty: When God created man, She was kidding!

Getting beyond quips, there are two contradictory answers to your questions. One: most of Jewish law and Jewish text are the product of men, so there is a certain bias built into Judaism. Answer two: many of these sages and Judaism in general held women in high esteem. The intention was and is to honor women in Judaism, in part, precisely because women bring life into the world.

If this is so, then why all the "second class" treatment you describe in your email? I believe a big part of the answer is found by looking at the issue using the context of days gone by. The Middle East in ancient days was male dominated. Society was tribal and clan based and was often headed by a male chief or leader. Still today, in many of the countries in the region, much of this old tradition exists and the status and treatment of women in those countries is appalling.

But the Middle East was not unique, the whole world was male dominated—and still is! Only now and only in the Western world are women beginning to get equal rights. Historically speaking, the gaining of these rights is a relatively new phenomenon. In the U.S., kicking and screaming, men finally granted women the right to vote in 1920—not exactly ancient times!

For thousands of years, Judaism, like the rest of the world, has been led mostly by men. But in the last fifty years, Judaism has changed a great deal regarding women. Today, the Conservative, Reform, and Reconstructionist Movements have made huge strides in granting woman rights and power. All three movements ordain women rabbis, allow women to read Torah, pray with men, have worked to make their prayer books gender neutral, speak of the Matriarchs [of Judaism: Sara, Rachel, Rebecca, and Leah], and encourage women to wear *kippot*, *tallis*, and *tefillin* [skull cap, prayer shawl, and phylacteries — all traditionally reserved for use by men]. Obviously, individual synagogues handle these practices differently, but in general these three movements view women as deserving rights equal to men.

"But," you may be thinking, "what about the Orthodox?" Within Orthodox circles there are certainly women speaking out for changes, but by and large, I would refer to my point about our tradition holding women in high esteem. You may not agree with the following rationale, but our tradition says that women are "released" from many obligations because of the important role woman play as mothers and wives. The home is viewed traditionally as a holy place with the women bringing in the spiritual light (this is why women light the *Shabbat* candles). Many of these women feel respected as, in the words of our tradition, "women of valor with a worth higher than rubies."

Sexist garbage? Not according to many observant women who view their role with comfort and happiness. Before you dismiss this as brainwashing, think for a moment about the reverence we have for "Jewish Mamas." All kidding on the subject aside, we Jews deeply value our mothers and grandmothers.

Unfortunately, in the space of this column, I cannot get into greater detail explaining more of the rationale behind Jewish law's views toward women. But, as I said at the outset, much of the rationale is motivated by respect for women.

I see this and admire the intention; at the same time I have problems with some of our tradition's views toward women, especially the issue of *agunot* — women trying to get divorced. But today, within Judaism there is a wide latitude of practice relative to women, and

I feel very comfortable partnering with my wife to raise our two daughters, just as we raise our two sons, to become proud, equal, and fully participating first-class Jews.

Thanks for writing!

Gil

**Email Responses to
"Why Does Judaism Discriminate Against Women?"**

Subj: re Woman as second class citizens.
Date: 6/8 10:46:27 PM CDT
From:
To: GilMann@aol.com

I saw a program on 20/20 about the women in Iran and how they are treated. When interviewed, one woman said she is content because she had to be. Similarly when orthodox women say they are happy, it makes me wonder. Yes in some ways they may be, but I have to ask, how can they not feel suppressed in other ways?

I just saw the movie, *Woman at the Wall.* If Orthodox women are so content, then why have some of them fought so hard for equality at the Wall? [The writer is referring to the Western Wall in Jerusalem, the holiest site in Judaism, which has designated sections for men and woman to pray separately, according to traditional Judaism.] I think there can be some kind of equality within the confines of Jewish Law, but I myself would be hard pressed to not feel the laws were set up to keep women under male control.

Subj: re: women in Judaism
Date: 6/9/ 7:14:08 AM CDT
From:
To: GilMann@aol.com

Gil,

As a woman I appreciated your reiteration of the historical perspective and Judaism's advanced (for the times) proposition of respect.

I appreciated your very considerate discussion of the denominational differences within Judaism, and the fact that women today frequently have the freedom to choose their own desired level of religious accommodation.

Finally, thank you for briefly mentioning the agunot [women who cannot get a divorce because their husbands will not agree to one]. My heart goes out to these women.

Name (female)

Subj: Women as Second Class
Date: 6/9/ 5:34:39 PM CDT
From:
To: GilMann@aol.com

Dear Gil:

My grandfather is ULTRA Orthodox. When I was 8 years old, I asked my grandfather why women were not allowed to read from the Torah, Pray with Men or Sit with men (including spouses). My grandfather responded "it is because some men may find a woman's voice "enticing" and then they are not praying, but rather concentrating on the woman's voice.

As I got older I did a little research and found that some men have found a woman's voice "enticing" and some have acted upon that. Also the reason for separation in the Shul is the same reason men and women don't shake hands. During the woman's monthly cycle, the Torah states (on three separate occasions) that at that time she is "niddah" [menstruating] and even her husband is not allowed to touch her. Therefore the separation is required, so as not to break rules of the Torah. Growing up Orthodox and now am Conservative, I still continue with some of the Orthodox traditions, as I find them very meaningful and not offensive.

Subj: women of the wall
Date: 6/10/ 6:11:28 AM CDT
From:
To: GilMann@aol.com

Gil:

Please answer me as to how it is an "honor to women" to hurl insults and violent threats at them because they wish to read and pray and hold services from the Torah at the Wall Please tell me how it is an "honor to women" to exclude them and oppress them and call them unclean. I don't get it.

Years ago, I studied Native American spirituality, and traditional NAs believe much the same as the Orthodox Jews about women. Once, when I asked a teacher about WHY it was not okay for a menstruating woman ("unclean") to be around a man, he gave me an answer that I think comes closer to the truth than anything I've heard.

"When a woman is on her 'moon time', she has an enormous amount of power — more than usual. Her power is so strong at that time, she could kill a medicine man — at the very least, make him sick." Interesting, hmmm?

Shalom!
Name (female)

Subj: Second class — hardly!
Date: 6/10 1:48:38 PM CDT
From:
To: GilMann@aol.com

As far as I'm concerned, no more comment necessary. A woman can find her place if she really wants to do so...

Subj: E-mail of the week
Date: 6/10 9:55:56 PM CDT
From:
To: GilMann@aol.com

Dear Gil:

Re: the status of women as 2nd class citizens. In explaining the orthodox view, you left off a very key element in your answer. You did mention that women are exempt from certain things. They are exempt from time related miztvos [Biblical command-ments], such as specific prayers (3 times daily) that must be said at certain intervals. This issue has nothing at all to do with male dominance or any such line of reasoning. The element you missed is; anyone who is exempt from the performance of a mitzvoh can not be the source of helping another fulfill their obligation.

The women's role in raising her family, critical for the continuity of our people, is ridiculed in today's times. How tragic that this is so. Just look at the deterioration of society, how so many children are neglected and the tragic results and then decide which role is more important.

Name (non-gendered)

Subj: Judaism Where Do I Fit In
Date: 6/11 1:18:41 PM CDT
From: E
To: GilMann@aol.com

I thought your comments were excellent. Yes, women are told they are spiritually higher than men and are exempt from time bound mitzvot, but we are not prohibited. Now that women are living longer and child bearing years only account for less than half of our lifetime there leaves much of a lifetime in which we have time to participate more fully in our religion.

Subj: it is me Name
Date: 6/11 1:40:43 PM CDT
From:
To: GilMann@aol.com

dear Mr. Mann

the simple issue is very plain.

God divided the partnership of man and women half. The most important part is with the mother. She raises the next generation of the future of the Jewish people. The most important job for woman is not to daven [pray] but to take care of the next generation. So who got the important part? The women. your friend Name (male)

Subj: Women as equals?
Date: 6/12 9:31:27 PM CDT
From:
To: GilMann@aol.com

In my shul [synagogue,] we are discussing this problem women being counted for a minion [prayer quorum — traditionally ten

men still observed in Orthodox and some Conservative syn-
agogues] and being called up for an aliya [ritual honor] right
now. A few dedicated women who attend services fairly regularly
feel left out. Sometimes we are short a few men to make ten.
It seems that a woman who is dedicated and wants to help
make a minion on a regular basis is better to include than the
many men who chose not to come to services even though they
are able to.

Subj: Good Reply!
Date: 6/13 5:41:24 AM CDT
From:
To: GilMann@aol.com

Dear GilMann:

Enjoyed your reply to the women re: Women 2nd Class Citizens
in Judaism. Good Reply!

Just one quibble — I lead a Renewal havurah [a small group of
people that often self-organize for prayer, study, or to celebrate
the Jewish Holidays and the Sabbath] — I noticed, and was
pleased — that you pointed out to her that Reform, Conservative,
and Reconstructionist movements would treat her fairly. But
please, next time, don't forget to mention the Jewish Renewal
Movement — we now have 80 rabbis, many of them female, and
shuls and havurot all over the world. See "www.jewishrenewal.org"

also: www.aleph.org

Those are our two primary websites. Our movement is probably
bigger on equality for women than even Reconstructionism.

Also, please don't forget to mention the Humanistic Jews —
while I don't share any of their views — Renewal is very, very,
very G-d and Kabbalah-oriented, in a New Age sort of way — the
Humanistic Jews have kept a lot of Jews who don't believe in

God from leaving Judaism altogether, and they have good attitudes towards women.

Cordially,
Name (female)
Name of Havurah and city

Concluding Thoughts to Copy, Cut, Paste, and Save

When I sent this book out in manuscript form to readers from many backgrounds (Jewish, non-Jewish, observant, non-observant, male, female), they rated this chapter's topic at the top of their interest list. The issue of women's role in Judaism obviously touches a sensitive nerve.

The evolving role of women is not unique to Judaism. The news regularly features stories about the role of women in all major religions. Islam, Christianity, and Judaism are all grappling with women's issues such as equality, ordination, attire, marriage, and divorce.

As for Judaism, from my perspective, some of the most creative and refreshing developments have women at the forefront. I refer to such innovations as healing services and centers, work to include the disabled, new liturgical and folk music, art, dance, poetry, and literature. I feel strongly that Judaism is enriched and strengthened by women's leadership and contributions. I'll say more about this in the conclusion of this book.

Some Jews may feel uncomfortable with this movement away from tradition, but Judaism has always been a way of life that has evolved. This evolution has been a result of events in history and the influence of different societies.

History and society today dictate that men and women have access to education and information as never before. This will only increase the impact of women and rate of change for women in Judaism and probably in all religions. The Internet is very much a part of this momentum.

On the web, resources for Jewish women grow daily. For example:

www.jwa.org
www.jewishrenaissance.org/

Some may feel threatened by equalization of women's rights and roles in Judaism because they see the trend as unraveling an entire tradition and upending a world order. For them, and everyone else, I'll end with the following joke… which, naturally, someone emailed to me:

> God looked down on Eve and saw that she was lonely. God spoke to Eve saying: "I will provide you with a companion. He will stand by you, love you, and protect you."
>
> Eve said, "Sounds good."
>
> God said, "I should mention that he is going to be rather insecure and so he'll always insist that he's the stronger and more important sex."
>
> "I can live with that," said Eve.
>
> God said, "There is one other little thing. He'll also insist that he was created first. But you and I will know the truth. It'll be our little secret… woman to woman!"

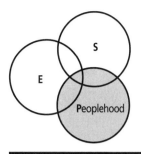

Section III: Peoplehood

As the former Soviet Union fell apart in the early 1990s, there was a huge wave of emigration by Jews anxious to leave the persecution and prison of the USSR. Most of the Jews who escaped emigrated to Israel and a smaller number came to the United States. When a call went out to the Jewish community in my city for host families to help these people get settled in town, my wife and I volunteered to adopt one such family.

Shortly thereafter we met them, a husband, wife, and two young children. The night we met, the wife, Asya, told us she was anxious to have her two boys circumcised now that they could live freely as Jews. Asya told us that she had no Jewish education and had almost no exposure to Judaism in her life because of the indoctrination by the Communist government. There were few synagogues, and attending one was asking for serious and official trouble. Given this background, I asked her, "How did you know you were Jewish?" I'll always remember her response. For a second, she just stared at me. She seemed puzzled, as if I had just asked the most idiotic question. Then she realized my question was asked in earnest, and explained that Jews in Russia always knew they were Jews, because of the anti-Semitism of their neighbors. It was simply a part of life for a Jew, she said, encountered on the bus, at the university, and at work. It was constant, it was everywhere, it was always a problem, and sometimes it was dangerous.

What she described to me that night is a negative part of Jewish Peoplehood: the insecurity of being a minority, a feeling of being different, a feeling of discomfort, and in her case, a feeling of being threatened. For centuries, these have been some of the predominant feelings Jews have felt wherever they have lived. For them, the Peoplehood circle was literally a circled ghetto.

A large part of Jewish identity and Peoplehood has always been defined by others who are not Jewish. A classic example is that the first person in history to call Jews a people was Pharaoh. While many label Jews as a people, in my experience, this Peoplehood aspect of Judaism is not well understood by Jews and non-Jews. Simply put, I describe Peoplehood as extended family. If you think in terms of extended family, you can also understand why Jews feel pride or shame if they read in the news of a fellow Jew who has done something good or bad.

But Jewish Peoplehood or extended family is really a bit more complicated. Unlike a biological family, a person can also convert to Judaism, thereby becoming a member of the Jewish people or family. Converting means accepting certain beliefs and behaviors. Yet, as you saw in the sections on Ethics and Spirituality, the range of belief (and nonbelief) and behavior within Judaism is large. Despite this range, every Jew is still a part of the Jewish people. Additionally, as I mentioned in the introduction to this book, anti-Semites like Hitler did not care about what a Jew thought of Jewish Ethics or believed or did not believe about God. These enemies of Jews have never asked for a faith statement; they zeroed in on Jewish Peoplehood.

Largely because of Jewish Peoplehood and a sense of being different, Jews often connect to other Jews — even if their beliefs about God are totally different or if neither practices or observes much Judaism. I liken this connection to being overseas and meeting someone who happens to be from your hometown. The feeling is wonderful as you share and compare common backgrounds, landmarks, and memories. Not much needs to be said; you "just know" what the other person means, and you feel a sense of connection... even if you are very different people. Jews often feel this way about each other. This is the positive side of Peoplehood.

Another positive side is that because of Jewish Peoplehood, Jews for centuries have emphasized the importance of helping each other (as in hosting a family of new immigrants). A famous line in the Talmud sums this up: "All Jews are responsible one for another." Anti-Semitism has made this teaching a necessity.

Anti-Semites have far from disappeared from our planet, but today fortunately, for most Diaspora Jews, their non-Jewish neighbors (with glaring exceptions like in France) are not a threat and are often accepting and kind. These amicable relations are so far reaching that in many places, especially the United States, non-Jews and Jews are falling in love with and marrying each other in great numbers. (Studies show about 50 percent of Jews in the U.S. are now marrying non-Jews, which casts a whole new light on the idea of Peoplehood.) This acceptance has given Jews, for perhaps the first time in history, the luxury and challenge of trying to define themselves as a people.

This acceptance is new, but the main Peoplehood problem that Jews outside of Israel wrestle with is age-old: namely, how to fit into societies and a world where they live as a minority. The opportunity to explore the issues of fitting in via the Internet is also new. In addition, because there are few barriers to entry on the Internet, the cyber community discussing Jewish Peoplehood includes Jews and non-Jews. Almost without exception, the non-Jews who write to me are courteous and respectful when they submit their questions or comments about Jewish Peoplehood topics. They often offer an insightful outsider's perspective. In addition, many non-Jews want to learn more about Jewish Peoplehood to better understand their own identities.

Generally, I'd divide the emails I've received about Jewish Peoplehood into two conflicting questions: What do Jews have in common with the larger community around them? And what distinguishes or is different about the Jewish people? These questions can create conflicts that are difficult to reconcile. For example, many Diaspora Jews feel this conflict very tangibly during the Christmas season. Few people like the feeling of being left out or excluded (think of yourself in high school), and at the same time, most do not want to lose all that's unique about themselves by assimilating into the majority.

Stated another way, the chapters in this section all ask, How do I belong? How can I understand and connect to Jewish Peoplehood... in a world where most people are not Jewish? The tension and struggle caused by these issues of Jewish and non-Jewish identity can be seen in the emails in the following chapters in the Peoplehood section:

A Christmas Tree in My House?
You Don't Look Jewish!
I Am Catholic and Dating a Jewish Guy
Are Converts Treated as Second Class?
Are Non-Jews Anti-Semitic or Are Jews Paranoid?
Returning to Judaism

Chapter 14
A Christmas Tree in My House?

Shalom Gil:

I have a problem. My kids from my first marriage are 9 and 15 and are Baptist. I converted to Judaism four years ago. I am now married to a wonderful Jewish man.

My children are supportive of MY choice for my own religion but have made it clear to me that they are Baptist and will not change at this point. I don't press that issue. They do however, share Shabbat *candle lighting on Fridays when they are here with me (every other week) and they do celebrate the other holidays with me as far as getting together for dinners but not going to synagogue or anything like that. We always have a* Seder *on Passover and we do celebrate* Hanukkah *with some presents and celebrate* Rosh Hashanah.

Now that they are getting older, they are saying that I don't share THEIR holidays with them, like allowing a Christmas tree in the house. What makes this year especially difficult is that they are here with me this Christmas season and they are feeling cheated in a certain way. Usually they are with their Baptist father over the season and I have never really had to directly deal with this issue. Now I am and I don't know what to tell them.

I have told them that this is a Jewish home and that we don't have a tree. But now they are angry and hurt because I have not acknowledged them in their religion. I admit—I am feeling guilty. They do participate with me all of the time—how do I do the same for them? Honestly— I feel like I have abandoned them somewhat by not freely allowing them their religion when they are with me. Please help me if you can. I need some direction on this issue. Thank you.

H

Dear H:

First I want to compliment your conscientiousness and the attention you're giving this issue. You're clearly trying to be a good mom and person. Your problem is so intriguing and challenging that I plan to use it as an Email of the Week and encourage readers to send in their advice.

Personally, I wouldn't like having a tree in my home so you must know that I start with this bias. I don't buy the idea that a Christmas tree is just a secular or seasonal symbol (it's not called a holiday or winter tree.) In fact, I think your kids understand this completely, which is precisely why they want a tree — to celebrate Christmas! Additionally, I know that any advice I give on this most tender topic has the potential to upset somebody… but here goes.

I've come to these conclusions: You're correct to be sensitive to your kids' religious needs — after all, you converted, not them. The Jewish home where you live is designed to nourish you, but you also have an obligation to nourish the children you have brought into this world. Accordingly, I'd suggest the following course of actions. In this order:

First choice: Have the kids spend the holiday period with their dad… if this is still an option.

Second choice: See if you can give the kids a tree (or little trees) in an area of your house that can be for them (i.e., bedroom or loft).

Third choice: Let them have a tree in your living or family room.

No matter what you choose, I think you should have an honest and caring conversation with them — so all of you (including your current husband) can express your thoughts, desires, misgivings, and concerns. You may need to find some compromises (for example, how to handle decorations, crucifixes, etc.). Here, I don't mean to imply a compromise that is a mixture of religions — like Jewish ornaments on the tree. I think this is confusing and not true to either religion.

You should look at this issue as a situation that you must face in your home until your kids are 18 or so, meaning this is a temporary issue—not something for the rest of your life. In the future, though, I'd endeavor to have the kids spend this holiday period with their dad so you can avoid the discomfort of a tree in your home.

To further help you, I invite readers to email their comments to me at GilMann@aol.com and I will forward them on to you.

I wish you and your children a holiday season of love, understanding and happiness!

Gil

Email Responses to "A Christmas Tree in My House?"

Subj: convert and her kid's wish for a Christmas tree
Date: 12/9 6:10:34 PM CST
From:
To: GilMann@aol.com

I am a convert to Judaism, and feel fortunate that my wife and kids are Jewish.

I believe that the best solution is to allow these children to have a (perhaps small) tree in their own bedroom or other personal space. If they are Christians living in this home even temporarily, then they should have the space for their own religious observances.

But it is best to keep the tree out of the common space of the home, so that the home as a whole remains a Jewish home.

Perhaps she can also drive the kids to some spectacular public Xmas tree somewhere in her community. Just as she ought to drive them to church if they want to go.

Shalom,
Name

Subj: Christmas Tree
Date: 12/9 6:19:28 PM CST
From:
To: GilMann@aol.com

This woman certain has a difficult situation. I think that the 15 year old is in a more difficult position than the 9 year old, because being a teen presents special challenges. I have the following thoughts, on both this issue as well as the more general challenge of having a bi-religious household, which may or may not be helpful:

1. The teen years are when many people start to realize their own religious beliefs (for some of us it takes a bit longer...) It is important to talk with the 15 year old in particular about how to make sure that the child is being validated in his/her religious beliefs.

2. Nevertheless, I really think that, as a parent, it is her prerogative to determine the religious nature of her household. Since BOTH adults in that household are Jewish, it is NOT appropriate to have a Christian symbol (a tree or anything else) on display in the main living areas. The mother will ultimately present a better role model to her children by being firm in her own religious beliefs than by giving in to a "compromise" that makes her clearly uncomfortable.

3. I also worry that for both of the children, the decision between Jewish/Baptist may be one of mom vs. dad. It seems that dad has majority custody of the children, and the children may have chosen Baptism because they feel closer to their father, as well as because that was the religion of their childhoods. I would try to find out what the father (and the church they attend) may or may not be telling the children about Judaism when they are with him. I have unfortunately known some cases in my personal circle of friends where a bitter divorce between a mixed-religion couple turned the non-Jewish partner into an unexpectedly harsh anti-Semite. I hope that the mother has spent time talking

to the children about why she made her decision, what it means to her, and will keep those lines of communication open.

Subj: Christmas tree
Date: 12/9 6:33:07 PM CST
From:
To: GilMann@aol.com

Under no circumstances should a tree be allowed in that home. Because both the mother and father are jewish, this is a jewish home, Period. Children have to learn that some things are not negotiable. The mother should explain this to them and reward them in some way for not being allowed to have the tree. Name

---

Subj: regarding the Xmas tree issue
Date: 12/9 6:41:03 PM CST
From:
To: GilMann@aol.com

Hi Gil; I am somewhat going thru the same problem as the mother in this week's question. This is the first year that I won't have a tree in my home, I have just started the conversion process. I think it would be a good idea to let the kids have a tree in the room they stay in, while they are there. Or, maybe the mom has a Christian friend that the kids could spend some time with over the holidays.

I think it would leave a bad memory for the kids when they are older, if the mom is not sensitive to their needs now. They may even get a bad impression of Jews.

Just my opinion.

Sincerely, Name

Subj: Christmas Tree
Date: 12/9 7:52:48 PM CST
From:
To: GilMann@aol.com

Dear Gil,

I have a cousin who is very active at his synagogue. He has two children who are both Jewish. His wife is not Jewish, however, and is the daughter of a minister. While my cousin does not feel comfortable with Christmas, his wife celebrates Shabbat, fasts on Yom Kippur, refrains from bread on Pesach [Passover], etc. She is clearly a "friend" of the Jewish people but cannot convert and observes Jewish rituals for her family. Along comes Christmas and my cousin has a tree. Why? Because this is part of his wife's tradition. She loves Christmas, the decorations and music.

My cousin feels that since his wife observes all the Jewish rituals and even agreed to bring up his two children as Jewish, how can he deny her her ONE holiday. When the children were named in the temple and were bar mitzvahed, his entire non-Jewish family came. The children know that the tree is mom's and the menorah belongs to the rest of the family.

Just another take on the December dilemma.

Name, MSW, CSW

Subj: Xmas tree in my house
Date: 12/9 8:17:08 PM CST
From:
To: GilMann@aol.com

My only additional comment to the writer of this letter, in addition to your very sensitive response, is explaining to the children that the Chanukah miracle represents the survival of Judaism in the battle against the hellinist assimilation of the time. It would be antithetical to the spirit of the holiday to have an Xmas tree in the house, which represents the dominant religion of our time. Thank you

Name

Subj: Christmas Tree
Date: 12/10 4:15:26 AM CST
From:
To: GilMann@aol.com

I believe this issue could lead to a useful discussion about what it means to be Jewish and how this differs from other religions. An important part of being Jewish is having a Jewish home. Unlike other religions, Judaism is truly a way of life and so how one conducts oneself within his or her own home is part of the practice of Judaism. It is for this reason that a Jewish home — i.e. one that is run by a Jewish head of household — should not have a Christmas tree. I believe that the suggestion that a tree be made available within the room of the child or children is appropriate. IF this is not possible, perhaps the mother can arrange for the children to celebrate Christmas (with her) in a Christian home.

For years, I helped my Christian neighbors with their tree and opened presents with them on Christmas morning. In so doing, I recognized the non-religious nature of the holiday. But for better or worse, a tree remains a symbol of Christmas and, at bottom, Christmas is a celebration of Jesus' s birth. Having a tree can only lead to confusion; helping the children to understand the nature of Judaism should, one would hope, lead to acceptance of the mother's religious beliefs and her adoption of a way of life.

181

Subj: Where do I fit in
Date: 12/11 3:58:24 AM CST
From:
To: GilMann@aol.com

I am in the process of converting. My husband, however, is not. We have no children.

I have no aversion to a christmas tree in the house but I have long known that Christmas celebrated in our culture is mainly a commercial, secular affair. I lost the holy part of the day long, long ago. If the children need to have a tree in her Jewish home then a compromise might be what I am considering this year. I have suggested to my wife that we get a Rosemary herb tree. They are not large, 2' or 3', are fragrant and, not being botanically gifted, make me think of the Mediterranean area. I hope that this will make a bridge for me to be able to leave Christmas behind while letting my wife have some sort of semblance of a tree. They are also useful after the crowd leaves as the wonderful herb for cooking.

As I told my Rabbi, the only part of the "holiday" season that has sustained me all these years is the feeling of charity and decency that I have come to recognize as the real spirit of the time between Thanksgiving and christmas. I plan to let that be the guide for me. I also solved the gift giving at christmas time with my family by offering a compromise that was heartily accepted. Instead of giving gifts I suggested that they take the monetary amount they would have spent and donate to any charity cause they wish. There are no strings attached to the amount, fifty cents or fifty dollars, makes no difference. Someone who is in need gets something, my family members get into the habit of giving to others, and I get the satisfaction of knowing that I have made a difference to someone at Channuka. It seems to me that that is the real spirit of the season, Channuka, Christmas, Ramadan or whatever you choose.

Name

Subj: Christmas tree in Jewish home
Date: 12/11 7:15:22 PM CST
From:
To: GilMann@aol.com

Dear Gil,

Having faced a similar issue in the past, I would recommend that the mother do some research and explain to her children that "Christmas" trees are not Christian at all but originated with pagan rites. Have her read Jeremiah, chapter 10. She can then give the children two good reasons for not having a tree in their home: 1) it is the home of her and her Jewish husband and, therefore, a Jewish home, and 2) the tree is not Christian anyway being of pagan origin. To allow them to acknowledge their faith she could allow them to light candles instead of a tree.

Sincerely,
Name

Subj: RE: A Christmas Tree in My House
Date: 12/11/99 11:32:32 PM CST
From:
To: GilMann@aol.com

This is certainly a "teaching moment!" What a great chance to set the relationship between catholicism and judaism in perspective for her children. Jesus said something to the effect that he was there not to break the law, but to fulfill it. Jesus was an observant Jew, and that when the children help her with Jewish observance this should actually be helping them to understand many of the things he said and did. i.e. watching her observance should be religiously enriching for them. She should explain that observing Jewish laws and traditions do not break any catholic laws or traditions, but that some Catholic practices violate Jewish practices, and that where this is the case then in her home the Jewish practices take precedent. She can remind them that Pope John Paul calls Judaism Catholicism's older brother. She needs to take a no-nonsense approach without any guilt, with an approach toward educating her Catholic children with a deeper appreciation for the sources and origins of their own faith. And, as an unanticipated side effect, her own knowledge of and appreciation for Judaism will grow.

Subj: Christmas Tree in the Home
Date: 12/13 6:58:25 PM CST
From:
To: GilMann@aol.com

Dear Gil,

We are a Temple class of high school and middle school students. We often read your columns as a basis of discussion during our weekly meetings.

Student One: I consider myself to have a unique perspective on the subject because I come from a home where I go to my mother's on the weekends. She has remarried to a Catholic man and celebrated Christmas every year for the past two years. While I am strongly opposed to the tree, my mother has made it clear that I have no choice in the matter.

I feel that the lady who wrote to you should, first of all, call a family meeting with her children and husband to discuss the matter. Personally, I feel that a tree should be placed in the living room or other desirable room in the house. She must remember that it is not only her house but her children's as well. She should respect their wishes and their religion.

This is a difficult issue, I feel the easiest way would be to have the children go to their father's house for Christmas and visit their mother's on Chanukkah. Of course, sometimes Christmas falls on Chanukkah. The woman does not have to give the children presents, they just want recognition of their holiday and their religion. Which, in my mind, is perfectly fine and acceptable.

Student Two: I also have a unique perspective because my mother converted to Judaism from being a Lutheran but her family is still Lutheran. My family in my home celebrates Jewish holidays but we always go to my Grandparents (on my mother's side) house to celebrate Christmas. I think that this is a good idea so I can get a more diverse cultural experience by learning about different holidays or cultures. I don't give presents to my parents but I do give presents to my family on my mother's side so I am not really celebrating the holiday but helping them celebrate their holiday.

Subj: E-Mail of the Week — Christmas Tree
Date: 12/13 9:05:50 PM CST
From:
To: GilMann@aol.com

Gil-

It is wonderful that these young children are so sensitive to, and understanding of, their mother's new belief. She brought them into the world, she, and her former husband, caused suffering to these children by breaking up the family (for whatever reason), and now she wants to deny them a happy tradition, to which she also contributed, because she has a Jewish home? Gimme a break.

That tree belongs in the living room, not in the bedroom or loft. That is belittling the children's tradition. Their traditions are as important to them as her new-found traditions are to her.

I hope the new husband is sensitive to the children's needs. He made a choice when he married this woman.

Name

Subj: One more kibitz: Christmas tree
Date: 12/18 4:19:11 PM CST
From:
To: GilMann@aol.com

Frankly, the whole issue of the Christmas tree has more to do with a fear of assimilation than anything else. Jews who NEVER step into a synagogue, who've never observed Shabbat and eat shrimp and pork (but not, for some reason, ham) get into a lather about Christmas trees. It's totally hypocritical. I'm not saying we should now all buy "Chanukah bushes," but if your kids are still young and Catholic by birth and choice and they're living with you in December — and they remember beloved Christmas trees past — get a Christmas tree! It's for the sake of saving a family!

Name
City, State

Subj: In response- xmas trees
Date: 1/13 6:55:04 PM CST
From:
To: GilMann@aol.com

Well, I have one for you Gil. We are not Jewish. My Jewish about-to-be son-in-law informed us that no Xmas tree will be put in THEIR living room... but he called me three times to be sure we invited them over to decorate OUR house. I just love this kid and give him a lot of credit but this really made me laugh. Our daughter's mikva [ritual immersion bath upon conversion to Judaism] is on January 24 and we are looking forward to surprising her with an oneg [post-service celebration with food]. We got her a ring of 5 trees planted in Israel in her honor. Supportive? You bet. But being Native American and not christian, we STILL put up a tree every year and are happy to hear that my daughter and her family will still be having fun with us during this happy time of year... including my popcorn stringing, tinsel

Peoplehood: A Christmas Tree in My House?

hanging, light replacing, candy cane eating, stocking loving son-in-law. The Creator made us all and thankfully, made us all a family... the family of man.

Happy to be supportive of our daughter's conversion,
Name

Subj: christmas tree
Date: 1/13 7:50:33 PM CST
From:
To: GilMann@aol.com

I once read an article regarding a non-Jewish journalist who went to live in Israel with his family for a year. As Sukkoth [one of the three Jewish pilgrimage holidays prescribed in the Bible] came closer his children came home from school and asked when they were building their Sukkah [temporary shelter built to celebrate the holiday of Sukkoth]. The writer said they were not putting one up because they were not Jewish and it was not "their" holiday. For days, the children tried to convince their father that the hut had no real religious meaning, it was a symbol and really just a little house, and why couldn't they have one. This interaction made the author understand what Jewish families go through around Christmas time and how, even a tree can have religious associations.

Thanks, Name

Subj: Xmas Tree
Date: 1/14 1:34:16 PM CST
From:
To: GilMann@aol.com

Dear Gil:

I tend to get upset about the concept of an Xmas Tree being a secular symbol of good will and good cheer in the winter season.

Yes, I know its origins. I understand that it was a pagan symbol adopted by the Catholic Church. But whatever the religion or non-religion of a family, to display an Xmas Tree in one's home during the winter season and to decorate it with ornaments makes it a Xtian symbol.

As a committed Jew, I would not have such a symbol in my home, no matter how beautiful, how lovely, how fragrant or how significant it might be to a member of my extended family. Fortunately, I married a Jewish man and we are raising our child to be a committed Jew so the issue for us is far removed.

I do know Jews, however, who have Xmas Tree Envy and have chosen to have a tree in their own home. I find this repugnant. I too keep a kosher home and would not have someone bring tref [non-kosher] food into it. While I do not claim to keep the entire gamut of mitzvot (I see myself as a Reconstructionist Jew), I can not see actively embracing the symbol of another religion, no matter how it has been "dumbed down," commercialized, or trivialized. I have too much of a sense of history and feel a shiver down my spine for all my ancestors who died fighting and rebuffing the imposition of just such Xtian symbols in their lives.

Name

Concluding Thoughts to Copy, Cut, Paste, and Save

Christmas and the holiday season touch many nerves. I'm going to end this chapter with some additional examples of this. Before sharing them, here is a short email I received from the mom who originally wrote to me:

Subj: Re: Dual religion home
Date: 12/3/ 2:26:04 PM CST
From: H
To: GilMann@aol.com

Thank you so much Gil for your input — I greatly appreciate it. I will be talking with my family and making a decision. I have also spoken to my rabbi over this also. It looks as though we will probably opt to let the kids have little tiny trees in their own rooms. Seems like a comfortable compromise to all. I've thought about having them spend their holiday with their Dad but my family, who is Anglican, would miss them terribly. Also, my 15 y/o stays with me exclusively and won't see her father presently, so she is the one really, that has brought this about. Actually it is she who suggested a tree in her room, which I thought was extremely considerate of her and that made me feel really special. Thanks you for all of your help.

Take care and Happy Chanukah to you also!
H

Next are two additional columns I wrote as a result of emails from readers who reacted to the column at the beginning of this chapter. The first follow-up column is called: "Lousy Christmas Tree Advice?" which is a dialogue I had with a non-Jewish writer. The second is called "The Jewish Christmas Tree." I hope these columns give you inspiration that you'll "Copy, Cut, Paste, and Save."

First follow up column to "A Christmas Tree in My House?"

Lousy Christmas Tree Advice?

Dear Readers:

Now that the intensity and emotion of the Christmas season is behind us, I am sharing an edited exchange of emails I had with a non-Jewish reader. He wrote in reaction to a column discussing placing a Christmas tree in a Jewish home to accommodate young non-Jewish children from a prior marriage. I don't normally get into these kinds of lengthy exchanges with writers (I wish I had the time), but I found his comments especially thought provoking, so I did... hope you find our debate of value...

Dear Gil:

Your article regarding the Christmas tree in a Jewish house has prompted me to respond for these reasons:

1. I disagree with your premise that a Christmas tree is a sign of some Christian belief. My family (Catholic background) does not practice any belief system but enjoy the tree, lights, etc.

2. When our son first invited his special Jewish friend (who became our daughter-in-law) to our home for the Christmas holidays we asked her to bring her Menorah which we placed in a "prominent" location in our home. When Jewish holy days are celebrated we willingly participate and encourage the activity. It is our practice not to fear what others choose to believe and do. Respect for the differences in people is a major consideration of all religions and should not be denied to the children in your article. Their belief system should be encouraged and not be relegated to some inferior status as you have suggested.

Do you think the rigid ideals you and others put forth make people better?

O

Hello O:

Thanks for your email. As I wrote in my column, a Christmas tree is not called a winter tree or a holiday tree. You can view it as a secular symbol if you wish—many Jews or Muslims would disagree with you.

As to your second point, I am not sure what you are calling a rigid ideal. I think you would agree that ideals are worth believing in.

They are standards we try to live up to because they will make us better people. Using the word "rigid" is certainly a negative spin. How about lofty? In gray areas (like much of life) we must find ways of balancing our lofty ideals with the pragmatics of life and individuals. That is why I suggested to the mom who wrote that she provide a place for a Xmas tree — even a prominent place — in the home for her children's spiritual needs even if they cause her discomfort. Hope that clarifies things a bit. Thanks for writing.

Gil

Dear Gil:

Thanks for your response. Can you tell me why some people are afraid to have a different religious/secular symbol in their home when they allow a person of different faith in their home? Would you ask a guest in your home to sit in some obscure area of your home because they were of a different faith... after all they are a living symbol of their faith? It really is about "heart," not some academic exercise suggesting lofty ideals... Gil, the kids are confused and hurting... loosen up!

O

Hello again O

We all have different thresholds... including you. Perhaps you would not care to have your kitchen koshered so a strictly Orthodox Jew could eat in your home. Or perhaps if a devout Muslim insisted that he perform one of his daily prayer sessions to Allah in your living room and asked you and your family to leave so he could do that. How about a Wicca or witchcraft worshiper insisting that you or your children or grandchildren join him or her in some pagan worship before breaking bread?

I am being extreme on purpose. I am all in favor of respecting and learning from other religious traditions... but my home is my home. I would happily welcome a person of another faith into my home and discuss his or her beliefs and faith system — I would not be happy, however, if they brought a ham sandwich into my home.

Jews have over the years developed a sensitivity to having other religions forced upon us... even to the point of death (e.g., the Inquisition). Symbols like crucifixes and, yes, even a Christmas tree mean a great deal to many of us.

I have tried to loosen up... which is why I ultimately suggested that for the children, a tree be placed in the living room if that is what is necessary to nourish and enhance their faith and well being. I would ask of you to please be mindful of the sensitivity of many Jews who have been hurt and scarred by countless generations of persecution... in the name of other religions.

Gil

Dear Gil:

I am well aware of the hurt that peoples have experienced because of differences in perception or cognition... be it the color of skin, religions or political ideology. You ask me if I would allow people to conduct a worship behavior in my home and if I would participate... YES. When I am invited to a Jewish Temple I am honored... and to a Muslim Mosque... I am honored... this is so, because I understand the common fears of mankind, and the variety of tradition/custom to ask for relief from the fear of sickness, old age and death... there are others! I maintain we all should "Lighten Up," and not take ourselves seriously... from a distance, it's all very comical, and at the same time, very sad. What is not funny is the way we treat each other because of those fears and the belief systems we develop.

Be Kind... Be Good... Be Jewish if it suits you... practice any faith at the time it suits you, but don't take it to be license to claim a special significance. There are no Gods in my system because I would be hard pressed to select one or more of the many prayed to each day by millions of people.

O

Hi O!

You raise some good points though I think you downplay significant differences between religious systems. Religion can be a godsend and a curse. In my experience, few people have the thoughtfulness, open-mindedness, and conscientiousness that you have about life... and respecting other life. If everyone in the world could be as introspective and desirous of kind behavior as you appear to be, perhaps we wouldn't need religion and perhaps the world would be a better place. As for me, I embrace Judaism largely because I dream of a better world for adults and children of all religions — with and without Christmas trees.

Peace!
Gil

_____

Second follow up column to "A Christmas Tree in My House?"

The Jewish Christmas Tree

Dear Gil:

When I was a little boy, until I was about 8 years old, we had a Christmas tree in our home. Looking back, I believe that it was a "very Jewish" thing to do.

Years earlier, my parents were very close to the next-door neighbors, the Johansons. This family was a "good Christian" family with 3 boys (older than the three children in my family.)

My mother was especially close to Mrs. Johanson, who was also a fairly young woman at the time. Mrs. Johanson died after a terrible battle with cancer. As a "dying wish," and since she had no other family, she asked that my mother continue to provide a place for her boys to gather for the holidays, until they were old enough to provide for themselves. So, after Hanukah, we would briefly put up a Christmas tree so that the Johanson boys would have a place to meet and be with "family." This only went on a few years, until they met at one of their own families' home. All three boys became successful, including one becoming a state senator. One of my brothers by the way, became a rabbi.

So, I continue to believe that this act of kindness by my mother meant that having a Christmas tree was, indeed, a mitzvah [a good deed or fulfillment of a commandment]!

Respectfully,
C

Dear C:

Many Jews have strong opinions about the appropriateness of having a Christmas tree in a Jewish home. They contend, as do I, that the tree is not a generic holiday symbol but a Christian ritual object that, generally speaking, does not belong in a Jewish home. I know this topic can stir emotions because I have written about Christmas trees in the past and received much email afterwards.

Your unique and moving story is different than anything I have ever seen before. I suspect many people (including me) would agree with you in saying that having a Christmas tree in your house was a mitzvah… a good deed.

Some might say that your mother's act was misguided in that she first had a responsibility to her own three young Jewish children. The argument could be that having a tree in a Jewish home was wrong for numerous reasons, including the message it sent about accepting Christianity in your home and the longing this might have created for the three of you to have a tree of your own.

I could see these points, but I admire your Mom and think she did the right thing. She sent a message to the three of you all right—a message that deeply imprinted on you. That message was that Jews should treat others with goodness and kindness whether they are Jew or Gentile.

I suspect your mother's decision was not flippant. The fact that after a few years a tree ceased to be in your home suggests to me that having a Jewish home mattered to your Mom. From what you have written, having the tree in your home for those few years was also most consistent with having a Jewish home.

Recently I wrote a column called: Religions: The Cause of the World's Problems. I responded to a writer who made that assertion. In a sentence, my column said that religions have certainly brought some bad things to our world... but I would not advocate ridding the world of religions.

For ultimately I believe the major religions of the world try to teach us to treat each other as your mother treated the Johanson boys. This is why she wanted a Jewish home... to raise three boys of her own who would grow to become *mensches* [decent human beings] (one of whom became a rabbi). Three Jews who would go out into the world someday, be kind to others and treat those in need with compassion.

Much is made of brotherhood at this time of year. Thanks to your mother, you really know what it means. I want to believe that the Johanson boys do as well as they recall with warmth how at a time of pain and loss, they were welcomed and comforted by a Jewish family at Christmastime.

Thank you for sharing your touching story. Happy Chanukah!

Gil

Chapter 15
You Don't Look Jewish!

Dear Gil:

I have heard the phrase "You don't LOOK Jewish!" as long as I can remember, when asked about my religious beliefs. It is true, I do not have the typical dark hair, (mine is red), my eyes are grey-green, and I have missed out on the typical "Jewish" nose, too.

I do not ask anyone their religious preference, but when they ask me & I respond in truth, I am always stunned by THAT PHRASE. My initial response is to say, "You don't LOOK Methodist (or whatever), but I can't — it is too disrespectful, in spite of how they have reacted to me. Any suggestions??? By the way, I wear Jewish jewelry every day. Thanks for taking your time reading this email.

N

Dear N:

Personally, I have had similar experiences as not only do I not look "stereotypically" Jewish, but also, my name is WASPy sounding. The irony in my case is that Gil is not short for Gilbert. I was born in Israel and Gil, my given name, is a modern Hebrew name — pronounced in Hebrew more like "geel." (As an aside, Israelis have often asked me how I, an American, ended up with an Israeli Hebrew name.)

If people are surprised because I "don't look Jewish," I am not offended (if anything, I am amused). I don't give their comment much weight, viewing it as neutral, though I know that, in reality, their attitude could be a positive or negative toward Jews.

My response has been: "You should go to Israel. There you will see Jews of every color, shape, and size. This is because Judaism is not a race. Judaism is a way of life — anyone can convert and become a member of the Jewish people."

A second response that I offer to you is a recommendation to see the movie: *Europa Europa*. The movie is an amazing true story of a

Jewish boy in Germany who gets involved in the Nazi youth movement during World War II. Much of the movie deals with the physical description of Jews according to Nazi and Aryan ideology. Some scenes are so absurd and powerful that anyone watching the movie would have to reexamine their thinking about the way Jews "look."

Having said that and having met Jews from all over the world, I will confess that in my experience most of the Jews I have met have dark hair and brown eyes. HOWEVER, my own son is blond! In the summer, he looks like one of the Beach Boys! (My wife and I and the rest of our kids all have dark hair.)

Looking at him every day reminds me of the problem of stereotypes. For a further reminder of the inaccuracy and trouble of stereotypes, I'll end with this email that I recently received that came under the subject: Black Jews.

Dear Gil:

I welcome the day when I as a Black Jew will walk into a shul and be readily accepted for who I am… a Jew. I hate always having to explain all about me. I hurt sometimes to feel the eyes, trying to figure me out. I look forward to the day when all Jews will be warmly welcomed… until then… I guess I'll keep pressing thru.

I have received other similar emails from Black Jews. There are lessons to be learned from all of these emails. As Jews and as people, our appearance is not what matters. Judging others and being judged based on looks is often inaccurate and hurtful. I thank you both for writing and reminding us!

Gil

Email Responses to "You Don't Look Jewish!"

Subj: No Subject
Date: 3/9 8:52:16 PM CST
From:
To: GilMann@aol.com

the story about the woman who did not look "jewish" amused and intrigued me. for years people reacted to me in the same way (all gentiles). i've been told i look very jewish by my german friend. i've been told that i look swedish by most gentile people though. i have to laugh at the stereotypes that most folks have about how we are supposed to look. i do have blonde hair that is very curly and light hazel eyes. i guess this means i look "somewhat" jewish (the curly hair). most people assume we all have curly hair, or so i've been told. i even had a close friend's husband tell me, "you look really good for a jewish girl." i could not believe that one! he went on to say that most jewish women were not attractive. i was not angry so much as dumbfounded. where has he been all his life? oh well, i just wanted to share my thoughts.

shalom and todah (thank you), name

Subj: "You don't look Jewish"
Date: 3/9 10:24:01 PM CST
From:
To: GilMann@aol.com

I was in a class for converts and/or engaged "inter" couples where the first thing the Rabbi did was pick a person at random, instruct her to go quickly through the class saying "Jewish/Non-Jewish" based solely on looks. He reminded the class not to respond. Afterwards he asked for hands from all those identified correctly. The total was 35%. This was a powerful lesson in stereotyping.

I am a blond, blue-eyed Norwegian-American Jew. Once I was in an elevator on my way to a Jewish book store when the middle-aged lady in the car looked at my Star of David and asked if I knew what I was wearing. Then, in my own synagogue, a very short older gentlemen (whom I did not know) looked up at me and asked how I knew the prayers since "you don't look like a little Jewish girl." All I could think of saying was "I'm not so little."

Subj: But you don't look...
Date: 3/9 10:35:53 PM CST
From:
To: GilMann@aol.com

Hi, Gil.

I'm a convert, and I've heard it all, too. Sometimes, when you KNOW the comment is anti-Semitic, you are tempted to say, "Isn't that strange! And you don't look like a bigot.";

Subj: "not looking Jewish"
Date: 3/10 2:46:22 AM CST
From:
To: GilMann@aol.com

Dear Gil,

I have a funny story apropos to "not looking Jewish." I have blond hair, hazel eyes, I was born on St. Patrick's Day and my middle name is Kate. My entire name sounds Irish.. Needless to say, I have no trouble passing as a non-Jewish woman, for sure.

My mom looks just like me. So, one day we were on the subway together and two elderly Jewish people sitting next to us started talking in Yiddish to each other condescendingly about us "shiksas" [a derogatory term for non-Jewish women]. Well, it took every ounce of self control to keep from smiling. Little did they know that we understood everything they said. When our station was coming up, my mom bent over and whispered "Ich bin nisht a shiksa" (I am not a shiksa) to them in Yiddish. Well, you never

199

saw a sharper color of red that their cheeks turned as we departed the train. It made our day!

I love being able to pass. Especially in that situation. When people tell me, "you don't look Jewish" I am tickled pink. I usually say, "really?" and launch into Hebrew or Yiddish.

On the flip side, I have been a silent party to many an anti-Semitic comment when the inconsiderate person doesn't realize that I am Jewish. This recently happened in bank. The woman was complaining to the teller how she had a cold and how her Jewish doctor, who should have a close relationship with his miracle-working God, failed to make her better. I am always stunned to hear things like that out loud. And since I pass, I don't feel obligated to fix her anti-Semitic mentality. Nothing I could say would make a difference anyway. Anyway, those are my stories, for your interest and amusement.

Shalom,
Name (in English and Hebrew)

Subj: Looking Jewish
Date: 3/12 10:25:00 AM CST
From:
To: GilMann@aol.com

Dear Gil:

This letter on stereotypes was very interesting. When I was in college at Arizona State University, I lived with 3 women who had never met a Jew before. In November, a woman who lived down the hall passed out questionnaires for a psychology experiment she was doing on Jewish stereotypes. Basically it was just asking about big noses and penny pinching types of things. My roommates, who had seen me with my rather ordinary nose pulling change out of my pocket that fell on the floor which got left there until the end of the month when I really needed the cash and saw me lending money when asked (if I had it), said that they knew that I was different, but they still had to agree that Jews were... accepting all the stereotypes.

I don't know how to change people's minds except by being who I am, but when trying to show by example doesn't work — how do you change stereotypes?

Name

Subj: Hi!
Date: 3/12 6:02:35 PM CST
From: Christian Salzman
To: GilMann@aol.com

Hi!!

I read your column about "YOU DON'T LOOK JEWISH"! It was very good! I have the same problem, i live in Sweden where most people have like blue eyes and blond hair. I am one of those people, but I'm also Jewish! No one believe me when i say to them that I'm Jewish, it's very strange my mother is dark and my father is also dark so... When i go to the temple all old and orthodox people look at me like i was an invader or something. I don't like that stereo type picture of a Jew!

Kind regards
Christian Salzman (name used with permission)

Subj: I don't look Jewish
Date: 3/16 12:03:28 PM CST
From:
To: GilMann@aol.com

Dear Gil:

Thanks to Clairol, I have red hair but in my youth my hair was naturally blond. My eyes are gray and I too do not look Jewish.

I always thought that the comment, 'you don't look... ' was just a manifestation of the racism around us in the US.

In the near future, I will be moving to Philly to do my post grad work. I was looking through the personals for people to hook up with via the Net before moving there so I would not be a "total" stranger. Without exception, all the men asked for a JWF — Jewish White Female. I think this to be a very sad commentary indeed on the mental state of the Jewish community when we have to specify color of skin in our potential associates.

B'shalom [in peace]
Name

Concluding Thoughts to Copy, Cut, Paste, and Save

We all know that we shouldn't judge a book by its cover, but we do it anyway. Human nature, I guess. Really, I think this is our animal nature.

Animals quickly size up situations by the first sensory data they receive. For animals, this is probably a survival mechanism or a defensive measure to quickly identify friend or foe. Humans also do this with the first sensory data we receive, which is usually visual. Sometimes we are served by this ability; for example, if we see a dangerous situation, like a person with a gun, we can react quickly.

But most of the time, after a quick look at others, we make decisions about them that have nothing to do with danger and more to do with stereotypes. Theoretically, we humans are above animals because we have the ability to take advantage of our intelligence to stifle our impulse to hastily judge based on another's appearance.

But, alas, we humans often stifle our intelligence and revert to our animal impulse to judge others based on what meets our eye. This chapter shows that looking at a person, Jew or any other, and then judging based on stereotypes is often inaccurate or worse.

Judaism maintains that humans can either act like animals or rise above this nature to divine behavior — elevating ourselves to behavior that is holy. This includes the commandment in the Torah to judge others fairly.

Rabbi Joseph Telushkin points out that on *Yom Kippur,* Jews confess the sin of judging others hastily. In *The Book of Jewish Values*, he emphasizes how wrong we can be when we judge unfairly based on appearances with this poem by Roger Bush:

On the Street

She was pretty and she smiled at the men approaching.
I could see her in profile. A sweet thing and cheeky, too.
Embarrassed males turned away.
Quickened their pace; looked guilty, some blushed.
But undaunted, she met with an expectant smile and the next,
only again to be refused.
Soliciting, I thought; a prostitute; in broad daylight;
Until she turned,
And I saw she was selling buttons for charity.

He staggered down the steps and fell, Lord,
A crumpled mass on the footpath.
His bottle broke and the liquid spilled across the walk.
He's drunk, I thought. Disgust. Disdain. Until…
Two girls rushed from a nearby car and cried,
"It's Daddy. Please help. He's ill."

He caught my gaze. This greedy-eyed young man,
He too had seen the open handbag on the aged arm,
With the few dollars exposed to view.
He stalked the prey, and the old woman just window shopped.
He'll grab and run, I thought, but no,
Quietly, he tapped her shoulder, pointed to the bag,
Exchanged smiles.
They went their way.

O Lord, forgive me, forgive me.
Why do I always think the worst of your children?

Next time you feel the impulse to judge another based on their appearance or a stereotype, hopefully this poem and the emails in this chapter will help you to avoid the urge.

Chapter 16
I Am Catholic and Dating a Jewish Guy

Dear Gil:

I am a young adult, Catholic by birth, but within the next few years will be starting the process of converting to Judaism. Recently I have begun dating a Jewish man. His parents only know of my Catholic upbringing and are very much against our relationship. It upsets me that they are not willing to accept me.

I would be interested to know if things would be different if they knew of my plans to convert. I don't want to throw it upon them or have them believe that I am converting just because I am dating their son, since I have intended on converting for over a year now. How do parents feel about this? Would I be accepted if they knew of my plans to convert? Would they accept a convert as they would a Jew by birth? It is very frustrating to me because I fully intend to marry a Jew after I convert and I don't really understand why it is such a problem if I am dating one now. I would like to hear what Jewish adults think about this and also young adults who may have experienced this before. Thank you.

D

Dear D:

You ask a number of good questions that are difficult to answer with certainty. I will try to answer the best I can. I must start, however, by saying that every parent is different so their reactions will differ.

With this stated, I will try to give you some insight into why some Jewish parents do not react warmly to their children dating non-Jews. (I will get to the conversion issue a little later.) The first reason is that, over the centuries, the experience Jews have had with the non-Jewish world has not been a happy one—to put it mildly.

Generations worth of experience with anti-Semitism, persecution, and physical harm have left deep scars on many Jews. For these Jews, the idea of having a Gentile in the family is a very difficult adjustment... regardless of how nice the individual is. This may be challenging for you to deal with… but should not be taken personally. I should add, however, that if I was the one being rejected I think I would probably feel offended, hurt, and maybe angry as well.

Personalities aside, statistical studies show that most children of intermarriages are not raised as Jews. This particularly pains many (potential) grandparents, especially considering that Jews today are struggling to survive numerically. Recent demographic trends are discouraging, and don't forget we lost over a third of our people during the Holocaust.

"But Gil," you may be thinking, "I told you I am planning to convert to Judaism. I still don't know if I will be accepted!"

Here, I must tell you that I have heard from others who have wondered the same thing. I have also heard from some Jews after they converted who told me of being accepted and from some who still were not accepted.

The best explanation I can offer for lack of acceptance has to do with skepticism about the sincerity of or the motivation behind the conversion.

For example, I have heard from Jews who have told me that they knew so and so who converted for the sake of convenience in order to get married. Later, they got divorced and went right back to Christianity.

As a rule of thumb, I reject this kind of skepticism… as do many other Jews. On top of that, personally, I don't really care why a person chooses to become a Jew. To be a Jew is plenty hard as far I'm concerned, and I consequently view those who convert and embrace Judaism ("Jews by Choice" — as converts are now called) with respect.

In fact, according to Jewish law, Jews are supposed to show favor to converts because "they have left their father's house, their people, and all Gentile people to join us. They are to be afforded special protection!" Further, when a convert is blessed we customarily refer to them as the "the son/daughter of Abraham and Sarah," the first patriarch and matriarch of Judaism. To me this is a high tribute.

There is much more in our tradition that is positive toward converts, such as the fact that King David is the descendent of a convert (Ruth), but I won't get into all of that here.

According to Jewish tradition, initially, potential converts to this difficult way of life are supposed to be discouraged. But if a potential convert insists, we are to welcome them. My posture is to be welcoming. And so I say to you with warmth, I hope Judaism and the man you someday marry bring you fulfillment and happiness.

Thanks for writing,

Gil

Email Responses to
"I Am Catholic and Dating a Jewish Guy"

Subj: Response to D's question of the week.
Date: 6/14 10:23:25 PM CDT
From:
To: GilMann@aol.com

Dear D,

I too am a "Jew by choice." I too felt initially, that I was not being accepted by my inlaws. They were concerned that their grandchildren would not be raised Jews. My husband too, was very adament about the need to marry into his own faith.

I was also raised Roman Catholic, but was non-practicing at the time that I met my husband. I believed in G_D, I prayed, I asked for forgiveness for my sins, what more could anyone want?!

I met my husband 5 years after graduating college. I was never really exposed to the Jewish faith prior to that. Meeting him gave me the opportunity to explore this faith. I found myself really liking the traditions and family oriented practices! We together decided to attend conversion classes, and really learned a lot. I converted in a reform congregation, but did go into the mikvah, therefore my conversion is fully recognized by conservative congregations. We were married by the same Rabbi who converted me. What a wonderful person he is! He made me feel very welcome, and comfortable with the whole process. He made the conversion process easy for me.

We now have 4 wonderful children, and are very happy that we made the decision we did at the time. The children are aware of their being Jews. They are also aware that mommy chose to be Jewish, and as they grow older, they will know the whole story of my conversion. We belong to a conservative congregation, because it is the only temple in our city. I would have initially prefered to belong to a reform temple, however we have become accostomed to our temple, and it's workings. We have been here 6 years now. I have over the course of time found out that many of the congregants in our temple are "Jews by choice"! I was pleasantly surprised that so many of the couples had one convert! I feel very much a part of this temple now. People are very accepting of converts here. We have made many good friends through the temple.

My inlaws and I get along very well now. They understand that we are committed to raising the children in the Jewish faith, as well as living it in our home. I felt initially after getting married, that they were not as accepting of me as I would have liked. I believe they were waiting to see how it would all play out. My mother-in-law has even said recently, and I quote "you are the best thing that has ever happened to my son."

So, it has been a long and sometimes a scary journey, but well worth it in the long run. I am married to a wonderful man, and we have a very good life together.

I hope your difficulties with your potential in-laws get easier. Perhaps it would be wise to let them in on you plans to commit to the Jewish faith. It may ease their mind about the future!

Hope my experiences help you gain perspective on the bigger picture, and how the future may look much brighter! Good luck!

Feel free to E-mail me directly, if you have other thoughts or questions, at ____@____.com

Name

Subj: Convert
Date: 6/11 10:41:26 PM CDT
From:
To: GilMann@aol.com

I applaud this person's wish to convert, and feel that if she is going to marry this man she definitely should inform the parents. Also what is his reaction. Does he want her to convert? How religious is he? Does he plan to send his children to Hebrew School? I know several converts and they are more religious and observant then the Jews I know. Another question comes to mind will she end up a Messianic Jew. It is very hard to give up your belief in Jesus as the messiah. I always question the person's motive. It is difficult enough growing up a Jew, and many wish they were not. I am Jewish married to a man who converted, but he didn't really have a strong belief in any religion before we married. Our children are Jewish and married to Jews. We have been very happy and he finds great satisfaction in the rituals. Another question how do her parents feel about the conversion? My husband's were never told, because they would have objected. His father was a Methodist Deacon and objected to me anyway. Good luck to this person and I hope her motives are pure.

Shalom
Name

Subj: convert
Date: 6/11 10:40:28 PM CDT
From:
To: GilMann@aol.com

There is also the question of the method of converting. Orthodoxy does not recognize non-orthodox conversions. Also, according to orthodoxy, if a person converts and does not keep the laws like shabbos [as in not working, driving, or using electricity on the Sabbath] and kashrus [keeping kosher], the conversion is not valid. Therefore, there are lots of question for potential in-laws to ask of their children's dates if they are converts.

Subj: Follow your heart!
Date: 6/12 9:27:45 PM CDT
From:
To: GilMann@aol.com

I feel not only fullfilled by being Jewish, but grateful that it is the first word I would use to identify myself. I am in an interfaith marriage, yet all three of our sons are being raised as Jews.
I love being a practicing reform Jew.

If this choice to convert to Judiasm feels right to you then by all means do it! Do not let anyone stand in your way. Many people of another generation will never change their archaic beliefs. We have many converts at my temple in Florida and they are very much welcome.

Good luck to you in whatever your choice may be,
Initialed

Subj: Conversion: Response to D
Date: 6/13 1:23:40 PM CDT
From:
To: GilMann@aol.com

Dear Gil:

I am a convert or a Jew by Choice. Have been for 26 years.
I call it a Jew by Conviction, but that is using a Baptist or
evangelical word

Anyway — My question to the young lady is: Why are you waiting
to begin your conversion studies? Why do you think you want to
marry a Jewish man "someday"?

I don't know why you want to be Jewish, but I say, if you REALLY
do, then get busy, Jewish boyfriend or not. It might be good for
you not to date him right now. If he cares for you, he'll wait until
you have your spiritual life straightened out and your conversion
is complete. If not, then he is not the one for you anyway. You
need to get your own self in order before you even think about
marriage. I don't know how old you are now, but you need to
examine your own motives for whatever you do regarding your
religion. I would be happy to correspond with you, and Gil may
give you my name and address. I wish you well, and I will help
you in any way I can, but you MUST BE SURE IN YOUR HEART
AND SOUL that you understand what you are doing and that you
are strong enough to take the abuse you will get from your own
family if you proceed with this. My best wishes to you in your
quest.

Sincerely,
Initialed

Subj: Catholic Girl
Date: 6/22 7:43:52 PM CDT
From:
To: GilMann@aol.com

I sympathize with this young lady, for she has a long hard road
to go as you pointed out to her with all the horrible things that
were done against Jews in the name of Christianity. After saying
that, I must tell you that 30 years ago, I, a Christian Lady,
married that most wonderful man who happened to be Jewish.
I had very hard times with his family even though I was well
educated in what the Jews had to endure. (My father had many
Jewish friends) To no avail, I suffered. We had a son and had
to sneak him to the Church to have him baptised because my
husband decided that i had more faith and knew my religion
better than he. To make a long story short, my son is a 27 year
old lawyer who has recently embraced his jewish heritage by
himself. We taught him both religions and he chose and is very
happy. Unfortunately my Mother-in-law died 4 years ago and was
unable to see it but I believe she knows it. Shalom, Name

Concluding Thoughts to Copy, Cut, Paste, and Save

This chapter raises two sensitive issues: conversion and interfaith
dating/marriage. The issue of conversion is discussed further in the
next chapter, so I'll only comment here on intermarriage.

First, a definition: If one spouse converts to the religion of the other
spouse, this is NOT an intermarriage in my view, since both of them
now share the same religion. A Jewish intermarriage therefore
includes one spouse who is not Jewish.

Interfaith dating between Jews and non-Jews is widespread today, and consequently so is intermarriage. The actual statistics are debated (some say 50 percent or more of Jews today intermarry). The numbers may be debatable, but the trend is clearly in the direction of increasing rates. The statistics also say that most of these couples do not raise their children to be Jewish. This data is considered an alarming Jewish demographic time bomb by many Jews.

There is a positive spin to these statistics. They show that Jews have achieved a level of acceptance in society that was unimaginable just 50 years ago. I used to say that when a Kennedy marries a Jew, we will have finally "arrived." Well, a Kennedy has a married a Jew, and the acceptance this represents is worth celebrating. I feel lucky to live in a time when my Gentile neighbors are such nice and good people. But I'm also worried. I'm disturbed by the rising intermarriage percentages, and especially the child-rearing data, because I think Judaism is worthy of preserving and the population trends don't bode well. This is not to say that Judaism is better, but rather that Judaism is good and should continue.

What to do? First, I believe our synagogues and other Jewish institutions need to find every possible way to make interfaith couples and their children a part of our community. I understand the constraints, the arguments, and the Jewish laws that make these efforts difficult. Still, when faced with policy decisions, I've concluded that we should lean toward the more liberal solutions in an effort to say "welcome." I don't think finding ways to encourage participation takes great creative thinking... but when it does, I believe the Jewish community should be creative.

Now some will argue with me that such "concessions" to intermarried couples encourage intermarriage. I used to think this way as well. In fact, I once even declined to stand in the wedding of a close friend who was intermarrying. Here's a shocker: they got married anyway. They did not "fall out of love" as a result of my stubborn position. My relationship with my friend did suffer though... perhaps irreparably.

Over the years, I've made a 180-degree change in my position because I decided that resolutely "holding out" against intermarriage and ostracizing others does not stop intermarriage. In fact, it hurts Judaism in the final analysis because the attitude often convinces the couple to have nothing to do with Judaism. Being obstinate, angry, and creating distance sends the unintended message that Judaism is cruel and intolerant. Who could blame the couple for saying, "We don't want that tradition in our lives or for our children."

Judaism in reality is a rich, wise, and kind way of life (which is why I work so hard on "behalf" of Judaism). One of the reasons we have intermarriage, however, is that many Jews don't know a lot about Judaism. Jewish education for most Jews consists of preparation for a Bar or Bat Mitzvah… and after the age of 13, the education ends. I could write a great deal about overhauling Jewish education, but won't do so here. I will say, however, that we must start educating Jews to see the value, relevance, beauty, and practical application of Judaism in their day-to-day lives. There should be so much meaning in Judaism for Jews that removing it from their lives would leave an unfillable void. They would then be more inclined to seek a Jewish soul mate.

Even if we were able to successfully fill Jews with this kind of inspiration, guidance, and affection for Judaism, intermarriage would continue outside of Israel for a simple reason: Jews are a minority. Most of the people around them are not Jewish, and people fall in love with the people around them because, as the Lou Reed song says, "Love is chemical." I've heard many interdating couples and young intermarrieds say (and believe) that their love for each other is so strong, they will be able to conquer any religious issues if and when the time comes. That usually means when the kids arrive. Well, my experience has been that "love does not conquer all," especially when children arrive, because kids bring religious issues to the surface, often in painful ways.

To conclude, I suggest that people be mindful and honest about these realities of society and family life. Dating may well lead to marriage, and anyone considering a serious relationship should be very conscientious about the choices they are making. These are not issues that should be dismissed in the heat of passion. Many experts say that a couple should raise their children in one religion—rather than saying, "We'll raise the kids in both religions and then we will let them choose." There are numerous other ways to handle the issue, from agreeing to raise the children in one of the parents' religions to one of the parents converting.

These few paragraphs cannot do justice to this complex and important subject. I'll end this chapter by providing two websites that specialize in intermarriage as further resources: the Jewish Outreach Institute: www.joi.org and www.interfaithfamily.com.

Chapter 17
Are Converts Treated as Second Class?

Dear Gil:

I always had a deep fascination with Judaism since I could remember. I believe my parents both have Jewish blood in their veins. My mother's maiden name is Lewin. Further evidence is that my late father's hometown, Siedlce, Poland, was populated by 17,000 Polish Jews before WW2. It's geographic location is between Treblinka and Warsaw. Siedlce Jews were killed. Unfortunately, any genealogy information is probably most likely lost or destroyed during the war.

I am wondering should I or shouldn't I convert to Judaism? I always get the feeling that born Jews are more resentful and distant to the Jews by choice. I think the Jews by birth feel offended when Jews by choice convert. Do Jews treat Jews by choice like second class citizens?

V

V Shalom:

In my experience, sadly, the answer many times is yes. This is a shame on various levels, not the least of which is that the founding father of Judaism — Abraham — converted to Judaism and King David is a descendant of a most famous convert: Ruth!

In addition, Jewish law repeatedly prohibits mistreatment of converts. One of the greatest rabbis of all time, Maimonides (known as the RAMBAM), wrote: "Toward father and mother we are commanded honor and reverence, toward the prophets to obey them, but toward proselytes (converts) we are commanded to have great love in our inmost hearts."

In keeping with this teaching, I am also able to answer your question with the response that many Jews accept converts fully. I have heard from converts who were so warmly welcomed that their feelings of conviction about conversions were only strengthened as a result of their wonderful reception from Jews by birth.

As for the second-class citizenship reaction, I offer several possible explanations. First, many Jews carry the hurt of centuries of persecution from Gentile neighbors, and this colors their view of non-Jews. I think many also feel that this pain is something we Jews own and a person who converts (and whose relatives did not suffer anti-Semitism — or worse, whose relatives may have persecuted Jews) does not have the same kind of "ownership" of Judaism as a Jew by birth whose ancestors suffered.

Also, I have heard Jews by birth express skepticism and cynicism about the sincerity of a Jew by Choice's conversion. Converting "just to marry" a Jew is often cited. Marriage is one of many possible events or "stirrings" in a person's life that might motivate them to convert to Judaism. I am fine with marriage being one such event. Marrying someone is a huge life decision that should involve deep soul searching. If part of that soul searching includes a reevaluation of one's faith and an embracing of the Jewish way of life, then I say "Welcome!" Becoming a Jew is a huge sacrifice and commitment, and I greatly honor any Jew by Choice who sincerely embraces Judaism. As I have written in the past, I wish all Jews by birth would be as serious about their Judaism as many of the converts I have met! ("Jews by chance" is a term I've heard that sadly describes many born Jews.)

A problem arises in the eyes of many Jews (including mine), however, when a person converts to Judaism because they are marrying a Jew but, following the marriage, practices no Judaism or even continues to practice his or her original religion (e.g., actively celebrating Christmas). Still, in my experience this is the exception. In fact, I have found that in couples where one of the partners has converted to Judaism, the convert is often more committed to Judaism than the Jew by birth.

I must say in closing that the danger in all that I have written is that I am generalizing. Whenever a person generalizes, they are asking for trouble because there are so many exceptions. Still, I offer these answers to you in the hope that you will not be dissuaded from your interest to pursue Judaism. And I offer these words to others, in the hope that the "distance" often felt by Jews by Choice be eliminated. Instead, we should welcome converts as a blessing to our people with the following RAMBAM teaching in mind: Peace be unto converts... fellow pupils of OUR father Abraham.

Thanks for writing!

Gil

Email Responses to "Are Converts Treated as Second Class"

Subj: Converts
Date: 10/12 8:19:12 PM CDT
From:
To: GilMann@aol.com

It is always deeply painful to me to hear someone speak about a person as a convert. This happened just last Sunday morning at our Chabad [an Orthodox Chasidic denomination] minha [afternoon] prayers. When I heard it, I immediately reminded my dear friend (who should have known better) that, first of all, it is a sin to refer to anyone as a convert. Secondly, the 600,000 of us at Mount Sinai were all converts. Also, Ruth, the mother of Messiah (may He come soon) was a convert. To think that we might not have Meshiach [messiah] coming if it hadn't been for a convert. May Hashem [God, literally meaning The Name] bless all converts and may these despicable comments cease.

Name

Subj: Convert Response
Date: 10/12 8:50:12 PM CDT
From:
To: GilMann@aol.com

Dear Gil:

First, I commend your answer. It was very thorough and on target. From my experience in our Orthodox community, converts are treated no different that Jews from birth. Great care is given not to remind them of their background so they shouldn't feel second class. There are many converts in the community where I live and their former status is never given a second thought.

I wish her well in her search.

All the best.
Name

Subj: (no subject)
Date: 10/13 10:44:45 PM CDT
From:
To: GilMann@aol.com

I am a Jew by birth. First, I'd like to say that I would never make a converted Jew feel second-class or act or say anything to differentiate them from born Jews in my interactions with them. However, I have a difficult time accepting converted Jews as "real" Jews. I am middle-aged and have the fondest and most loving memories of holiday traditions, dinners, etc. with extended family during every Jewish holiday since my early childhood (and I'm sure these family celebrations existed for me since my birth). I also know what Judaism has meant to me from the time I was a child in Sunday and Hebrew school and through different phases of my adulthood. I have memories of my personal commitments of following Jewish law and how those interacted with my family's commitments. I remember and have stories shared about how my grandparents spent all day in synagogue on the Sabbath and festivals. I remember as a young child my dad being so cautious not to leave evidence outside our home of our Jewishness; two of his uncles died in the Holocaust. My grandparents were Bubbi and Zedah and my Mom is now the proud Bubbi. My Bas Mitzvah at the age of thirteen was very important to me, and so have been the Bnai Mitzvahs of family and friends both while growing up and now. I remember how I would stay at synagogue all day with friends on Yom Kippur and have continued to do so as an adult. I remember as a child that on Jewish holidays, classes at school were almost empty and often staffed with substitute teachers. I have a Jewish father for whom I light a Yahrzeit glass [memorial candle lit on the anniversary of death of close relatives] and for whom I say Yizkor [memorial service] and other Jewish ancestors whom I also remember.

Judaism also encompasses practicing in the heart, at home, with family, in synagogue, in the community, and commitment toward Israel. A converted Jew as well as a born Jew can have all of these. I admit it bothers me somewhat when converted Jews are on the board of a synagogue. Converted Jews lack the foundation of years and years of Jewish ancestors, practices, traditions, get-togethers, and identity. For me, that history and foundation is the backbone of my faith and is there even if circumstances prevent me from practicing my Judaism as much as I'd like.

I am normally a very accepting person. However, as I already mentioned, I have difficulty accepting a converted Jew as having as much Jewishness in him/her as a born Jew. I'd like some feedback, even different points of view concerning what I've said. Good Shabos [Yiddish greeting wishing a Good Sabbath]!

Subj: Good column
Date: 10/14 12:28:03 PM CDT
From:
To: GilMann@aol.com

I appreciated your recent column about Jews by Choice; thank you for showing both sides. I converted one month ago after being married to a Jew for 8 years, and everyone has been very nice to me. Maybe Reform Jews are more accepting? You should have seen my temple filled with congregants and 50 of my friends and relatives from both sides from across the country, singing "Siman Tov u Mazel Tov" [a traditional song of congratulation sung at happy occasions] loudly and happily for me! I try to proudly set an example by being more observant than the average Reform Jew, getting my husband to join a temple after not attending for 25 years and now enjoying weekly services and many rituals he never experienced, getting his relatives to temple and learning Hebrew, showing born Jews that their faith is rewarding and fun and interesting enough for someone to spend a year and a half reading 100 books and taking private tutoring to convert. If I ever do experience any resentment, now I'll know more about where it's coming from and some things to say in response. Todah rabah [Hebrew for thank you very much]!

Shalom,

Subj: No Subject
Date: 10/12 9:14:37 PM CDT
From:
To: GilMann@aol.com

Shalom, Gill Mann

I am a Jew by chance, however I honor that chance opportunity, I was given. I'm not a very religious Jew, and married a girl who was not born Jewish. Unfortunately, our marriage did not last, no fault of hers, but she was a better Jew by choice, than I by chance. Even though we did not live together, she raised our two children as Jews, sent them to Sunday school, and kept a Jewish house.

Thought this might add to your collection of converts who BECAME Jews.

Name

Subj: (no subject)
Date: 10/12 9:17:11 PM CDT
From:
To: GilMann@aol.com

As a long-ago convert, I was quite taken with the responses concerning this. I had a Jewish father (nonobservant) and a Catholic mother (also nonobservant), so why did the little synagogue in my little town seem so appealing to me? I don't know, but it did — it was where I belonged. Now 45 years later I can only say that I am delighted to be who I am, to have 4 wonderful Jewish children and five Jewish grandchildren and 2 Roman Catholic grandchildren who are delightful, as well. In all the years since I converted, I've had only two people who were churlish about it — neither of whom would I invite for a cup of coffee anyway. It's a lovely life.

Name

Subj: (no subject)
Date: 10/12 11:30:41 PM CDT
From:
To: GilMann@aol.com

My father, too, told me that as a convert, I would never be considered a Jew by born Jews. I have been most fortunate in that I have always been warmly embraced and supported by Jews. I can relate to what the writer of this week's email is saying. And it is not fair to generalize that only Jews have suffered. My father was taken from school at age 12 because he was a Pole. He was placed in slave labor situations, tortured and sentenced to execution, and lived without his family until he grew into a wonderful adult. People throughout Europe suffered from persecution for one reason or another throughout history, as have those on every other continent. Persecution is not an excuse for any group to carry it like a medal and exclude others.

That is only a reverse form of discrimination and Jews, of all groups, should understand the pain of exclusion.

Thanks for the forum
Name

Subj: conversion
Date: 10/13 9:55:05 AM CDT
From:
To: GilMann@aol.com

Great answer to the person about converting. Since we are considered "the chosen" people," who is to say converts are not chosen too, just later in life.

Subj: Re: Are Converts Treated as 2nd Class? Email of the Week
Date: 10/11 8:56:25 PM CDT
From:
To: GilMann@aol.com

Gil,

Another reason for the second-class citizenship reaction is some Jews have an ethnic based Jews identity. They can't understand someone joining a different "people." For example, I, (writer's name), can't become a Chicano. I hate that attitude, but it exists.

Name

Subj: Re: Jews by choice
Date: 10/13 6:46:07 PM CDT
From:
To: GilMann@aol.com

I'm glad that people like you and I welcome new comers to our community!

Name

Subj: are converts allowed to hurt when jews hurt?
Date: 10/26 7:55:16 PM CST
From:
To: GilMann@aol.com

Gil,

I have a comment on your question about converts (I prefer the term "Jews in Progress" to "jew by choice").

I was very welcomed by our community at my conversion (my conversion service was very public and took on more the air of a bat mitzvah than a conversion... party and all). This was almost 4 years ago. It wasnt until two weeks ago that I finally realized in everyone's minds I will always be slightly less of a Jew.

Two weeks ago tomorrow we had a terrible event happen in our community. Our synagogue was torched by an arsonist. As a result all jewish institutions in my city are under police guard. The entire community was shaken by this event and we all had to do our best to help the children at religious school where I teach, make sense of it and cope with the emotions. It was tough on top of my own emotions and by the end of class I was visibly upset. Someone who knows I was a convert asked me what was wrong and I voiced how upset and unsafe I was feeling and I was totally floored to be told "I don't understand why you are so upset, you haven't been a jew long enough for this to involve you."

It's funny for me I feel MORE connected to my Judaism than many of the people I worship, teach and study with (born jews) yet in their mind I am not jewish enough to be hurt when jews are attacked. I have had similar comments made regarding my feelings on what is going on Israel. I have not yet "earned" the right to cry for the Israelis because I am not really a jew or haven't been a jew long enough.

How long do we have to be a Jew to feel when antisemitism is involved?

Name

Subj: conversion column
Date: 10/28 1:58:10 PM CST
From:
To: GilMann@aol.com

The article on conversion hits home with me because I am married to a woman who converted to judaism. It was a decision she made, I wanted the conversion but I never influenced the decision because I wanted the decision to come from the heart. It has been 4 years now since my wife's conversion. She is a devoted Jew. The holiday dinners, the teaching of Judaism to my children, and the respect of ancestors is all there. She has proven to be a stronger Jew than many of my family members. I agree with you, many times the convert is stronger than the natural born. I believe it is in the heart, not always the blood. Please keep the articles going, they are interesting and many times helpful.

Name

Subj: Considering Conversion
Date: 10/12 8:33:53 PM CDT
From:
To: GilMann@aol.com

As I read several of the other e-mails I noted that many have some sort of link to Judaism through family. I have none. My lone link is my heart.

I was raised in a strict Christian environment, but since I was a teenager I have felt that something was missing in my life. I have been drawn to Judaism for more than a decade. I feel for my life to be complete that I must find someone who will listen to me and help with the decision making process concerning conversion.

I am 43 years old. I live in the South, directly in the buckle of the Bible belt. I have wandered for so long. I desperately need to find my home.

I appreciate your listening. Thank you for making yourself available to me and others.

Sincerely,
Name

Concluding Thoughts to Copy, Cut, Paste, and Save

Very often, I receive inquiries like the last email above from readers asking how one converts to Judaism — so often that I devoted a column to the question. As a natural outgrowth of the emails in this chapter, I end with that column. But I would be remiss if I didn't first state that Judaism has never been a proselytizing religion. In fact, traditionally, a person who inquires about converting to Judaism is to be turned away three times. This discouragement is to ascertain the individual's seriousness and also because the Jewish way of life is not easy. Jewish tradition encourages potential converts to take their time and carefully deliberate before making their decision to become a Jew.

Converting to Judaism

Dear Gil:

I am 39 and have just recently been told that my grandfather escaped Russia and was Jewish. My siblings and I were raised in a Christian family, but for some reason I never felt like I belonged.

My adult life has been spent searching for something I felt that I have lost. The need to find out everything I can on Judaism is insatiable. I cannot absorb enough information. How do I make the decision to pursue my heritage? Is there anyone I can consult on the feelings I am experiencing? Are there more of us out there? The conflict within me is very strong and this inner battle needs to come to an end. Thank you for reading my e-mail.

L

Dear L:

Take comfort in knowing that there are many others like you. I know this because I have received a number of emails from others that are similar to your letter. Technically you are not Jewish unless you formally study and embrace the Jewish way of life—in other words, unless you convert to Judaism. Perhaps this is an option for you.

In the course of my travels and lecturing, I met a most extraordinary gentleman who shared some circumstances with you. He grew up in Germany to a Jewish father and Protestant mother. When he was six, the Nazis came to power. He received no religious education, but to protect him, his parents had him baptized. The persecution was so severe and the situation so desperate that his mother committed suicide during the war. After that, he and his father were thrown into labor camps. When the war ended, he had no family, and because he was not Jewish, he got no help from Jewish relief agencies.

With the help of a Protestant organization, he was brought to the U.S. He got involved in the church and eventually became an ordained Christian minister. But like you, he always felt a piece of himself did not quite fit. When he was almost 65, he decided that he needed to be true to himself and he converted to Judaism — the religion of his father.

By converting, he is far from alone. A little known fact is that in the U.S., there are an estimated 200,000 converts to Judaism, or to use the more beautiful term, "Jews by Choice." This is an especially impressive number when you consider that there is a total of only between 5 million and 6 million Jews in the U.S. Their contribution to our people goes beyond numbers. As I've written elsewhere, I wish that all Jews by birth were as serious about their Judaism as most of the Jews by Choice I've met.

PLEASE don't misunderstand me, however; I am NOT trying to pressure you! On the contrary, I would suggest you carefully and slowly consider whether or not you want to convert. But your letter indicates a yearning to me that might make conversion a correct decision for you. To help you decide, here are five suggestions:

1. Continue to learn as much as you can about Judaism. Read, explore the web, go to lectures, take introductory courses on Judaism, which are offered by many colleges and Jewish congregations, and talk to some Jewish friends.

2. See if Judaism's basic beliefs and practices make sense to you. Remember, though, that Judaism is a faith of deeds, not forced creeds. Nonetheless, here are some general Jewish beliefs that are widely held among Jews:

   • Judaism introduced the world to the idea that God is one, not many, and is kind, loving, and personal. In Judaism, you pray directly to God and can receive help, guidance, and understanding. You can pray on your own and with a prayer community in a Jewish congregation.

- Judaism doesn't accept the idea that people are born evil. Rather, people have free will to choose between right and wrong.

- Judaism encourages religious freedom of thought. Judaism welcomes probing spiritual questions.

- Judaism has, for 4000 years, emphasized a strong sense of family and the value of a close community.

3. Experience Judaism as it is lived. Visit a Jewish congregation to sample a service or attend a Jewish ceremony, such as a Passover *Seder* or a Sabbath meal. Visit a JCC and a Jewish bookstore.

4. Talk about your thoughts and feelings with your partner, your friends and your family. It is common to experience some moments of doubt or fear of the unknown. It is also vital that you stay in touch with your birth family. Converting to Judaism does not mean you are abandoning your family and friends.

5. As early as possible, but especially as you get more serious about actually becoming Jewish, you should talk to rabbis of the different Jewish movements.

These suggestions come from Dr. Larry Epstein, a leading expert on conversion who manages a very helpful website that I highly recommend: www.convert.org. There are far too many resources there than I can list here, but I feel confident you will find many answers there to the questions you are so earnestly asking. Please keep me posted on your searching. Good luck!

Gil

Chapter 18
Are Non-Jews Anti–Semitic or Are Jews Paranoid?

Mr. Mann:

Do you think there is such a thing as Jewish paranoia, and that one can find anti-Semitism even where it isn't intended or lurking?

Do not some Jewish people, those of a lower socio-economic level, sometimes walk around with a "Chip on their shoulders," screaming, "I'm Jewish! Do something to me."

L

Dear L:

First, please call me Gil. I answer by saying I definitely think that some Jews are paranoid. I don't think it has anything to do with socio-economic status, however.

Rather, I believe it is based on the overall status of Jews in history. Objectively speaking, as you look at what has happened to Jews over the last couple thousand years, who could blame Jews for becoming paranoid? Kinder or more positive terms would be "pragmatic" or "realistic" or "alert to danger."

Famed Author Tom Clancy, in his thriller *The Sum of All Fears*, gives a good explanation of why Jews might feel this way when he describes Israelis as having an:

> "us-and-them mentality... [that is] understandable. They all think like front-line grunts. What do you expect? Hell, man, their whole country is a free-fire zone for the other side. They have the same way of thinking as us line animals had in 'Nam. There are two kinds of people — your people and everyone else... The Israelis think that way 'cause they can't think any other way. The Nazis killed millions of Jews and we didn't do [anything] about it."

This description I think might apply not just to Israelis but to many or even most Jews. The Nazis, of course, are only one part of many centuries of horrible abuse, threats, and harm that Jews have suffered. Consequently, I think many, maybe even most, Jews are paranoid to some degree. I know I am — but I don't think there is anything wrong with that. As opposed to clinical paranoia — Jewish paranoia is very much grounded in reality.

Now having said all of that, I am going to depart from my line of reasoning to say that while I understand "Jewish paranoia," I also think there are Jews who take this way too far.

I think there are some Jews who do have, as you put it, "a chip on their shoulder." Most of those who I have met have actually experienced severe anti-Semitism in their lives — or their relatives have. Hearing their stories I can understand why they feel as they do.

However, in my opinion, their thinking is wrong if it reaches the point of saying (as I have heard): "Scratch any Gentile deep enough and you will find an anti-Semite." I find this kind of thinking revolting.

Going back to the Holocaust again, there are numerous examples of Gentiles risking their lives to save Jews. These courageous and generous people are models of ethical and dignified behavior. Imagine being literally faced with execution if you tried to give a hand to a persecuted minority person. Could you honestly live up to the model set by these incredible non-Jews?

Less dramatically, today in America, Jews have experienced unparalleled acceptance from our non-Jewish neighbors. The best example of this is that non-Jews are choosing to marry us in unprecedented numbers. So much so that some say the biggest threat to the long-term existence of the Jewish community is no longer hate, but ironically love!

So where does all this leave us? I conclude as follows: I still fear anti-Semitism, but I do not fear it from the vast majority of Americans. Yes, I do remember seeing signs during the 1973 Arab oil embargo that said "Burn Jews Not Oil" and I have certainly seen and heard some American anti-Semitism, so I am always a little wary. Still, in my adult life, my being Jewish has not been an obstacle for me in any serious way — for example, when I have chosen where I wanted to buy a home, work, or study. I have also met many non-Jews (including online) who have embraced me together with my Judaism. I hasten to add that I recognize that my parents' and grandparents' generations were not able to say that about America when they were younger. In addition, I recognize that in many parts of the world today anti-Semitism remains vicious.

But that is outside America, and so my other conclusion relates to those (American) Jews who walk around with "a chip on their shoulder." These Jews I believe are doing a disservice to themselves, to Jews in general, and to non-Jews.

Fortunately, I believe most Jews today do not subscribe to such thinking. We have risen above any paranoia we might feel to become proud Jews and proud contributors to the non-Jewish society where we live.

So to sum up: I think we should stay ever alert to those who would harm us — they definitely do exist. At the same time, we should appreciate how lucky we are to have so many non-Jewish neighbors who accept us as Jews and as human beings.

Thanks for writing,

Gil

Email Responses to
"Are Non-Jews Anti-Semitic or Are Jews Paranoid?"

Subj: Judaism
Date: 4/23 1:27:55 PM CDT
From:
To: GilMann@aol.com

Dear Gil,

When I was a teenager, I had a sage cousin, older than I, who told me that one could be born a Catholic and die a Presbyterian; born a Methodist and die an Episcopalian; etc.; but if one was born a Jew, one would die a Jew.

He also told me the story of how the Czar of Russia and the Emperor of Austria were having a meeting just as the Czar had caused a Pogrom [a violent anti-Jewish riot] to be loosed in his country, and the Emperor had just given his Jews civil rights, allowing them to hold public office, own property, vote, etc. The Czar was teasing the Emperor about this, and the Emperor's response was, "you destroy your Jews your way, and I'll destroy my Jews my way."

All of this is to answer your question about anti-semitism which brought me here in the first place. The answer is somewhere in the middle; indeed, there is anti-semitism out there and frequently it surfaces, depending on the culture; but we Jews do from time to time get a little paranoid and overreact.

And as far as the ultra right is concerned, I hate extremists of any stripe; that is, the kind of people who say, "if you're not with me, you're against me."

Keep up the good work.
Name

Subj: Re: Anti-Semitism or Paranoia?
Date: 4/23 7:56:42 PM CDT
From:
To: GilMann@aol.com

I have not experienced much if any anti-semitism in my life, although I will admit I am very assimilated. I don't often go to temple, and I am very bad about observing the sabbath — but I am proud of being a Jew, and being a part of Judiasm's great history, and I certainly have never hidden the fact I am Jewish. So maybe my perspective is distorted.

However, I have often felt that many Jews ARE paranoid. It's not that I don't think anti-semitism is out there, it is just that many Jews seem to almost define their existence by it. We are not a community of victims!

I believe a lot of anti-semitism comes from ignorance. I will not spoil for a fight, nor will I let the ignorance of others define me.

Name
City, State

Subj: Anti-Semitism
Date: 4/23 8:54:22 PM CDT
From:
To: GilMann@aol.com

Dear Gil,

Reading this week's response, I am reminded of the old saw: Just because you are paranoid doesn't mean that they aren't out to get you!

Best wishes,
Name

Subj: Paranoia
Date: 4/23 9:32:48 PM CDT
From:
To: GilMann@aol.com

I think that some Jews do indeed find antisemitism where none exists. I think many more jews ignore antisemitism where it does because American jews have adopted the "go along to get along" philosophy — precisely the attitude that encouraged the holocaust. I think there is danger even here in America, and that Jews should at least be armed against the time when that danger will rear its ugly head.

Name

Subj: Anti-sematism
Date: 4/23 11:41:53 PM CDT
From:
To: GilMann@aol.com

Dear Gil,

As a young child, I experienced anti-semitism first hand in my nice quiet neighborhood in Indiana. My brother defended and then befriended an overweight, unpopular boy in our neighborhood. Being close in age to my brother, I hung out with them too. We built a go cart with this friend. When the boy's father found out we were Jewish, he forbade his son from playing with us and made us dismantle the go cart. This wasn't enough. He then came to our house (his son chose to still hang out with us) and told my father to "keep his Jew bastards away from his son." And then proceeded to sucker punch my father. We were shocked to see a "grown" man behave this way. This experience made me turn to my mother and ask, "Mommy, is it bad to be Jewish?." This was my first, but not last, experience of anti-semitism.

In public school all Jewish Holidays were an "unexcused" absence. My social studies teacher ridiculed me in front of the class for not writing the word G-d "what's the matter with you Jews anyways?."

As an adult and in the work environment, I have heard many derogatory comments from co-workers about Jews. You see I don't "look" Jewish, so people always say things around me.

Having said all this, I wouldn't consider myself paranoid but certainly more aware of the ignorance that anti-semitism stems from. It is because of these experiences, I am constantly pursuing more knowledge of my religion so I may shed some understanding to those intolerant of differences.

I am a mother myself now, and I am instilling in my children a pride of being Jewish. I never want to hear the insecurity that I once felt, "Mommy, is it bad to be Jewish?."

Proud to be Jewish and still learning,
Name

Subj: Jewish Paranoia...?
Date: 4/24 6:28:34 AM CDT
From:
To: GilMann@aol.com

Dear Gil:

I had to write about this commentary because it's a question I've asked about myself many times. I think perhaps the appropriate terminology for many Jews would be 'hypervigilant' — sensitive to nuances of experiences.

In my own experience in Houston, I have met several outright anti-Semites, mostly right-wing Christians. However, what frustrates me the most is the basic ignorance of many Gentiles here to who we are and what we are, and a blind and mildly hostile attitude toward us in general. As my teenage daughter says — they just don't get it!

I have worked in positions of authority in both the energy and insurance industries here — and this blankness on the part of some seems to cross all socioeconomic boundaries. It has been an ongoing frustration that Christian holidays are observed, but for Jewish holidays I've had to take vacation, even though as a salaried employee I work many more hours than standard.

So, yes, there is hypervigilance or paranoia, but, as the old saying goes "just because you're paranoid doesn't mean you don't have enemies." Thankfully, there is also some progress — local behavior differs from one area to another.

Shabbat Shalom!
Name

Subj: Jewish Paranoia
Date: 4/24 10:57:49 AM CDT
From:
To: GilMann@aol.com

I am not a Jew but I have studied Hebrew with Jews for over 20 years. I have enjoyed most of the people I met. Only a few have acted, one on one, as if I were an evil being (and two of those call themselves "rabbi," one an ultra conservative, one an ultra reform, go figure.)

I think hatred begets hatred. While it is important to remember our history (lest we have to repeat it) it is also important to release the negative emotions attached to events in our histories. Every people, every culture, has some version of the Holocaust. We can argue that "my horror was bigger than your horror" and we can say, "but you can never, never understand how I feel." But these thoughts are, one, not true, and two, not helpful in getting along with each other.

Recently there was a series on the American Indian on the History channel. It presented massacre after betrayal after horror, perpetrated mainly by the "white" culture on the Native Americans. I could empathize completely with Indians who hate whites and feel very angry over what was done to them and to "their" land. Where do we go from here? How can I as a nominal white person relate to a Native American?

As a child, looking at the pictures of the Warsaw ghetto, the ovens, the bodies, the piles of shoes... I was filled with horror and sadness. It was not necessary to *be* Jewish to feel those feelings. I think it is important to allow others to share the pain and to allow the idea that, indeed, it IS possible for a non-Jew to understand those feelings. To say, "you could never understand," is to create a barrier to the bond we share as human beings and to violate the commitment each should have to peace and to "never again" allowing such an atrocity to happen.

It takes a village to raise a child, but it takes the entire human race to raise ourselves by our bootstraps out of the morass of our past.

Name
City, State

Subj: Personal experiences with antisemitism
Date: 4/24 12:43:10 PM CDT
From:
To: GilMann@aol.com

Dear Gil,

I have experienced anti-semitism in several very different scenarios.

As a child I grew up in a predominantly black "ghetto" of New York City. I found anti-semitism there as a form of escapism. Black people were down, jews were "rich,"... clearly jews must be responsible for black people being down. The lower the IQ, the higher the level of anti-semitism. I also noticed that those who thought this way were a very small minority of the black community.

When I went into the service, I encountered a different kind of antisemitism. I was in officer training in 1967. The training was hard, and I was ordered not to go to temple for rosh hashanna and yom kippur [the Jewish High Holy Days marking the new year], as it would "put an unfair burden on my fellow cadets." My response was a very polite "screw you." There were no repercussions, and the officer who I willfully disobeyed seemed to respect me more for it.

As an upper classman in Officers Training School i got the names of all the incoming classmen who were jewish (about 12 out of 800). I went to each of them and urged them to attend services and ignore any external pressure not to. I don't know how successful I was, and my perception was that most of them wanted to forget that they were jewish.

As an officer on active duty, I would occasionally sit at the officers club with a newcomer, who would rail about the jews to me, thinking me a sympathetic soul. As I said before, the lower the IQ, the higher the level of antisemitism, as the typical profile of such an officer was a "barely" high school graduate who had gotten a commission way back when when a college degree wasn't required. I never encountered any anti-semitism from senior officers, who seemed to have an unusually high regard for Israel and, especially her military.

I toured Europe after the service, and wound up sitting in a wine cellar in Vienna next to a german who, in german (I speak some german), went on about how hitler was right about the jews. I noticed the reaction of the germans and austrians around him, it would have been the same if they just found out he had bubonic plague. That made me feel good about the new Europe.

What have I learned from my experiences? Well, for one thing I learned that any kind of racial bias is an indication of a low IQ. I am especially sensitive to bias against our new immigrants and our african american community. If I encounter it publicly, I will not let the speaker get away with it, my inhibitions about that are long gone.

My experiences have taught me that the confrontation of anti-semites will send them back to the holes they crawled out of, while silence will be taken as fear and will only encourage them.

Name

Subj: My love for Jewish people and Israel
Date: 4/27 11:42:08 PM CDT
From:
To: GilMann@aol.com

Dear Gil,

I am not Jewish. I think it is only fair that I tell you that up front. I was raised Irish Catholic in a small town in Ohio. I am now a born-again christian and attend a large non-denominational church in the south.

It has never been my intent to "convert" jews. I have over six Jewish people whom I hold as the dearest of friends as they do me. I revere and respect the fact that for thousands of years Jews have survived demonically inspired behavior by some of the lowest of the human race. I also believe that I and anyone who believes that the bible is the inspired word of God are eternally indebted to them for the scriptures preservation.

Jesus came through the Jewish race and for me He is the Lamb that was slain for my sins. To hate or hurt anyone, especially a Jewish person would be to spit in the face of God. If He loves the whole world how could I call myself a believer and harbor hate? Besides what is there to hate? People whose very existence originates in the scriptures? whose race preserved for generations the truth of God? who gave me hope in Jesus? That would be crazy... and hitler was crazy and anything but a christian. Many Christians sacrificed to help save the Jews as regrettably many did not. I would like to believe that I would have laid down my life like Corrie ten Boom for the lives of God's people.

Only God can reveal truth to anyone. I pray for God to make Himself known to all Jewish people as He did in days gone by. I pray that they will finally seat Elijah at their Passover table. I pray for the peace of Jerusalem and Psalm 91 over all my dear Jewish friends and their loved ones.

I taught my three sons about the Holocaust before they were ten years old so that they would know the truth. I was just ten when as a young girl with the chicken pox I sat up and saw on TV the "Diary of Anne Frank." When it was over I sat in the big chair in the living room and sobbed my heart out. I promised the Lord that when I grew up if He would help me I would do what I could to see that the horror the Frank's experienced would never happen again. To the best of my ability I have kept my promise.

One thing that I notice about the Jewish people that I have met, even my dear friends is that only one I know actually reads the scriptures on a regular basis. In that regard they are a lot like Catholics. They leave it all to their religious leaders.

If I had influence over the Jewish youth I would teach them to seek the Lord with all their hearts everyday in prayer and honor the two most important commandments of the scriptures. Love the Lord your God with all your heart, mind, and soul; love your neighbor as yourself. I respectfully sign off praying for God's best for you.

Your gentile believing friend,
Name

Subj: Re: Question
Date: 3/1 10:40:52 PM CST
From:
To: GilMann@aol.com

More and more I learn that I live in a Utopia/Nirvana, but it may be due to the socio-economic/educational level of the areas. I have never experienced anti-Semitism. I make it well known that I am Jewish. I teach at a Catholic university, where, in religion courses, students are reminded that Judaism is their parent religion and the religion of Jesus.

I moved to a new area last November and most here are new to this state. I'm not. Most of the neighbors don't know anyone so I made Christmas dinner for them. They all knew I had never done it before and there were no Christmas decorations — of course. I would guess that some were never in a Jewish home before that day. It was wonderful!

Maybe, a great deal is one's attitude. The small amount of time I spend in Jewish chat rooms on AOL, I "hear," the most awful things. When TWA, Flt. 800 went down, one person typed, "Who cares? They were all goyim. [derogatory term meaning non-Jews]. I witnessed the same kind of responses during the Oklahoma City bombing.

Why do I "see" so many Jewish people, in chat rooms, who truly believe they are superior, only because they are Jewish. More times than not, these are the same people who use sexually graphic language in a public area or use swear words. It's an area of people 50+. Is it, simply, taking on an attitude of superiority when one feels inferior and using Judaism for that superiority?

The Jewish online people, with the ghetto mentality, practice the same discrimination and bigotry that they complain about others are doing to them. (Ignore the syntax there. You can, also, ignore my typos.)

Thanks
Name

Concluding Thoughts to Copy, Cut, Paste, and Save

Anti-Semitism and Jewish paranoia are perhaps the most tangible aspect of Jewish Peoplehood. Writers in this chapter attributed anti-Semitism to different factors, ranging from low IQ to poor socio-economic status. Much has been written on the subject. I believe that at the crux of most anti-Semitism (like Pharaoh's) and for that matter, discrimination against any group of people, are two things: insecurity and ignorance.

I've concluded that humans simply have a heck of a time with other humans who are different. History is replete with conflict between peoples of different religious, racial, and ethnic backgrounds. Atrocities of the last decades in Europe, Africa, and Asia are tragic cases in point. We humans are such tribal animals. This wouldn't be so bad if we didn't react so poorly to those who are different than us.

The pattern starts at a young age, when kids and then teens seem to naturally ridicule individuals who are different. When we see a kid who appears different, or speaks or acts differently, or has atypical interests or attractions, the reaction is to make fun or worse. Adults don't seem much better. I've never understood why the human animal is so insecure. When we encounter a person or a group that is different, the first instinct for many people (including some Jews, as the writer of the last email in this chapter pointed out), is to perceive a threat and to defend ourselves by lowering the other or artificially raising ourselves.

This has been the history of anti-Semitism as well. Over the centuries, when anti-Semitic non-Jews encountered Jews, every difference was compared unfavorably, from appearance and work ethic to religious philosophies. In the process, Jews have been accused of being insular, dishonest, cheap, heretics, deniers of God, and many other hateful traits. Most of what has been said is based on total ignorance or a fragment of information blown out of proportion.

On the other hand, when reading the emails from non-Jews who have fond feelings for Jews, you can see open-mindedness and knowledge, or if their knowledge is lacking, a desire to learn. These people do not feel threatened by differences between themselves and Jews. They often write that they are studying or have studied some aspect of Judaism. These people do not fear Jews; they fear ignorance. They seek to understand how and why we are different and how and why we are the same.

If all of us would model ourselves after these admirable people, our differences would no longer be a source of paranoia or anti-Semitism. With such fear gone, we would have the potential to take what distinguishes Jew from non-Jew and turn these lessons into a source of growth and blessing for all.

Chapter 19
Returning to Judaism

Dear Gil:

I grew up in a very non-religious, atheist, Jewish family. I was always confused about my religion, because my parents liked to emphasize to me that although they didn't believe in God, Judaism is still very important. I have never understood this. I am 27 and am just now starting to explore my Jewish heritage.

I know very little about my culture, and I don't even know what the major holidays represent. Having read on AOL your brief excerpts on the importance of recognizing "our" heritage, I feel compelled to learn more. I just thought I would let you know that I feel inspired to become more informed about my Jewish background, and that it will answer those many questions I've stored in the back of my mind.

P

Dear P:

Your email reminds me of an unusual Jew I heard about. This fellow was a poor, nearly illiterate agriculture worker who worked for a wealthy Jewish rancher. The unskilled laborer fell in love with the boss's daughter. The daughter loved him too, but said she'd only marry him if he studied Judaism.

He agreed even though he could barely write his own name and was already 40 years old. Study he did, and he became one of the greatest rabbis of all time. His name was Rabbi Akiva and he lived about 2000 years ago. Many schools today are named for him in part to honor the value of learning in Judaism and that Jewish learning can begin at any age.

Now here we are 2000 years later, and thanks to the Internet, Jewish learning has never been more accessible. I suggest you enter the words "Jewish learning" into any search engine and you will find resources that can keep you going for years.

I constantly receive email from others like you who are exploring their Judaism anew. This sort of good news does not make headlines in this day and age of angst over our diminishing numbers, assimilation, intermarriage, etc.

So, I decided to feature your email, precisely to make a headline called: Returning to Judaism. I am doing this for two reasons. First, to give you and others encouragement. I want you and others to know that you are not unique in wanting to examine or re-examine Judaism. I have even heard from senior citizens who are looking at their Judaism seriously for the first time in their lives!

Know that there are many other adults like you, who have "questions stored in the back of their minds." Further, the "stuff of Judaism" is adult material, says Rabbi Harold Kushner, and he is right. For example, Judaism has much to say about such adult topics as: how to deal with work problems, aging parents, raising children, health, friends, enemies, etc.

There is a second reason I wanted to feature your email: There has been a running argument amongst Jewish academics, rabbis, and leaders about whether to expend Jewish communal resources on Jews who are active (the core) or Jews who are disconnected from Jewish life (the periphery).

Some argue that the Jewish community should invest its resources on the core Jews and not waste time and money on Jews on the periphery. Your email and contacts I have had with countless other Jews like you lead me to reject this argument.

My experience is that Jews may and do come to their Judaism for many reasons at many times in their lives: a birth, a death, a career issue, a marriage issue, a hunger for spirituality, an exposure to Israel, meeting an impressive Jew, reading an influential book, and on and on.

We can never know what will motivate a Jew to further delve into their Judaism — regardless of how connected or disconnected they are to Jewish life. I have found the same approach works for any kind of Jew. The approach is simple: a personal touch, a warm welcome, and a willingness to genuinely entertain any questions, no matter how intelligent, ignorant, or challenging.

I don't believe we can afford anything less. Besides, the next Rabbi Akiva may be out there... perhaps it is you? I hope so. Thanks for writing!

Gil

Email Responses to "Returning to Judaism"

Subj: Returning
Date: 5/4/ 3:49:49 PM CDT
From:
To: GilMann@aol.com

Hi Gil —

Your column today made me think about how far I've come in the six months that I have been on an active journey back to Judaism.

In the last six months, I have crossed over the line from non-belief in a higher power to a definite belief in something, although I'm not sure what, I'd call it "forces of spirit in the universe" at the moment. I went from viewing prayer as superstition to viewing it as an opportunity to reflect and connect with that spirit (rather than to ask favors as is popularly portrayed). I went to Passover Seder at a Unitarian congregation, had a lovely time and decided I am too Jewish to belong there.

And I have finally found a rabbi I can relate to. I read in our Federation [similar to a Jewish United Way organization] paper about a new congregation forming in our area that had a woman rabbi. I went on the web and found her pictured with her husband and preschool-age children. I went to meet with her a couple of weeks ago and it was a meeting of minds and hearts. She is willing to guide me in my study.

The rabbi suggested I start reading some traditional texts to complement my contemporary readings. Last week, I found myself in Barnes and Noble trying (unsuccessfully I might add) to buy a copy of the Torah she suggested. So, I need to go online and order one this weekend.

I feel so good being able to say out loud and with pride that I am Jewish and catching up on the study of my own tradition.

I guess the time will come when I will be able to at least visit a congregation. The rabbi told me she would meet with my husband and daughter to determine what would make them feel comfortable. My daughter is very excited about meeting a rabbi who is a mom, and to meet her little children.

I'll write again from time to time. Thanks for rooting me on. It is wonderful to be at a new stage of growth in midlife!

Name

Subj: response to your column
Date: 5/5 7:10:47 PM CDT
From:
To: GilMann@aol.com

I am on a search for my Jewish roots. This has been stimulated by 2 things: recent mission to Israel and secondly, my new computer.

I now subscribe to jewish.com newsletter, get an interpretation of this week's torah passage from a rabbi in Israel and subscribe to some web sites that help fight the media's pro Arab reporting.

I grew up in a family that acknowledged some of the holidays in a very minor way. We did enjoy a seder at my uncle's home, he was observing, kept kosher, sent his sons to yeshiva [an Orthodox day school, often a rabbinical seminary], etc. I went to hebrew school for 2 weeks at age 9, had my tonsils removed and never returned. I have always identified with Jewish history in the 20th century. Perhaps it was reading "The rise and fall of the third Reich" when I was a teen. Perhaps it was wonderful

Jewish teachers at my public school in Brooklyn. They discussed the meaning of prejudice and discrimination. Perhaps it was the stories my mother told me when she worked for an older couple who were holocaust survivors. Perhaps it was the stories my father and the rest of the family told about discrimination they had experienced. The civil rights struggles of the 60s helped. My participation in feminist struggles helped.

I've always known I'm a Jew. Now I'm learning more about what this really means.

I enjoy your column and read it weekly.

Name

Subj: Returning to (or trying to re-discover) Judaism
Date: 5/6 7:09:28 AM CDT
From:
To: GilMann@aol.com

When I was 7 1/2 years old my parents moved away from Detroit (leaving all of our relatives) and relocated in a very rural area in Michigan. At the time (1966) my father believed that his religion would have been used against him (out there) and he decided that we could no longer "practice" our religion and "became" Unitarian. We celebrated Christian holidays and went to church and Sunday School. I was too young to understand what was going on or the impact this was having on my entire family.

As I grew up I knew I was Jewish but recieved no religious education. This was very troubling to me when I learned that my parents had both been Hebrew School teachers in Detroit.! My Dad's family was more "observant" than my Mother's, and all kept kosher homes.

When I was 14 we moved back to the Detroit area where it was "ok" to be Jewish again. By this time my Father was a full fledged agnostic and my Mother was guilty... and seemed to join a synagogue just "for show." I was just confused!

In college, I started to have a crisis of faith and have been on a 25 year (off & on) journey to discover my heritage and define my beliefs. I have never lived (as an adult) in an area with much of a Jewish population. I have been building a library and done a lot of reading. For the past 5 years I have lived in a tiny town in what used to be called the "borsht belt." While this would lead one to believe that there must be a large Jewish population, that's far from the truth. I am one of a handful. The closest synagogue doesn't have a large enough congregation to support a rabbi and doesn't have weekly services. BUT, I was able to take an Intro. to Judaism class through the synagogue and continue to discover "where I fit in."

Thanks for "listening" to my story.
Name

Subj: Searching out Judaism
Date: 5/6 1:59:14 PM CDT
From:
To: GilMann@aol.com

Dear Gil:

When my brother committed suicide when I was 14, the rabbi asked me if I was as withdrawn and strange as my brother when he was gathering information for the eulogy. I had always felt like an outsider at our synagogue & was thoroughly outraged by the rabbi's comments. My mother was an atheist Jew whose being Jewish was important ethnically but not religiously. When my brother decided to keep kosher, my mother wanted to know where she'd gone wrong. I just searched many other religions until I decided to research Judaism as I had the others. I found Judaism closest to my beliefs, but the synagogue here was as unwelcoming as my home one had been. It wasn't until a new younger rabbi came that I found the same kind of welcome and joy that I'd found in many churches around religion. Because of him, I decided to come back to Judaism, although I still do a lot of questioning. My rabbi left our synagogue due to politics within, and I again feel disenfranchised but I think I'll keep going until at least they finally hire a new rabbi. Maybe I want to see if my new rabbi was an aberration or what Judaism is really about.

Name

Subj: (no subject)
Date: 5/6 8:04:18 PM CDT
From:
To: GilMann@aol.com

Gil:

I just want to weigh in on providing info for the Jews on the periphery. They may forever remain there if the core does not reach out.

I was raised in a rather awkward situation. My mother is from a conservative Jewish family, as is my father. My parents divorced when I was about seven and when I was ten my father decided to marry my stepmother. She was an antisemite. She terrorized my three sisters and me. She made us feel like the lowest of the low and often warned us how lucky we were that she was not putting an end to our filthy Jewish lives. We were forbidden to discuss our birthright and always reminded of how repulsive our people are and how disgusting our heritage is. I went through most of my life afraid to tell anyone my "secret." I did not tell anyone that I was Jewish until I was in my early twenties and even then, I was scared to death.

I still live in fear, although now I believe that some amount of fear is normal for Jews. I live in fear, now in my early thirties, but I have reclaimed my faith and, although I am married to a Protestant woman, we raise our three girls as Jews — as it should be. It boggles my mind to listen to my six year old proudly proclaim her birthright! She loves being a Jew and loves to talk about it. She wants me to come to school to discuss Chanukah and Passover. Can you imagine?!

I try very hard not to pass on the fear. I try not to let her know how afraid I am to have a mezzuzah [the small ornament containing an important passage from the Torah that Jews are commanded to put on their doorposts] because, who knows what the mailman believes? I have been very fortunate to fall into a wonderful Jewish community in California. Were it not for the openness of this congregation I would have been a lost Jew as would my children — four Jews less for the Jewish community. I grew up in Chicago where there should have been plenty of opportunity to find resources to investigate my faith — quite honestly I could not put my finger on one. I don't even think that the Hillel [college organization for Jewish students] at my college tried to contact me. But only if someone had.

The Jews on the periphery may be the neediest of all. And also the ones with the most hope.

Subj: Briefly my story
Date: 5/6 10:34:13 PM CDT
From:
To: GilMann@aol.com

Gil,

I thought you'd be interested in my story. I grew up in a Jewish household. We were Kosher at home, attended a Traditional Synagogue every Saturday. I wanted to become a Cantor (I sing). The Rabbi at this Synagogue (I'd rather not say the name of either) told me how Cantors are the "bane" of Judaism and that the best thing for Judaism is for Cantors to be struck from the religion completely. This turned me off and I began giving every excuse I could not to go to shul on Saturdays

I sang in the High Holy Day Choir as a soloist, however that was the only time we ever went. My parents stopped going on Saturdays. I started to drift from Judaism, the singing during High Holy Day time was a "gig" for me and I got paid for it... that was all...

I ended up going to a Christian College and met a wonderful Lutheran girl who basically stole my heart. She never asked me to change for her and I never asked her to change for me. We eventually got married and were married by a Rabbi and a minister. At that point I wouldn't have had the Rabbi, but I knew that it was important for my parents, and out of respect for them I did it.

As the years flew by (and 3 children later), because I enjoyed singing, I ended up singing in a couple of Synagogue High Holy Day Choirs. But I was still far from the religion. I was attempting to go every Saturday, but it still didn't feel right. It wasn't me.

Then I found my present synagogue. The congregation has a lot of Ruach [spirit]. We went there one Saturday and were "hooked." My wife and boys eventually converted to Judaism and now we are "regulars" attendees. The Rabbi has become a friend and we love the community.

The point: our synagogue and the support we've had as a family, has re-awakened old feelings in me. I decided that I want to be a Cantor. I'm 36, and planning to sign up for HUC's [Hebrew Union College] Residency Program to become a Cantor. In the mean time, I've been studying on my own and with help. My Rabbi has been a font of knowledge for me and gives me books as gifts. I guess the main things that brought me back to Judaism were: A loving wife and children, finding a Synagogue and a Rabbi who was willing to accept us in their community, a desire from myself, and the reality that I had to let go of the past, and that one Rabbi's opinion of Cantors is not the reality. My goal is to be a "learned" Cantor. I don't want to just sing, but I want to understand and learn all I can, and be able to pass on that knowledge to other people. Who knows, maybe I'll find a young person like myself and can help them get through their own confusion.

Thanks again.
Name

Concluding Thoughts to Copy, Cut, Paste, and Save

Widely reported today are stories about Jews who have returned to Judaism and become very observant or Orthodox. A Jew who does this is called a *baal t'shuva* [literally a "master of returning"]. The number of Jews who have become *baalei t'shuva* [the plural of *baal t'shuva*] is impossible to calculate, but it's a tiny percentage of the Jewish population.

Although the stories are less sensational, there are probably many more people like the Jews in this chapter, who are exploring their Judaism anew as adults—most of whom, I suspect, will not become Orthodox Jews. Again, calculating a number is not possible, but based on my experience online and in other writing and lecturing around North America, I believe the number is significant and growing.

These Jews are difficult to quantify, and their stories do not make a lot of headlines, but they are out there. This is to say nothing of the many non-Jews who want to understand Judaism because they are spiritual seekers or because they want to understand their own faith or religion better. I've made this the last chapter leading into the conclusion because I believe there is a hunger and curiosity for Judaism that is not being addressed adequately.

What to do? Read on...

Conclusion

So you have read all these emails. What are the writers seeking and saying? They're certainly not apathetic about Judaism. I believe that these writers are expressing a desire for Judaism to provide guidance and meaning for their lives.

While the writers ask their questions in a Jewish context, they reflect universal questions asked by people of all faiths. They express a desire for answers to great human faith and existence questions: How do I lead an ethical life?, What is ethical?, Is there a higher Force?, How do I connect to this Force?, How do I connect to others?, Why are there tragedies?, Why does evil exist?, and so on. Ultimately, they ask: How do we find meaning in our short little lives?

My focus has been Judaism, so in this conclusion, I won't to speak to these questions for other faith systems. Still, as I discuss Judaism, I hope that there are ideas here that hold value for adherents of other faiths as well.

Can ancient Judaism provide what people are asking for and respond to the challenges of modern life?

I emphatically answer Yes! However, much work must be done. The emails in this book, taken together, show evidence of how the world has changed, and how Jews and non-Jews have changed.

How should Judaism respond to these changes? An email sent to me essentially asked that question. For this book, I've written a conclusion that is an in-depth response to that email and is also a reaction to all of the email I've received. My response addresses what I think Judaism and Jews must do to have a bright future in this rapidly changing world.

Is Judaism Keeping Up with the Times?

Dear Gil:

The gist of my personal Judaism is on page 15 in the Sim Shalom *prayer book. Instead of mourning about the loss of the Temple, the sage comforts his younger colleague by saying that God does not need animal sacrifice any more, but wants "gemilat chesed" acts of loving kindness — visit the sick, bury the dead, help your neighbors to rise up — without thought of reward.*

I have a personal relationship with God. The biggest problem with some of Rabbinic Judaism is to me, continuing to build fences around the Torah, until lay people can no longer reach it. I reject the fences, and personally tear them down for myself.

Instead of daily praise of God for drowning 30,000 Egyptians in the Red Sea, we should say thanks for the modern miracle of 1948, the emergence of the State of Israel, which I witnessed, and know to be a real miracle.

When Rabbinic Judaism keeps up with the times, and changes, I may agree with them.

P

Dear P:

You obviously take your Judaism seriously and I salute you. Being a serious Jew is not easy. I'll say more about this challenge later, but first I'd like to address three important questions raised by your email:

1. Is Judaism keeping up with the times?

2. How can Judaism be relevant and accessible?

3. Can Judaism evolve in a changing world?

To answer the first question, I'll use a business scenario. Imagine that 75 years ago, Procter and Gamble discovers a miraculous ingredient that eliminates tooth decay. They incorporate this ingredient in toothpaste, call the toothpaste "Godsend," and introduce it to the marketplace.

The toothpaste is a disaster. The taste is bitter, and something is wrong with the tube and users get toothpaste all over themselves. To make matters worse, people are offended by the name "Godsend."

After a year of dismal sales, Procter and Gamble convenes their board of directors, consisting of their corporate counsel, their banker, and CEOs of other large *Fortune* 500 firms. The company reports that the customers are idiots and management has decided to spend millions of dollars to educate customers using the advertising campaign slogan: "You don't know what is good for yourself."

Big surprise: sales get even worse. After another year goes by, P&G reconvenes their board of directors and reports that management has underestimated the stupidity of the customers. To fix this problem, management has decided to add guilt to their advertising campaign. So now customers will be told: "You don't know what is good for yourself and YOU SHOULD BE ASHAMED OF YOURSELF!"

This situation, of course, is absurd. What would Procter and Gamble really do? They would not wait a year. Within weeks or even days of sales not meeting projections, instead of convening their board of directors, they would convene focus groups and hear directly from customers why they were not buying.

Rather than bringing in their corporate banker or lawyer, they'd bring in their product people and say, "Keep the miraculous ingredient, but make the toothpaste taste good! Sweeten it up. Add some mint." They'd bring in their packaging people and say, "Fix the tube!" Finally, they'd bring in their brand people and say, "Change the name!"

Seventy-five years later, Procter and Gamble would have "Crest." Yet as we enter a new millennium, the Jewish community is experiencing "crisis" because, although the first scenario is ridiculous, there are parallels of similar behavior in the Jewish world.

Demographic studies of the Jewish people show that Judaism is in trouble. Many Jews have stopped buying "the product." Statistics show that huge numbers of Jews are opting out or barely participating in Jewish life. For example, most Jews do not belong to synagogues. Those who do belong, seldom attend. Jews are marrying non-Jews in ever-increasing numbers, (estimates are in the 50 percent range). About two thirds of these intermarried couples are not raising their children as Jews, (as I mentioned in the chapter on conversion). These trends are a demographic time bomb that has been called the "continuity crisis." In response, blue-ribbon committees, task forces, and panels have been convened to study Jewish identity and continuity.

Who sits on these committees? The CEOs of Jewish institutions: executive directors, principals, rabbis, and the most committed lay leadership in Jewish life, who sit around the table and say, "The customers don't know what's good for them... Judaism is good for them!"

I've purposefully exaggerated the Jewish scenario, and I don't mean to tarnish the efforts of these dedicated people. In fact, I must say that in my own city, I was Chairman of our Jewish Federation's Identity and Continuity Committee. From serving on these types of committees, I know that many initiatives have resulted that have been fruitful and praiseworthy.

Is Judaism Out of Touch?

Yet I'm concerned that the voices of "Jews on the street" are not being heard. Too often they are discounted or ignored altogether by leaders of Jewish institutions (synagogues, Federations, Jewish Community Centers, schools, etc.). Often the voices are dismissed as being "out on the fringe."

I disagree. Since 1996, when my first book was published, I've heard from thousands of Jews of every stripe and level of commitment, including very involved Jews. The issues they raise and their hunger for meaning are similar—often identical. For example, I've often heard the complaint that synagogue services are boring and meaningless, from both non-attendees and those who regularly attend services. Airing peoples' voices was one of the main reasons I wrote this book.

These voices lead me to conclude that Jewish institutions are not adequately aware of what's on the minds of Jews and consequently are not sufficiently responding to the way Jews live today.

A true story that dramatically demonstrates what I mean is told in the book *The Jew in the Lotus* by Rodger Kamenetz. The book describes a meeting between the exiled Dalai Lama of Tibet and seven prominent Jewish rabbis and scholars. The Dalai Lama invited them to come to India to teach him "the secret of the Jews." He wanted to know how the Jews had survived for thousands of years while living in exile.

The seven share much wisdom with the Dalai Lama. They decide among themselves that they would ask little of him in return, with one exception. Many new adherents of Buddhism from the west were born Jewish (the book calls them JUBUs). The rabbis gently say to the Dalai Lama that losing these Jews is painful and a loss to the Jewish people. The gist of his response was: I already tell students not to abandon their home tradition—but you must make sure there is something offered to them at home.

Today the phenomenon of Jews neglecting, straying from, or totally discarding their Judaism is well documented. And then there are huge numbers of Jews who proudly consider themselves to be Jewish, may even join synagogues, but really don't practice much Judaism. Why are so few Jews committed to Jewish life? In my experience, the main reason is that they don't find enough that is compelling about Judaism to make the effort. For many Jews today, Judaism consists of practices, rituals, and beliefs that are at best cumbersome, at worst, outdated, meaningless, and foolish.

Relevant Judaism

I believe one word should guide the thinking of all who care to perpetuate Judaism: *relevance*. Judaism's teachings must be relevant for dealing with real-life, day-to-day problems and issues.

After all, why does a "seeking" Jew travel to India to learn more about Buddhism? That's the extreme case. Why would a "run of the mill" Jew search on the Internet for information about Judaism?

They are craving ESP—Ethical guidance, Spiritual nourishment, and a sense of belonging to a community or People (I believe most people crave these basic human needs).

When Jews seek these needs outside of Judaism, or outside the walls of conventional Judaism, ask skeptical questions, or simply do not participate in Jewish life, too often the response I've heard from Jewish lay and professional leadership is a variation of these comments:

"What's wrong with these people?" Or "We'll just concentrate on the core that is interested." I'd summarize this attitude with the following marketing slogan:

"Judaism only on our terms, only on our turf!"

Can you imagine a company succeeding with this kind of attitude? For example, if only 15 percent of a synagogue's membership regularly attends services, my question is not, "What's wrong with 85 percent of the members?" I ask, "What's wrong with the services?"

In the non-profit world, somehow this seems to be a bold approach! But like my Procter and Gamble example, if you ran a company that had a great product but most customers were not buying, would you say, "What's wrong with them?" Would you be happy with a puny market penetration? Of course not! You would go out and try to understand your customers. You would ask how they lead their lives and you would listen attentively. With this understanding, you would then sell your product in a way that shows them how the benefits can match their needs.

Some critics call this approach "pandering," "watering down," "dumbing down," or weakening Judaism. What weakens Judaism, in my view, is when Jewish institutions and leadership are out of touch with Jews! Making Judaism accessible, understood, and relevant strengthens Judaism! My goal is far from watering down Judaism. I seek to enrich Judaism by clarifying what it teaches, explaining the benefits, and urging people to take Judaism seriously.

Marketing Judaism

Some might respond, "You can't equate Judaism to a product... and toothpaste, of all things!" My response is that Judaism is obviously not a tangible product like something you buy at the drug store. A nontangible analogy would be to think of a teacher standing before a class. The teacher is the seller, the knowledge is the product, and the students are the customers. In the case of Judaism, the product is a way of life consisting of Ethics, Spirituality, and Peoplehood.

For those who would say, "You can't use a business model for Judaism," I suggest they read the Harvard Business School's Study of the Willow Creek Community Church (January 23, 1996, No. 9-691-102). In fact, this study should be required reading for any Jewish lay or professional leader.

The study describes the remarkable growth of the Willow Creek Church of Barrington, Illinois. Listening to members and potential members drove this growth, or as the study states, "knowing their customers and meeting their needs." The results: In 1975, the church started with about 100 people. By 1991, services were drawing close to 14,000 people per weekend, with 5,000 of them returning a second time during the week for another service. The church cultivated a volunteer corps of 4,500 people and had annual revenues exceeding $12,000,000.

Harvard clearly viewed Willow Creek Church as a "business" that sold a "product." Do I equate Judaism with toothpaste that fights tooth decay? Of course not! I consider Judaism to be an infinitely greater and more noble product—literally a Godsend. Judaism is a most remarkable product that fights human decay. Why aren't more people buying this fabulous product?

I know that Jewish institutions are becoming increasingly mindful of their customers. Creative, innovative, and collaborative programs are now common: Jewish college students have been given free identity-forming trips to Israel, some synagogues are experimenting with music and other creative services, high-caliber and expertly marketed adult study series have been formed, and there are many other examples. But from my perspective, the pace and range of innovation is far from enough. The Jewish people and the world are changing. Jewish institutions must keep up!

The Evolution of Judaism

P, as you noted in your email, the loss of the Temple forced Judaism to change. Many scholars and books discuss this period of Jewish history, so a few words cannot capture what transpired. Still, here is a brief summary.

Over 2,000 years ago, the Jewish world faced a challenge that changed Judaism forever. A calamity of epic proportion occurred: Jews were cast out of their country into the Diaspora and the Temple was destroyed. The Temple had been a major focal point of Jewish life. Seven days a week, sacrifices were offered to God at the Temple. Three times a year, as commanded in the Bible or Torah, there were national pilgrimages to the Temple.

Suddenly, the Jewish country and Temple were gone. Over the next centuries, the most learned Jews — rabbis, sages, and teachers — exerted their influence and leadership and essentially saved Judaism. These scholars articulated Torah, oral law, and commentary into a written code of law called the *halacha* (which means "the way") that covered literally every aspect of human existence. These laws filled many volumes. To master this information, Jewish education became highly valued. The brightest students became rabbis. The word rabbi actually means "my teacher." The most educated and wise rabbis became judges of the law. Over time, the rabbis evolved into the leadership of the Jewish people.

During Judaism's evolution from the Temple Era to the Rabbinic Era, the core values and beliefs of Judaism were successfully preserved. To use the Procter and Gamble analogy, the rabbis preserved and repackaged the essential ingredients of Judaism (Ethics, Spirituality, and Peoplehood) for the "new" Jewish marketplace that no longer had a Temple and lived in the Diaspora. For close to 2,000 years, the Jewish people followed this new system called Rabbinic Judaism (some also call this *Halachic* Judaism.)

But in our modern day and age, this is no longer the case. Most Jews on the planet today do not use or consult Jewish law or rabbis as a part of their everyday life, nor do they have any interest in doing so. The few who do for the most part are Orthodox — and they are only about 10 percent of the world's Jewish population.

The Next Major Era of Judaism

So what is to become of Judaism? I agree with scholars who assert that Judaism has evolved into a new third era. This assertion is not a value judgment about whether Jewish law is good or bad or whether or not Jewish sages were wise. Instead, this assertion is an observation: The reality is that there's a major disconnect between the way most Jews live today and Rabbinic Judaism. How should individuals and Jewish institutions respond?

Some say the solution is obvious: Jews should just return to observing Jewish law. That may be desirable to some, but it's not very realistic. It's about as likely as Jews sacrificing animals in a Temple again—though a few still desire that too.

Others might respond by saying the problem is not new. Being Jewish has always been difficult, and the pressure to assimilate and be like everyone else has always been part of Jewish history. This, in effect, is the story of Chanukah.

The world today, however, is very different than at any time in history. There have been at least six radical and interwoven changes in the last century (for the most part, in the last half of the 20th century) that today monumentally influence the Jewish people and indeed the whole world:

1. Mobility: Almost all Jews alive today live in a country other than the country of their great grandparents. This modern exodus is many times greater than the Biblical exodus from Egypt. In addition, the way people regularly move from city to city today is a smaller ongoing exodus.

2. The Holocaust: The post-traumatic shock of losing a third of the Jewish people deeply affects Jewish and non-Jewish thinking, especially in matters of Spirituality (attitudes toward God) and Jewish Peoplehood.

3. Establishment of Israel: What should a free Jewish state be? This historic work in progress poses endless challenges, among them: Who is a Jew? How do democracy and theocracy coexist? How does a people that has been powerless for 2,000 years, ethically use its newfound power? What does a

Jewish homeland mean to the Diaspora? How does realization of the dream of a Jewish state impact Jewish theology, messianic thinking, prayers, holidays, etc.

4. The shrinking of the globe: Today, knowledge and travel are quickly accessible to an unparalleled percentage of the Earth's population.

5. The empowerment of women: Women in the West have unprecedented rights, education, and opportunities. As a subset, Jewish women are perhaps the most educated and influential women in the world today—for that matter, in all of human history! Today, Jewish women routinely are esteemed professors, doctors, lawyers, rabbis, judges, legislators, businesspeople, members of a myriad of other professions, and volunteer leaders. Some of the most successful innovations in the Jewish world today come from Jewish women: prolific writings, new and inspiring Jewish liturgy and music, new programs, and institutions such as the Jewish Healing Centers. Unleashing the talents of 50 percent of the Jewish people bodes well for a Jewish future.

6. The liberation of the Jews: Jews today can more freely choose where to live, work, attend universities, participate in government, and join organizations than at any time in history, (though anti-Semitism, especially outside of North America, is active and dangerous.) Jews also have great freedom of choice in deciding how, or even whether, to practice Judaism, another religion, or no religion.

   6a: Intermarriage: A significant aspect of Jewish freedom that deserves special mention is the loving embrace (literally) of non-Jews, such that intermarriage today is commonplace. The long-term effect of these marriages is not known, but there is little question that they will impact the future of Judaism.

A sociologist or historian might add to or subtract from this list. But taken in total, the result is that Jews today have realized their dream of freedom. The emancipation of the Jews has come a long way. Jews are now free to roam physically and spiritually as never before—although the memory of threat or actual threat is seldom far from

Jewish consciousness. Jews today have a range of choice from the Dalai Lama, to fundamentalism, to atheism, and everything in between.

New non-Jewish options and opportunities for Jews are so available and tantalizing today that, ironically, the realization of the freedoms Jews have dreamed of for centuries threatens the very existence of Judaism.

The Sovereign Self

The net-net of all this choice is that attempting to impose religion (or any beliefs or behaviors) on adults living in freedom is difficult. Modern technology is only increasing this challenge. The Internet, email, blogs, iPods, satellite TV and radio, cable TV, TiVo, podcasts, DVDs, CDs, and more give us unprecedented access to limitless choices and the freedom to tune in or tune out whatever we want. This trend will only grow.

All of this freedom and choice has given birth to the concept of "the sovereign self"—meaning that each person today is their own king or queen. We rule our own lives. Professors Arnold Eisen and Steven Cohen have written that the idea of the sovereign self can be seen in Judaism today as Jews, perhaps now more than ever, are deciding for themselves how (or if) they will live as Jews. The freedom individuals have today also partially explains why so many non-Jews write to me asking for explanations about Judaism, including regular inquiries about conversion.

When every individual is a sovereign, institutions in society have an enormous challenge to command the allegiance of members. As for Jewish institutions, they must strive as never before to "earn" their authority and prove their worth to individual Jews. No longer can the Jewish community dictate or use collective guilt to pressure individuals to "behave!" Jewish institutions are not dealing with loyal subjects.

Consequently, they can't expect "the people" to come to them. Institutions must actively go out there and "get the people." If what Jewish institutions offer isn't relevant, accessible, and beneficial,

Jews will simply choose to attend or do something else — they'll "vote with their feet."

The new era: Freedom Judaism

I feel confident that the Jewish people will survive. If for no other reason, because there will always be anti-Semitism and Jews have learned to use this adversity to strengthen themselves. Plus, there will always be a segment, albeit a small percentage, that will maintain traditional *Halachic* or Rabbinic Judaism.

Mere survival, however, is not enough. For Judaism to thrive in this age of freedom, choice, and the sovereign self, we cannot depend on anti-Semitism to band Jews together or on a small minority who religiously uphold *halacha*.

We live in a new era, that I call Freedom Judaism — typified by the Internet, a world of freedom, access, and choice. For Judaism to thrive in this era, the benefits of being Jewish must be so compelling that people freely choose the Jewish way of life. A person who converts to Judaism is known by the beautiful term "Jew by Choice." In this era of Freedom Judaism, really every Jew is a Jew by Choice. Judaism needs to respond and adapt to this age of the sovereign self, where little can be imposed on people.

This is particularly difficult for a way of life that relies on rules, standards, obligations, and subservience. Some will respond, "We can't just break, bend, or discard rules to accommodate every popular whim of the people. If we do, Judaism will deteriorate!" or "You can't have Judaism where everybody chooses whatever they want."

My reply is: I share this concern, but Jews are already picking and choosing what they want! My area of America Online was called *Judaism Today: Where Do I Fit?* As I've read all the email people have sent me, I've thought a more realistic name for the area should have been: *Me Today: Where Does Judaism Fit?*

The email in this book and demographic statistics of Jewish practices show that Jews today are effectively saying, "I will customize my own Jewish identity by choosing what I deem relevant and rejecting the irrelevant." Author and radio host Dennis Prager half jokes that, nowadays, every individual Jew thinks he or she has the genuine or correct recipe for Judaism, believing that "Everyone who practices Judaism to the right of me is a fanatic, everyone to the left of me is a Gentile." Put another way by Rabbi Leon Morris, the 5 million Jews in America today represent 5 million denominations of Judaism!

Preserving the ESP Essence of Judaism

Institutions may try to fight this independence or they can deal with this reality. This will require open minds, creative thinking, and hard work. As when the Temple was destroyed, Jewish leadership again needs to look to the core interlocking values and beliefs of Judaism — Jewish Ethics, Spirituality, and Peoplehood — and find ways to perpetuate this essence of our tradition.

How? The answers could fill books and articles and hopefully will. Rabbi Larry Hoffman has said that at the front of the sanctuary of many synagogues, emblazoned in Hebrew, are the words: "Know before whom you stand." Hoffman quips jarringly that the words could read: "We've always done it this way."

Jewish institutions today can not afford this kind of attitude. Leadership must creatively find as many ways as possible to help Jews access, understand, and benefit from Judaism. In other words: Make Judaism relevant!

With this in mind, at the end of this chapter, I've provided a number of suggestions for Jewish institutional leadership. They are under the following headings: Providing Relevant Content, Delivering Programs That People Will Want to Attend, Making Jewish Education More Compelling and Effective, and Additional Innovations and Opportunities. I hope that the ideas I've provided will be widely read, copied, shared with leadership, and discussed.

A Partnership

While the suggestions I provide mainly focus on institutions, for Judaism to flourish in this new era of Freedom Judaism, a partnership is necessary between responsive institutions and serious individuals. Unfortunately, most Jews today had a poor, dogmatic, or nonexistent Jewish education. Too often, what they are left with does not make for a very compelling case for Judaism.

The result—to use a phrase a Jewish professional once told me— is that for many Jews today, Judaism is akin to a "leisure time activity", squeezed in occasionally between work and play. But Judaism is meant to be more like a pair of glasses through which you see work, play—and everything else for that matter. This may seem overbearing, but personally speaking, by learning about Jewish thinking and practice, I've discovered the joy and even spiritual power of connecting to a wisdom tradition that existed for generations before me and will continue for many after.

Please understand me here: I'm not saying that all Jews should start keeping kosher and become ritually observant. What I am saying is that the Jewish way of life does require commitment.

That does not mean participation has to be a burden. It should be enriching. I've made clear that Jewish institutions need to make Judaism more relevant, accessible, and beneficial. At the same time, I must also say, that if you want Judaism to provide you with ethical guidance, spiritual nourishment, or a sense of belonging, you have a big role to play. A partnership goes two ways. I don't think it is fair to ask an institution, a rabbi, a spouse, a parent, or anyone else to provide you with Jewish fulfillment unless you are a willing and serious partner.

This requires effort that may not always be easy. But many worthwhile things in life are also not easy — such as work or personal relationships. We engage in them anyway though, because the benefits are worth the effort. We also know that these pursuits require time and serious commitment. Making Judaism meaningful to you is similar.

A good place to begin is your home. Some would argue that the home is the most important institution of all. Making your home Jewish can mean many things, from having and using Jewish ritual items, art, and books to personal Jewish practices.

Another part of being serious about Judaism is learning. If you don't understand something, be emboldened by the email you read in this book. Ask your own ESP questions and seek answers — find out what Judaism says, read books, take classes, and acquire knowledge. I've included a short list of resources at the end of this chapter to assist you.

An easy and friendly place to start is a website I've created called www.BeingJewish.org. Here, you will find many "hands-on" ideas and resources designed to show relevance and meaning in Judaism. I hope you'll visit!

I want to make one more important point for individuals living in this age of the sovereign self. Judaism has always emphasized the importance of community. An integral component of being a serious Jew means caring about the Jewish people and indeed all people. This means being willing to volunteer your time, money, and commitment to others. Although this is definitely an obligation, not only do I think the Jewish requirement to give to others is good, I have found it to be personally fulfilling.

I'm Optimistic

I'll end by saying that I love being Jewish. I think Judaism is relevant. I don't think Judaism is perfect or the only valid way of living in the world. I enjoy learning from other systems, discovering wisdom there, and also learning how Judaism differs and why.

In the course of my learning, I've concluded that Judaism is a good system—a very good system. Throughout history, Judaism has had an extraordinary track record of contributing good ideas and people to the world. I believe in the potential for ancient Judaism to continue to offer much to our modern world.

The email I have received from Jews and non-Jews shows me an intense hunger for and curiosity about Judaism. In this high-tech, complicated, and impersonal world, when faced with life's challenges, these writers are yearning for guidance on how to behave, Transcendence to have faith and believe in, and ways to connect and belong. In other words, they are looking for Ethics, Spirituality, and Peoplehood. In addition, my sense is that most Jews are proud to be Jewish. When I combine this with the remarkable history of the Jewish People to persevere, create, and evolve, I'm optimistic about a vibrant Jewish future.

Before signing off, I want to say that the suggestions I've made need not be efforts of Jewish "oy." They can be a source of Jewish joy. Jews have somehow always found a way to smile and even laugh in the face of suffering. If we were able to smile during pain, we certainly can find ways to do the same during this exciting time of opportunity.

There's much work to be done, but I feel lucky to be alive during this era and to have a chance to contribute. I hope I've made a bit of a contribution through these pages.

I am grateful to you and all who have sent me email.

Todah! [Thank you]

Gil

P.S. I welcome comments about this book or any other matter. Send email to GilMann@BeingJewish.org. Perhaps your email will appear in a future column or another book — anonymously of course. Thank you!

Some Resources to Further Explore Judaism

Books

How to Get More Out of Being Jewish Even if:
A. You are not sure you believe in God,
B. You think going to synagogue is a waste of time,
C. You think keeping kosher is stupid,
D. You hated Hebrew school, or
E. All of the above!
by Gil Mann, published by Leo & Sons Publishing

My first book was based on interviews and focus groups with all kinds of Jews seeking to find out what they do and do not practice in their Judaism and why. You can read this entire book in just a few hours and I guarantee you will find new and valuable information about being Jewish here. YOU CAN DOWNLOAD THE BOOK FOR FREE at www.BeingJewish.org.

To Life! by Harold Kushner, published by Little, Brown and Company

A very readable, sensible, and enjoyable explanation of Judaism, by the author of *When Bad Things Happen to Good People.* This book is especially good for anyone who had a bad Hebrew school experience.

The Nine Questions People Ask About Judaism by Dennis Prager and Joseph Telushkin, published by Simon & Schuster, Inc.

A skeptic's guide to Judaism that answers questions such as: Why do we need organized religion? How does Judaism differ from Christianity, Marxism, Communism, and Humanism? and seven more tough questions.

Unsettled: An Anthropology of the Jews by Melvin Konner, published by Penguin Group

This history of how Jews have been impacted by the world and vice versa is fascinating, insightful, and sometimes controversial. The author is a vivid storyteller, who is passionate, honest, and brilliant. Konner's personal Jewish journey and questioning adds a valuable dimension to the book.

Jewish Literacy by Rabbi Joseph Telushkin, published by William Morrow and Company, Inc.

This book contains 348 brief entries on the essentials of Judaism, organized by subject. This plain-English and entertaining book is a tremendous source of knowledge. Looking up one entry, it's easy to get caught up reading one after another — it's like eating Frito Lay potato chips — bet you can't read just one!

It's a Mitzvah! Step-by-Step to Jewish Living by Bradley Shavit Artson, published by Behrman House

If you think the Jewish code of behavior is outdated, this book will change your mind. It offers hundreds of modern, meaningful, and practical ways to practice Judaism — from protecting the environment to helping the homeless. It covers traditional ritual practices as well. As a bonus, it is filled with wonderful photos.

Internet

There are thousands of Jewish "places to visit" on the internet. One way to start is to go to the Jewish search engine: www.maven.co.il

Here are six Jewish websites I recommend:

www.BeingJewish.org

This is my website. Here you'll find practical, friendly information to help make Judaism relevant for your modern life. All of my past Jewish Email columns are posted here. Topics covered on the website include spirituality, intermarriage, holidays, conversion, parenting, cooking, environmentalism, and more. The site is designed to help you easily access the Ethics, Spirituality, and Peoplehood of the Jewish way of life. PLUS YOU CAN GET A FREE DOWNLOAD OF MY FIRST BOOK HERE! Please come visit.

www.myjewishlearning.com

Want to learn more about Judaism or find some "how to" information? You're in luck. A lot of resources have gone into this site to provide you with information (and even courses) on a myriad of Jewish topics. Major categories include holidays, lifecycle, text, ideas and belief, culture, daily life, practice, and history. This site offers something for everyone — whether you're insecure about your level of Jewish knowledge or want to add to your knowledge base — and you can learn from the comfort of your own home.

www.jewishfamily.com

This is a great Jewish online magazine you may want to check out produced by Jewish Family & Life. It has articles about parenting, answers to children's questions about Judaism (like "Can I visit Santa at the Mall?"), interviews with famous Jews, areas about food, travel, etc. You can also interact with the magazine and other readers through your computer.

www.convert.org

If you know somebody who is interested in converting to Judaism — or you simply want to learn more about Judaism — this welcoming site is a great place to start. Here you will find information about the differences between Judaism and Christianity, how to deal with sensitive relationship issues, the names of over 70 rabbis of all denominations who perform conversions, and much more.

www.interfaithfamily.com

Well-known today is the phenomenon of Jews marrying non-Jews. This website candidly addresses the challenges faced by intermarried families and their extended families (like in-laws and grandparents). The site offers a Jewish perspective while respecting the faith of others. Look here for resources and links covering many topics like religious holidays, lifecycle events, outreach programming, and more.

www.Jewish.com

This general Jewish site has a wide range of Jewish information covering many aspects of Judaism. Some of the topics you can pursue here are holiday information, Ask A Rabbi, recipes, book reviews, Jewish news, and more. They post many columns I have written in response to questions readers have emailed to me. To find these columns, enter "Gil Mann" in their search feature. They also have a Jewish store as a part of their site so you can find Jewish gifts for yourself or others.

Some Ideas for Jewish Leadership

Dear lay or professional leader:

Before offering one word of suggestion, I say thank you. The job of leading a Jewish institution is too often thankless. Professionals usually could have made more money by pursuing a career in the for-profit world. The work of a volunteer is obviously not even on the pay scale.

The motivation is not financial, but instead, to make a difference, to make a contribution that will positively affect others. I know this firsthand, after years of volunteering in non-profits and finding myself surrounded by *mensches* — very decent human beings who are trying their best to serve others.

The saying "no good deed goes unpunished" is often true for the well-intentioned leaders and volunteers of Jewish non-profits. So, again, I must begin any comments with thanks. I know you want your institutions to succeed and to provide for others.

Responding to a Changing World

Jewish institutions face a delicate balancing act in this era of Freedom Judaism, an age of choice and the sovereign self. They must simultaneously lead the flock and be led by the flock. This may sound like a contradiction, but many successful companies that sell products do just this. Think of how Apple introduced the iPod. They were responsive to customers while at the same time "driving" the marketplace. That is, they led and convinced prospects that the company's product was worthy of being chosen.

For Jewish institutions to do this requires a difficult examination of the standards, laws, rituals, and norms of Jewish behavior. Some will be maintained, some will be changed, some will be eliminated, and new ones will be created. This has always happened in Judaism and continues to happen today. Look at intermarriage, for example. Each decade seems to bring different standards and norms for Jewish/non-Jewish marriages in general society and Jewish life.

In the Rabbinic era of Judaism, *halacha* (which, again, literally means "the way") provided definitive traffic laws that guided Jews as they traveled the Jewish way of life. But today most Jews do not observe these laws. In this era of freedom and choice, *halacha* cannot be imposed on Jews. A more realistic application of *halacha* is not as enforceable traffic laws but as a guidance system, more of a compass or GPS for navigating through life.

I know such an idea upsets some, but I believe Jewish and world evolution is forcing these changes upon us. As part of this evolution, we will need to harness 2,000 years of Jewish wisdom and practice, together with additional knowledge that humans have learned about the world and life. Then we must infuse the Jewish way of life with rituals, rules, and institutions so meaningful and relevant that Jews will say Judaism is worthy of continuing. Ironically, part of this evolution includes re-adopting some rituals that were discarded earlier. This too is happening in Jewish life today.

With that said, the suggestions below are not meant as a critique; they are meant to help. I hope they will be read in this spirit. I base these suggestions on three bodies of knowledge. One is what I've learned from the thousands of people who have spoken to me via email, focus groups, and audiences where I've lectured. Second, I base these suggestions on what I learned in my successful business career as an entrepreneur. Finally, I rely on my experience as a volunteer in non-profits for more than 25 years.

I do not maintain that these suggestions are a panacea or amazing breakthroughs. They are meant to spur thought. I hope they will be copied and used as a blueprint for discussion. Even more so, I hope they will be implement and modified based on feedback from the customers.

Institutions Must Be Nimble, Responsive, and Relevant by Doing The Following:

Providing Relevant Content:

- New programming and institutions must be developed to address the relevant issues people grapple with on a daily basis.

Here a few programming ideas: ethics in the work place, healing and hospice centers, parenting and grandparenting skills, hands-on social action, community *mitzvah* or *gemelut hesed* [kindness] days, Judaism and environmentalism, Jewish art, and cooking projects and much more.

- New Jewish life-cycle rituals need to be developed for milestones and life events of today: examples are graduating from college, recovering from an illness, dealing with addictions, struggling with fertility issues, getting a driver's license, a major career move, moving into a new home, and retirement.

- Options need to be developed to address the reality that when it comes to spirituality, "one size does not fit all." Different people resonate to different expressions of spirituality. There is a broad range of preferences for such things as Hebrew, English, silent meditation, folk singing, organ, other instruments, dancing, traditional *davening* [Yiddish for praying], and more. In addition, we need multiple forms of expression for different affinity groups, such as young parents, older parents, bereaved, healing, singles, seniors, teens, men, and women.

- Prayer books should be more user-friendly and relevant. One of the best prayer books I've ever seen was for kids, filled with inspiring pictures and color. Why aren't adult prayer books like this? In addition, more contemporary and meaningful prayers are needed. Focus groups with end users (not scholars) should be conducted to gauge impact on worshippers.

Delivering Programs That People Will Want to Attend:

- Programming decisions should be driven more by the question: What will "they" (the customers) attend? as opposed to What do "we" want to offer? This requires creativity, but does not mean the content must be fluff!

- To learn what "they will attend," requires asking, really listening, tailoring programming, testing, modifying, and more listening. Surveys, focus groups, evaluations, and ongoing feedback mechanisms must be built into programming efforts.

- A human and personal invitation should be a part of reaching out for and then maintaining participation.

- There must be great sensitivity to people's insecurities about their Jewish competence, knowledge, and personal background. Nobody likes to feel dumb. We must be mindful that, in contrast to their Jewish knowledge, most Jewish adults are highly educated and competent in their careers.

- Scheduling and marketing of programming must be practical about the many competitive demands for people's time and attention. Think of your own busy schedule. How much time do you usually have available—one hour, two hours max? Then add commuting time. With all of this in mind, program packaging should revolve around these questions:

  What obstacles to participation can we remove? Examples: Frequency and length of programs, babysitting, convenience, formality, and dress code, etc. Costs, tuitions, and dues deserve special attention here. The expense of being Jewish is one of the biggest barriers to participation in Jewish life and needs to be seriously addressed by leadership.

  What benefits can we offer? Examples: You will learn and be able to harness x, y, and z to improve your life. You will receive fun, food, and spiritual and/or intellectual stimulation. You will see or meet friends, be welcomed into a warm community, etc.

- Turf must be shared. For example, nurturing spirituality is not exclusively the domain of synagogues. Institutions and professionals should look for ways to collaborate and eliminate competition when delivering Ethical, Spiritual, and Peoplehood programming.

- Programming must be delivered in creative new places: outdoors, at malls, at places where people work and play, in homes, and in retreat centers. As an aside, retreats and *Shabbatons* [group Sabbath getaways] have huge potential. Although they are a big and inconvenient time commitment, anyone who has attended can attest to their power!

Making Jewish Education More Compelling and Effective:

- The thrust of education for children and adults must shift to emphasize teaching "Why be Jewish?" much more than "How to be Jewish." For example, we should be teaching kids why they would want to *become* a Bar or Bat Mitzvah much more than teaching how to *have* a Bar or Bat Mitzvah. For adults, we should teach *why* they would want to observe rituals, not just *how*. There are many fascinating explanations. Most Jewish adults have never heard them (for example, explanations and theories of the "whys" behind keeping kosher).

   In other words, we should be teaching the ethical underpinnings that motivate Jewish behavior and ritual... the spirit of the law, not just the letter. If we do, people may find more "spirit"uality in Jewish practices and ethics.

- Education resources should be shifted from kids (pediatric Judaism) to parents and other adults. Educating a parent, future parent, or grandparent offers twice the bang for the buck, as this education then flows down to the kids. Plus, as Rabbi Harold Kushner says, the "stuff" of Judaism is adult material.

- Jews and non-Jews should be encouraged to learn with each other. We all need to better understand how we're different, how we're the same, and why.

- Pay for teachers should be increased. For this profession to attract the best and the brightest, salaries and benefits must be competitive with those of other valued professions.

- Education for rabbis and other Jewish professional should include training in market research, active listening, public speaking, and effective teaching techniques.

Additional Innovations and Opportunities:

- Jewish summer camps—a research proven success story—must have increased capacity and affordability. Studies show that less than 10 percent of Jewish kids go to summer camp and most camps have waiting lists. Also, more overnight camps need to offer 2 week options.

- Homes should be made into Jewish institutions. Tools, resources, and teaching must be created to help people make their homes their Jewish castles. This includes guiding people to acquire Jewish art, ritual objects, and a library. In addition, training should be provided so that in the comfort of their own homes people can learn to: better celebrate Jewish holidays, Shabbat, recite meaningful blessings, cook, and live Jewishly in ways that they can understand and find relevant in their lives.

- Media (such as radio, cable, satellite, and podcasts) should be used more effectively. Technology today allows us to laser in on specific audiences with specific content. We can and should target these audiences with what they want. Again, this requires genuine listening, understanding, and responding.

- The Internet should be further exploited. The anonymity, ease, speed, and low cost of the Internet offer opportunities to connect, educate, donate, and more.

- Israel/Diaspora relations need strengthening. Every possible opportunity to have Diaspora Jews and Israeli Jews exchange people, programs, ideas, and just plain old friendship should be pursued. To give just one example, there should be a large-scale high school foreign exchange program. Kids could live for a month or a quarter with a host family with other teens and then switch countries.

- Conversion should be encouraged. This is controversial in the Jewish world, but my experience is that Jews by Choice are a terrific asset to our people. At a minimum we should be more welcoming to those who have converted.

- Outreach to intermarried families must increase. A friendly welcome to these couples and their children should be the mantra in the Jewish world. The beauty, depth, warmth, and wisdom of Judaism should be on display to them.

To any professional or lay leader of an institution who looks at this list and responds, "We already do that," I say, *kol hakavod* [honor to you]! Do more! Show others! To those who say, "We can't do that," I say, come up with alternative ideas.

To those who say, "You can't put all the burden on Jewish institutions. What about the responsibility of individual Jews?" I agree! I wrote in the conclusion of my book that what is needed is a partnership between responsive institutions and serious individuals. And I said in no uncertain terms that individual Jews need to be responsible for finding meaning in Judaism and not put the onus on anyone else or on institutions.

At the same time, if institutions don't adapt to our changing world, they run the risk of becoming ex-institutions. I will leave you with the following challenge that was once posed to me by Rabbi Irwin Kula: Imagine the synagogue, school, JCC, Federation, etc., that opened up across the street from yours... and puts yours out of business. What would they be doing?

I challenge you to imagine what they would be doing — and then lead your institution to do just that, so that you will thrive, as will Judaism.

Kol Tuv [all good wishes],

Gil Mann

P.S. I invite you to my website www.BeingJewish.org, where you can find additional ideas and resources to use in your institution. I hope you'll come visit and I welcome your email!

A Note to Educators

Dear Educators:

Teachers hold a special place in my heart as my grandfather, mother and wife were all teachers.

With this in mind, I've been especially touched over the years to hear from many teachers who have told me that they have used my books and columns in their classrooms. Some have even sent me emails that students wrote as a result of classroom discussions. At least one of those emails is in this book.

I have been honored to know that teachers have used this material and I want you to feel free to reprint and use any material in this book. There are many additional columns that did not appear in this book. These archived columns can be found at www.BeingJewish.org (look under Jewish Email.) Also, you can download my first book for free there. All of this material is available for your use as well.

My only request is that you tell people where you found the material and invite others to visit the website.

Please feel to email me at GilMann@BeingJewish.org with suggestions on how others might use this material or any other comments. I read every email sent to me and promise to respond — at a minimum to let you know I've received your email.

Respectfully yours,

Gil Mann

PS Even if you are not a professional educator, please feel free to copy, use, and pass on material in this book and on my website.

Praise for Gil's first book:

By GIL MANN

HOW TO

GET MORE OUT OF BEING JEWISH

E V E N   I F :

A. You are not sure you believe in God,
B. You think going to synagogue is a waste of time,
C. You think keeping kosher is stupid,
D. You hated Hebrew school, or
E. All of the above!

"This book is a home run!"
Bud Selig
Commissioner
Major League Baseball

"This book is nothing short of superb."
Harold Kushner
Author
When Bad Things Happen to Good People

"'In these modern times, how can Judaism help me to find meaning in life?' This non-threatening book will be a great aid to many as they search for answers to that question... Covering profound and difficult Jewish questions, yet written in an extremely easy to read and accessible style."
— Jewish Book World

"There are many books on Judaism written from every possible point of view, but I have never seen anything like this. This is a marvelous piece of work." — Rabbi Herb Friedman

"This [is] a wonderful book for readers who are struggling with numerous questions about Judaism. The book is thought provoking even to those who believe they have a grip on what Judaism means to them."
— The Kansas City Jewish Chronicle

"This book gave me the permission to continue my Jewish searching... and not feel guilty." — Anonymous reader

---

Gil invites you to visit his website:
www.BeingJewish.org.

He welcomes your email.
Send them to:
GilMann@BeingJewish.org

To order his books go to the website or call
1–800–304–9925